George Bruce, author and journalist, spent a year studying the mass of both published and unpublished 19th century historical material about the First Afghan War before writing this book. He shows how the war began with the unjustified fear that Russia was then capable of overrunning India by way of Afghanistan; how counter-invasion by a British-Indian army in 1839 to place a pro-British puppet on the Afghan throne turned into a hated military occupation; and how the British adventure ended, three years later, with a sudden Afghan rising, swift defeat for the invaders and bloody massacre in the snowbound passes. A few prisoners apart, only one man—Doctor Brydon—survived out of the entire army. the women and the camp-followers, who undertook the ill-fated and bitterly ironic expedition to Kabul.

George Bruce

RETREAT FROM KABUL

HOWARD BAKER
London

George Bruce
RETREAT FROM KABUL

© George Bruce, 1967

First published by Howard Baker Publishers
Limited, 1969

Howard Baker books are published by
HOWARD BAKER PUBLISHERS LIMITED
47 Museum Street, London, W.C.1
Printed and bound in England by
Balding & Mansell Ltd, of London and Wisbech.

RETREAT FROM KABUL

Contents

Chapter One

General Sir John Keane was carried behind the cavalry advance-guard in a palanquin borne by relays of Hindu bearers across the plains, mountains and deserts of Afghanistan during the march from India. He was followed by a groom leading his charger and, in a long procession that stretched for 30 or 40 miles across country, by his staff officers, by columns of lumbering horse-drawn artillery, by more cavalry, endless lines of red-coated infantry and the still longer lines of lurching supply and baggage camels intermingled with the host of thousands of camp-followers.

Like a great migrating tribe, the army had marched on Ghazni, in central Afghanistan, at 4 a.m. on 21 July 1839, but four hours later, the fortress which dominated the route to Kabul was still not in sight. Shrugging aside normal military prudence and his dislike for riding horseback, General Keane had then called for his charger, mounted stiffly and, according to Major Hough, Deputy Advocate-General, had ordered his staff officers and a cavalry escort to accompany him on a reconnaissance far ahead of the army across the plain towards Ghazni. Certainly the risks he and his staff faced in this impetuous ride from Afghan marksmen who might be hidden about the plain were great. But Keane's misgivings must have been too strong to be ignored, and with good reason.

He had left his heavy artillery 200 miles behind at Kandahar, and those guns, the 18-pounders, were the only ones capable of blasting a way in for the infantry through walls at Ghazni that might be 15 or 20 feet thick.

Keane's political officers had told him that the Afghans were friendly and would open the gates of the fortress to the British invaders. And his artillery and engineer officers had reported that the walls of the fortress were so weak that the 9-pounder guns and the 24-pounder howitzers could together knock them down if the citizens there were to oppose him. Brigadier Stevenson, commanding artillery, had, moreover, insisted that the transport animals were too weak after the long journey from India to pull the 60-hundredweight 18-pounders and their wagons loaded with nearly a thousand shells.

The terrain ahead of Kandahar, where these discussions had taken place, was far easier than that already traversed, so there was no real substance in this argument. And Ghazni, the *Dar-oos-Sultunut-i-Ghazni*—'seat of the Sultan's power'—was renowned throughout southern Asia for the strength of its fortifications, in contrast to his officers' belief, based on secondhand information, that they were tumble-down.

Yet a month ago, when his army was halted at Kandahar, Keane had allowed his subordinates to persuade him, and in what was reported to have been a characteristic flash of temper had let them have their own way and had ordered his heavy artillery to be left behind.

But his predicament was far worse than the admittedly serious one of lack of heavy artillery. The army was dangerously short of food as well. Impetuously, Keane had led his troops and their long train of camp-followers into the middle of a hostile country with insufficient rations either to keep them there or to march them out again.

And now, he had food for his fighting-men for two days only—on half-rations.

This scarcity must have been frightening on top of his lack of heavy artillery. It meant that he *must* somehow seize the fortress and commandeer its provisions within two days.

A siege was out of the question.

To by-pass Ghazni and march on towards Kabul, the capital, was impossible too, because Dost Mahommed, the ruler he was to depose, had an army in the field somewhere ahead. Keane could not risk leaving another army behind

him in the fortress, ready to stream out and attack him in
the rear directly he engaged Dost Mahommed. Nor could
he retreat with rations for but two days across country
where he would face continual attacks.

These facts must have hounded and oppressed General
Keane appallingly as he rode with his staff officers towards
the crest of the last hill that overlooked the fortress, where
he would be able to judge of its strength for himself and put
to the test the alleged friendship of its inhabitants.

A heavy, somewhat dropsical man who rode his horse
badly, Sir John Keane was commanding the Anglo-Indian
Army of the Indus. It had been formed at the word of Lord
Auckland, Governor-General of India, to invade Afghanistan, the wildest, and—from the military point of view—the
most difficult country in southern Asia. Keane's objectives
were the overthrow of the present ruler, Dost Mahommed
Khan, and his replacement on the throne by Shah Shuja-
ool-Mulk, a former king whom the Afghans had expelled
some years before.

When Keane reached the crest of the last rise the fortress
burst into view a mile or two away. 'It looked formidable
with its fortifications rising up, as it were, on the side of a
hill,' noted Major Hough, who was at Keane's side.

Keane, through his telescope, could see the massive
fortifications, about 70 feet high, built on a steep mound
about 120 feet high surrounded by a wide moat—a very
much bigger and stronger place that had been put to him by
Captain Thomson, his engineer—and in good repair.

No record exists of what Keane said to Brigadier Stevenson and Captain Thomson at that moment, but neither by
nature not habit was he inclined to control his feelings. The
scene must have been an explosive one.

His only hope was that the Afghans in the fortress would
turn out to be friendly, or could be bribed to be. If not, it
would certainly seem that he and his army were doomed.

And at that moment hope returned. One of the political
officers, Sir Alexander Burnes, said in a message to Keane
that he had just learned that the Afghans had completely

abandoned the fortress. This was strange news from the very man who earlier had insisted that they would stay and welcome the British, but there was a chance it could prove true and Keane rode with his staff on towards the orchards and gardens that lay on the plain at the foot of the hill, about a mile from the fortress.

But when they were about 600 yards from the gardens this hope too vanished in sudden puffs of smoke followed by sharp reports and the slow whistle near by of almost spent bullets—hardly likely action from a friendly or from an abandoned fortress.

It must have been a very unhappy moment for Keane. He had allowed himself to be talked into treating the occupation of Ghazni as an insignificant episode in the 'military promenade' which Lord Auckland, the Governor-General of India, had light-heartedly called the entire invasion.

Now he was faced by a massive fortress which he had no guns powerful enough to breach; which he was unable to mine owing to the surrounding moat; which was impossible for his infantry to scale and to which he couldn't lay siege because he had only two days' food supply.

Chapter Two

Startling though General Keane's incompetence is, far from being singular it is part of a pattern of political and military ineptitude in the conduct of this war that is almost beyond belief. Afghanistan was, and probably still is, one of the hardest countries to invade in the world. In all directions it is ribbed by high mountain ranges cut by narrow passes. Most of its surface is mere rock and though the mountain valleys are very fertile only about five per cent of the total surface is cultivable. It is hot in summer and intensely cold in winter. In the first half of the nineteenth century there were no roads, only narrow stony tracks made during centuries by the feet of animals and men.

In theory Afghanistan was then a monarchy, but the Shah at Kabul was never in the nation's history more than the Khan of the most warlike tribe and his authority no more than what he could maintain by diplomatic intrigue and military force.

There were four main tribes composing this feudal society: The Duranis, the Khyberees, the Belooches and the Ghilzyes, the last numerically the strongest and capable of putting some 40,000 fighting-men in the field. The tribesmen held rather than owned the land, and paid their chiefs for it in kind, in cash and, when called upon, by military duties, as did the chiefs in their turn to the Shah.

Like the chiefs of the Scottish clans, the Afghan chiefs inherited their powers, but still needed to be accepted by both the Shah and the tribal councils of elders, upon whose collective agreement their power depended. A chief could be overthrown either by the Shah or by an alliance of his followers.

Rather than a unified kingdom, Afghanistan at this time

was more like a confederation of independent tribal republics, with the Shah ruling in the towns and country-side through governors and troops, but with less influence in the remote mountainous areas.

When the nation faced invasion, or if foreign war was planned, the chiefs gathered with the Shah in public council to debate a policy. Once this was agreed, they were ex-pected to obey the Shah's orders implicitly, but when the danger or the need had passed, they again ruled more or less as they wished in their own territories. And whatever the power of the Shah, a tribe never refused hospitality and shelter to a fugitive—to do so would have meant deep dis-grace.

The Shah also obtained revenue by taxing merchants and tradesmen and—when he could enforce it—the chiefs and their followers as well. Some of this money he used, when persuasion or threats failed, to purchase the agreement of the tribes to freedom of transit for merchants through the mountain passes that crossed their traditional strongholds.

The great masses of the townsfolk belonged to none of the main tribes. They were descended from the different races who, like the Persians, had at one time and another pene-trated the country and established temporary supremacy. But the Shah's court was Afghan, of the four tribes, as indeed was the army, the chiefs of whom were usually the largest land-holders.

The vices of the Afghans were at this time the primitive ones of revenge, avarice, cruelty, rapacity and jealousy; their virtues love of freedom, faithfulness to friends, kind-ness to dependants and, when led or inspired by fanaticism, considerable bravery. Colonel Dennie, who was later to die at their hands, wrote prophetically of them: 'Their whole life is one of violence, rapine and murder. They know no law but force and the sword; and every man among them is armed from head to foot, a state which they never quit by day or night so insecure is life and property among them and so little dare they trust each other.'

The British diplomat Mountstuart Elphinstone, noted in

contrasting tone: 'An European coming among them would scarce fail to admire their martial and lofty spirit, their hospitality and their bold and simple manners. He would admire their strong and active forms, their fair complexions and European features, their industry and enterprise . . . and above all the independence and spirit of their institutions. They endeavour to maintain that all Afghans are equal.

'I once strongly urged on a very intelligent old man . . . the superiority of a quiet and secure life under a powerful monarch, to the discord, the alarms and the blood which they owed to their present system. The old man replied with great warmth. . . . "We are content with discord, we are content with alarms, we are content with blood—but we will never be content with a master."'

Discord, alarms and blood—these form the pattern of Afghan history and it is worth going back to the turn of the eighteenth century to see how from it Dost Mahommed emerged as the ruler the British now sought to overthrow.

In 1800 Zemaun Shah reigned, son of Timour Shah and grandson of the illustrious Ahmed Shah who extended the boundaries of Afghanistan and gave the Dhouranee Empire its name. Zemaun Shah had numerous brothers from his father's countless wives, but in history the most significant of them were the two who became Mahmoud Shah and Shah Shuja.

Zemaun Shah spent much of his rule alternately marching armies to threaten the north-west frontier of India and rushing them back to defend his throne against brotherly would-be usurpers. The British, knowing nothing of the state of chaos and disorganisation that ruled in Afghanistan, let themselves be needlessly alarmed by the threats of what seemed an exceedingly warlike race, which they tried to counter by cultivating the friendship of Persia—an attack on Afghanistan from that quarter, they reflected, would discourage Zemaun Shah from marching on India.

The real ruler of Afghanistan at this time was, however, the Vizier, or chief minister, Wuffadar Khan, successor to

Poyndah Khan, the equally powerful but more able vizier to Timour Shah and briefly to Ahmed Shah as well. But Zemaun Dhah had preferred the more devious Wuffadar, had spurned Poyndah, the hereditary vizier, and allowed him to be murdered by Wuffadar.

In Afghanistan, where revenge was one of the highest virtues, it was not so easy to get rid of an enemy. Poyndah Khan had no less than twenty-one sons, of whom the eldest was Futteh Khan, and in the heart of this formidable leader, and his brothers, revenge for their father's death became the first object in life.

In 1801 Futteh Khan persuaded Prince Mahmoud to combine with him in an attempt to overthrow Zemaun Shah, who was Mahmoud's brother. Under Fetteh Khan's leadership they occupied the southern capital, Kandahar, then defeated Zemaun Shah and took possession of the throne in Kabul. Waffadar Khan was immediately executed and honour was satisfied. Shah Zemaun was then dealt with more mercifully—his eyeballs were punctured with a dagger. A blind ex-king could do no harm.

But there was to be no let-up in discord. When he heard the news, the Shah's other brother, Shuja-ool-Mulk, at once proclaimed himself Shah of Afghanistan and occupied Kabul when Mahmoud was busy fighting elsewhere, but lacking in soldierly qualities, he failed to consolidate and was easily thrown out by Futteh Khan. Not long after, in 1803, exploiting the discontent that Mahmoud's rule had sown, Shuja—who was thirty-five years later to become the British puppet King—again defeated the Shah's troops and entered Kabul in triumph.

Mahmoud was his prisoner and according to tradition Shuja should now have blinded him, but he let the fallen Shah keep his sight—and soon paid dearly for this act of mercy. Futteh Khan had meanwhile escaped to organise insurrection again, and making another mistake, Shuja stupidly made no move to come to terms with this dangerous and influential king-maker.

The next several years of Shuja's reign were marked by

the usual discord, alarms and blood—the outcome of a reign distinguished by foolish mercy towards rebellious khans and cruel oppression of the peasantry. Eventually, in 1809, when tribal chiefs and people had grown to hate Shuja's very name, Futteh Khan—still faithful to the deposed Mahmoud—overthrew Shah Shuja and placed Mahmoud on the throne again. Shuja fled with what wealth he could lay hands on, and turned up at the court of Ranjit Singh, the Sikh ruler.

In exchange for promises of help and some financial aid, Ranjit Singh procured from him the famed Kohinoor diamond—it now adorns the British crown—but the promised help failed to materialise. The Shah was stripped of everything he possessed and eventually, after many vicissitudes, entered India as a beggar and threw himself upon the mercy of the British.

The illustrious Futteh Khan now reigned supreme at the court of the King, Mahmoud Shah, but this power had made him many enemies. One of his younger brothers at this time was Dost Mahommed, fourteen, son of a relatively humble woman. Serving Futteh Khan as a menial, he brought water and lit his hookah, but being a subtle and ambitious youth, listened carefully and spoke little. One day, hearing that one of Futteh Khan's inveterate enemies was in the city, he went out and struck him down and killed him in broad daylight. Futteh Khan recognised a kindred spirit and Dost Mahommed became a firm favourite.

When the all-powerful Futteh Khan decided later to subdue the Persian tribes who were then nibbling away at the western frontier, he gave Dost Mahommed his first military assignment—the seizure of the independent principality of Herat in the same region, from Shah Mahmoud's son Prince Kamran.

It was a move which heralded unwisely that Futteh Khan and his brothers now outshone the Shah in the Afghan firmament. But in zeal and effrontery, Dost Mahommed now outshone Futteh Khan. Starting with treachery, he gained entry to the city by posing as a friendly emissary of

Futteh Khan, then massacred the unsuspecting palace guards, seized the Prince, put all who resisted to the sword, robbed the treasury and finally violated the royal harem, or *zenana*. There, among other abominations, he seized the jewelled waistband of Prince Kamran's favourite wife and in a spasm of greed tore it from her body.

After this memorable night's work Dost Mahommed took fright at the vengeance he knew would be exacted and fled with his loot to far-off Kashmir, ruled by another brother, Azim Khan. Prince Kamran's wife had meantime made him swear an oath of vengeance and Futteh Khan was chosen as the appropriate recipient of the humiliated Prince's thirst for revenge.

Notwithstanding the Vizier's power in the kingdom and responsibility for keeping his father on the throne, Kamran seized him as he returned to Kabul from Persia and blinded him forthwith. Honour was again satisfied, but there was a need for security too, in the face of the challenge from this band of formidable brothers.

Kamran took Futteh Khan before Shah Mahmoud. Futteh Khan was called upon to write to his brothers and order them to surrender to the Shah. Resolutely, he refused —he would *not* betray his brothers and whatever harm was done to him, his influence now he was blind was at an end. Mahmoud Shah thereupon ordered the Vizier, upon whom his fortunes and his crown had depended for so long, to be slowly put to death before him.

Captain James Abbott, who received the account from Summund Khan, one of Prince Kamran's courtiers, tells how the blind Futteh Khan was brought into a tent in which sat a circle of his greatest enemies, together with the Shah and Kamran. They began by each in turn accusing him of injuries they said they had received at his hands and hurling insults of the worst kind at him.

'Atta Mahmoud Khan then stepped up to him, and seizing one of his ears, cut it off with his knife. . . . Shahagaussie Nawab cut off the other ear. Each, as he wreaked this unmanly vengeance upon his victim, whom he would have crouched to the day before, named the wrong of which it was the recompense. . . . Another of the barbarians cut off his nose: Khana Moolla Khan severed his right hand; Khalook Dad Khan his left hand, the blood gushing copiously from each new wound. Summurdar Khan cut off his beard, saying, "This is for dishonouring my wife."

'Hitherto this high-spirited chief had borne his suffering without weakness. . . . He had only once condescended in a calm voice to beg them to hasten his death. The mutilation of ears and nose, a punishment reserved for the meanest offences of slaves, had not been able to shake his fortitude; but the beard of a Mahommedan is a member so sacred that honour itself becomes confounded with it, and he who had borne with the constancy of a hero the taunts and tortures heaped upon him, seemed to lose his manhood with his beard, and burst into a passion of tears. His torments were now drawing to a close. Ghool Mahommed, with a blow of his sabre cut off his right foot, and a man of the Populzye tribe severed the left. Atta Mahmoud Khan finished his torments by cutting his throat.'

Dost Mahommed now had two reasons for swearing to put down Shah Mahmoud and his son Kamran. Their own wish for more vengeance upon him and his brothers; and his own irrevocable need to avenge the blood of Futteh Khan. He swore that he would march on Kabul with an army of retribution. His brother Azim Khan, ruler of Kashmir, gave him a few lakhs of rupees to pay his troops, and Dost Mahommed soon occupied Kabul. In the interests of legitimacy, Azim Khan then invited Shah Shuja to reassert his claim to the throne, but the partnership was brief— Shuja offended his new supporter by his airs and graces and soon was expelled from Afghanistan again.

Dost Mahommed and his brothers now shared the country among themselves, Ayoob Khan being briefly the nominal Shah. Together Azim Khan and Dost Mahommed now planned a defensive expedition against the expansionist Sikhs, but Ranjit Singh, hearing of it, sowed hostility among the brothers by lavish bribery. Azim Kahn heard of the treachery among the brothers he had trusted and was said to be so filled with grief that his spirit was broken, he lost his formidable power of generalship and his troops deserted him. He died soon after, and Ranjit Singh occupied the Afghan city of Peshawar, thus sowing the seeds of enmity between Afghans and Sikhs. Rivalry and discord continued for another three years until, by 1826, Dost Mahommed emerged as the most capable ruler and military leader. His brothers accepted the situation and the once humble Dost Mahommed became supreme in the land, bringing Afghanistan a measure of peace and security, while the former king, Shah Shuja, lived comfortably as a British pensioner in India.

Then, in 1833, tired of inactivity, Shuja obtained four months' advance of his pension from the British, some 16,000 rupees (£1,600) and set out once again to try to reconquer the country. Raising an army and obtaining more money to maintain it while *en route* to Afghanistan, he entered the country upon a caparisoned elephant early in 1834 and attacked Kandahar.

Dost Mahommed and his son Akbar Khan easily defeated the luckless Shuja, who fled the country, leaving his guns and equipment to Dost Mahommed. To regain Peshawar from the Sikhs was now the Amir's greatest ambition and he began to dream of an alliance with the British to attain it. In 1837 circumstances beyond his control affected the issue. Rumours buzzed around the Kabul bazaars that a British emissary was on his way to the capital. His arrival in due course was to bear heavily upon the destiny of Dost Mohommed and the plans of the British in India. For they were to restore Shah Shuja and in doing so would drench the land in blood.

Chapter Three

The events which led up to Lord Auckland's decision to invade Afghanistan were complex. Auckland, a Whig peer —'unstable as water'—who had succeeded Lord William Bentinck as Governor-General in 1836, brought with him from England the anxiety of Lord Palmerston, Foreign Secretary, about Russia's presumed ambition to invade India through her north-west frontier—for Russia had by then succeeded Napoleon as the imagined ever-present threat to the British Empire in the East.

India was of course governed at this time by the East India Company—originally a commercial organisation— through the Governor-General and Council, responsible to the Board of Control in London, which, in its turn, was responsible through its President to the British Government.

What perhaps brought the issue to a head at this time was a letter from the British Envoy in Persia, Mr. Ellis, to Lord Palmerston, in January 1836.

'The Shah of Persia lays claim to the sovereignty of Afghanistan as far as Ghazni and is fully determined to attempt the conquest in the Spring,' Ellis had written. 'The success of the Shah in the undertaking is anxiously wished for by Russia; and their minister here does not fail to press it on to early execution. The motive cannot be mistaken. Herat, once annexed to Persia, may become, according to the Commercial Treaty, the residence of a Russian consular agent, who would from thence push his researches and communications, avowed and secret, throughout Afghanistan.'

But Ellis and Palmerston, too, had let their anxieties run away with them, for in reality, far from Afghanistan being a frontier for the defence of India, this frontier then lay 1,200 miles away across the mountains and deserts of the Punjab,

Sind and Rajputana—not then a part of British India. It was therefore not of vital importance to India whether Persia held Herat or not.

Lord Auckland, then fifty-one and not well versed in the mundane problems of military transport and supply, failed to understand the obstacle this vast tract placed in the path of an army invading India. Encouraged by irresponsible advisers, he saw the peace of his term of office threatened by war from the north-west.

His fears grew when in the later summer of 1836 he received from the Secret Committee of the East India Company in London a letter referring to Palmerston's anxieties about Russian advances towards Herat. It instructed him 'to watch more closely the progress of events in Afghanistan and to counteract the progress of Russian influence' in a quarter which could possibly interfere with the tranquillity of India.

The letter went on to say that he should deal with the situation by sending a confidential agent to Dost Mahommed and if necessary, on the basis of information later received, to decide 'that the time has arrived at which it would be right for you to interfere decidedly in the affairs of Afghanistan. Such an interference would doubtless be requisite either to prevent the extension of Persian dominion in that quarter, or to raise a timely barrier against the impending encroachments of Russian influence.'

'Interference', in this context could only mean war; and so the dispatch told Auckland that he should at the right moment decide whether or not it was advisable to invade Afghanistan. It put into the hands of this mild,'pacific and indecisive peer responsibilities with which he was unfitted to deal.

Responding to Palmerston's misgivings, Auckland decided at first that he ought to know more about the policies of the ruler of Afghanistan. In November 1836 he therefore assigned a young Scot, Captain Alexander Burnes, on what was said to be a commercial mission to Kabul, but which was in fact a secret political one—the assessment of whether Dost Mahommed sought friendship with Russia or England.

Brilliant and ambitious, Burnes is seen in portraits as a tolerably handsome person with watchful blue eyes and a perceptive expression in a round face whose dignity is marred by a small sensuous mouth. Though perhaps a little rash and impetuous for a diplomat, Burnes's exceptional linguistic ability, no less than a bold, enterprising spirit which went beyond bravery, had secured him rapid promotion in the East India Company. His travels in unexplored Afghanistan and Bokhara four years earlier had, moreover, brought him friendship with Dost Mohommed and made of him a celebrity while still in his twenties.

While Burnes was travelling unhurriedly to Kabul, Auckland was becoming more and more under the influence of three ambitious advisers in the Indian Political Service, each one of whom, besides such a confused and uncertain man, was dangerous. All three of them found themselves suddenly placed so as to be able to influence the great issue of peace or war at the side of this Governor-General who was utterly ignorant of India and its needs.

These three officials were William Hay Macnaghten, forty-three, Chief Secretary to the Indian Government; John Colvin, a much younger man, Auckland's official adviser on Indian affairs, and his private secretary; and third, Henry Torrens, his adviser on military matters. All three were former East India Company army officers, brilliant young men who had transferred to the political service, become specialists in Indian affairs and languages, and had become determined to influence the course of events.

Macnaghten was the most important of them. He had joined the political service from the Madras Cavalry in 1814. For fourteen years, from 1816, he had been first judge, then registrar of an appeals court. He had become a specialist in Hindu and in Moslem law and had published notable studies of the systems, while at the same time attaining fluency in Persian, Hindustani and four other languages commonly used in India. A hard-working intellectual, he was appointed assistant to the former Governor-General

Lord Bentinck in 1830 and chief of the Secret and Political Department—that is, of Foreign Affairs—in 1833. As Chief Secretary he soon became Auckland's most trusted adviser. His defect—an excess of ambition, optimism and impulsiveness—began to influence Auckland dangerously.

Burnes meantime, after a long and leisurely journey reached Kabul in September 1837. He was welcomed, and received, he relates, 'with great pomp and splendour by a fine body of Afghan cavalry, led by Dost Mahommed's son, Akbar Khan. He did me the honour to place me on the same elephant upon which he himself rode and conducted us to his father's court, whose reception of us was most cordial.'

Dost Mahommed had assigned Kandahar to Kohan Dil Khan, one of his many brothers, and, but for the independent principality of Herat, 400 miles west of Kabul, and about 100 miles from Persia, he had ruled the remainder of this turbulent country with a rod of iron for the past ten years.

Before his seizure of power he is said to have been as much of a philanderer as a warrior, addicted to sex orgies and drunkenness, but when once he held the kingdom he stopped the drinking. He also taught himself to read and write, made a public confession of past crimes, dressed carefully, sought to rule with justice by redressing wrongs and making himself accessible to the poorest petitioners. Such was his love of fairness, indeed, that people were said to exclaim: 'Is Dost Mahommed dead that there is no justice?'

Yet any monarch who ruled in Afghanistan had no choice but to adapt himself to the vices of the people. As the contemporary historian Sir John Kaye remarked: 'Once embarked in the strife of Afghan politics a man must either fight it out or die. Every man's hand is against him and he must turn his hand against every man. There is no middle course open to him. If he would save himself he must cast his scruples to the winds. Even when seated most securely on the *musnud*, an Afghan ruler must commit many acts abhorrent to our ideas of humanity. He must rule with vigour or not at all. . . . We cannot rein wild horses with silken braids.'

This, then, was the determined ruler by whom Burnes was received—a tall, muscular man whom portraits show with the marks of hardship on aquiline features, with large pensive eyes, benign expression and carefully combed beard all surmounted by a voluminous turban.

Flattered by his splendid reception, Burnes swiftly dropped all pretence that his interests were commercial rather than political, and thus seems to have played his hand too quickly.

He allowed the wily and experienced Afghan leader to sense that the British were anxious about Russia's ambitions in the region and the possibility that the Amir might encourage them. The outcome was that while professing sincere friendship for Britain, Dost Mahommed sought her help in regaining Peshawar from the Sikhs as the price of an alliance with him.

Then on 23 November 1837 events took a new turn. A Persian army, aided by Russian officers and artillery, laid siege to the independent Afghan province of Herat. The worst fears seemed now several steps nearer to being realised. The ruler of Afghanistan became more important in British plans.

Dost Mahommed at once gave concrete proof of his avowed feelings of friendship for Britain. His brother, Kohan Dil Khan of Kandahar, against the Dost's advice, had sent one of his sons to the camp of Mohammed Shah of Persia to welcome the invaders. Russian agents at the camp praised the emissary warmly for this action.

Realising that the British might believe he was behind this move, Dost Mahommed offered to Burnes to prove his loyalty by marching an army against his brother and deposing him.

Burnes advised against this, but his warnings, sent to Kohan Dil Khan with those of Dost Mahommed, caused the expulsion of the Persian emissaries there and forced Kohan Dil Khan to agree to act henceforward in harmony

with his brother and the British. Burnes, on his part, promised Kohan Dil Khan to pay his troops to defend Kandahar should the Persians threaten it. Here, he went beyond
what he was authorised to do, sound though the proposal
was.

At this juncture, the formidable Russian Foreign Minister,
Count Nesselrode was using Persia as the tool of Russian
ambitions and so avoiding committing his country directly
against Britain: the Persians were willing, with Russian
support, to seize what they could of their former territories
in Afghanistan; while Dost Mahommed wished to keep his
own throne secure, regain Peshawar from the Sikhs, if
possible with Britain's help, and make an alliance if he could,
with her rather than Russia.

Burnes, convinced now that Dost Mahommed was the
only man able to rule Afghanistan who could also be a
reliable ally of Britain, committed himself wholeheartedly
to this view in letters to Auckland. In one letter he wrote:
'The Ameer of Kabul has . . . declared that his interests are
bound up in an alliance with the British Government which
he will never desert as long as there is a hope of securing
one.'

Then, while awaiting Auckland's reactions, having inherited from his ancestor the poet Robert Burns a passionate
love of women, he enjoyed himself to the full with beautiful
Afghan and Kashmiri girls.

A Russian agent, Captain Viktevich now arrived in
Afghanistan, claiming to be an envoy from the Tsar.
Burnes was alarmed, but Dost Mahommed took little
account of it, refused to give the Russian more than one
formal audience and calmed Burnes with assurance that he
was sure his wished-for alliance with the English would
materialise.

But the interests of too many other people were at stake
for the hopes of Burnes and Dost Mahommed to materialise.
One of them was Claude Martine Wade, the pro-Sikh
British resident at Ludiana, in the Punjab, who strongly
favoured the restoration of the former Shah Shuja, mainly

because Dost Mahommed was a sworn enemy of the Sikhs. Wade seems to have set himself firmly against any British alliance with Dost Mahommed and thus he supported instead the restoration of Shah Shuja by military force.

Through Colonel Wade's hands passed all the letters of Burnes to Auckland in support of Dost Mahommed. Wade read the letters, sent them on together with flat contradictions of the facts and contrary arguments.

Thus, while Herat was under siege by the Persians—while a Russian agent was in Kabul, and while the Afghans in Kandahar were known to have shown friendship to the Russians and Persians, Wade's arguments—to which Burnes had no chance of replying—inclined the vacillating Auckland against Dost Mahommed. And an alliance with him would certainly have offended the Sikh leader, Ranjit Singh—whose friendship was necessary to the East India Company.

At this decisive moment, when peace or war hung in the balance, Auckland turned his back on the wiser voices of his Council in sweltering Calcutta and took himself off to the cool hill-station of Simla with Macnaghten, Torrens and Colvin—all of whom, by now, had a vested personal interest in an invasion of Afghanistan.

The initial results were first a letter from Auckland to Burnes, rebuking him for his wise offer of assistance to Kohan Dil Khan of Kandahar were he to be attacked by a foreign power and ordering him to revoke this promise. And secondly, to Dost Mahommed a rude and dictatorial letter —while Burnes was still assigned to Kabul—refusing mediation with the Sikhs over Peshawar and warning him not to ally himself with any other powers without the good offices of the Indian Government.

Dost Mahommed now understood that the Governor-General no longer thought of an alliance with Afghanistan. At once he feared the truth—that an attempt might be made to put Shah Shuja back on the throne.

Negotiations from that moment became hopeless, but Burnes stayed on in Kabul, openly cohabiting with Afghan and Kashmiri women and thus so offending the Muslim Afghans that his assassination was openly spoken of in Kabul. At the same time, in face of Russian promises, their agent Viktevich was paraded in triumph through the streets.

Burnes eventually decided to leave and on 26 April 1838 turned his back on the capital, seeing all that he had accomplished in his career destroyed. His efforts had come to nothing, his mission had in effect been sabotaged. War had begun to threaten.

Lord Auckland had let himself gradually be pushed from a policy of friendship with Afghanistan to a completely contrary one. Only a year before, in April 1837, he had written that 'the British Government had resolved decidedly to discourage the prosecution by the ex-king Shah Shuja-ool-Mulk, so long as he may remain under our protection, of further schemes of hostility against the chiefs now in power in Kabul and Kandahar'.

In repudiating Dost Mahommed's offers of friendship and inclining himself towards Shah Shuja, Auckland had moved far from that position. He was to go farther still. His advisers, alone with him at Simla, persuaded him that the time had now come for him to 'interfere'—as the dispatch from the Secret Committee termed it—in the affairs of Afghanistan. The next decisive step was taken. Colvin looked after the political and Torrens the military side of plans for a projected treaty between the Indian Government, Ranjit Singh—the Sikh ruler—and Shah Shuja, whereby with the co-operation of Ranjit Singh and a parcel of Sikh troops led by British officers of the Indian army, Shah Shuja should invade Afghanistan, depose Dost Mahommed and rule in his place. William Macnaghten took the proposals to the Sikh ruler and on 26 June 1838 the treaty, guaranteed by the British was signed.

Burnes arrived at Auckland's headquarters at Simla, on 20 July. He was met by Colvin and Torrens, who speaking of the Governor-General said anxiously: 'Please don't say anything to unsettle his judgement now that we've got him to go to war.'

Burnes, who might still have been able to impress the truth of Dost Mahommed's pro-British feelings upon the uncertain Auckland, and so avert war, unwisely said nothing to stop the military preparations. He had contemplated resigning, but a careerist first and foremost, he stayed on, co-operated, was rewarded with a knighthood. But eventually, in the disaster that was to come, he would pay for it with his life.

Chapter Four

The sheer logic of events soon forced Lord Auckland to commit British troops to the invasion in a way he had at first never contemplated. It was intended that Shah Shuja, having no troops of his own, should be assisted by Sikhs, who were not only hated by the Afghans but also, it soon transpired, unwilling to face their bullets in the grim confines of the Khyber Pass. So it looked as though the Shah would be dependent upon untrained irregular troops recruited to march into Afghanistan and secure the throne for him.

Burnes, who had now joined Auckland's Simla headquarters, assured the Governor-General and his three advisers, that this plan would surely fail—these troops would be unable to face Afghan opposition. British troops must be used to make the force effective.

Two British regiments, he suggested, would be enough to guarantee the safe return of the deposed monarch to his former kingdom. But this scheme, which to the non-military mind looked so easy, was vetoed by Sir Harry Fane, the Commander-in-Chief in India. He went to Simla and told Auckland that he would not allow so small a force to embark upon so dangerous an expedition, and that if the British intervened at all it should be with a powerful force. Apart from restoring Shah Shuja to this throne it would later have to move against the Persian army besieging Herat.

Auckland, who still lacked any clear-cut policy directive from England, and was in any case not the kind of man who could decide major issues for himself, now came under strong pressure from his advisers—Macnaghten, Torrens and Burnes, especially. The issue was simple, but difficult: commit British troops to the invasion, or give it up entirely.

Doubtless Auckland felt he had already gone too far to retire without loss of dignity; and in any case, the voices of prudence were far away.

So Auckland, this quiet, respectable peer, who had no taste whatsoever for war—who had been a makeshift political choice as Governor-General by the Whig government, replacing Lord Haytesbury, Ambassador in Moscow, named by their Tory predecessors—pallid Auckland then, yielded completely. He directed the assembly in India of a substantial British army for the invasion of Afghanistan—without consulting his Council in Calcutta and against the advice of Sir Harry Fane, who wanted consolidation of the British position in India before extension in the west.

India had now been at peace for many years. Liberal-minded Englishmen had high hopes that it would continue, so that England could do more for unhappy India than she had yet attempted. By assembling a big army and embarking upon a costly war Auckland banished such hopes. Having now to justify his war plans in face of hostile public opinion, he issued with bare-faced dishonesty a proclamation pompously named the Simla Manifesto, composed mostly of lies and evasions.

Having no genuine reasons for war with Dost Mahommed, he argued falsely that he was forced to send British troops against him because he had allied himself with the Persians in their Russian-inspired attack on Herat; because Dost Mahommed had attacked Britain's ally, the Sikh ruler Ranjit Singh—whereas he had in fact defended himself against a Sikh attack; and because his schemes and ambitions were a danger to India's north-west frontier.

All these events, he said, had caused a crisis, and after serious and mature deliberation, he was satisfied that pressing necessity as well as policy and justice warranted the British Government supporting the return of Shah Shuja to the throne—who, though in fact hated by the Afghans, he claimed was popular, in contrast to the present ruler Dost Mahommed, who he said was unfitted under any circumstances to be Britain's ally.

This monstrous document, practically made up of lies from start to finish, then ended hopefully: 'His Majesty Shah-Shuja-ool-Mulk, will enter Afghanistan surrounded by his own troops and will be supported against foreign interference and factious opposition by a British army. The Governor-General confidently hopes that the Shah will be speedily replaced on his throne by his own subjects and adherents; and when once he shall be secure in power, and the independence and integrity of Afghanistan established, the British army will be withdrawn.'

In England, a wave of indignation followed. Nearly everyone whose experience in war or politics counted, opposed it. Lord William Bentinck, Auckland's predecessor, called it 'an act of incredible folly'. Lord Wellesley, one of the greatest of Governors-General, pronounced 'this wild expedition into a distant region of rocks and deserts, of sands and ice and snow', an 'act of infatuation'. The great Duke of Wellington declared with prophetic insight that the result of once crossing the River Indus to settle a government in Afghanistan would be 'a perennial march into the country'.

But Auckland, who knew nothing of war, persisted, encouraged by the three officials at his side.

And then came an event that still could have saved the day—the news two weeks after his proclamation of 1 October that the Shah of Persia had raised the siege of Herat and that the Persian army had retreated. The immediate danger was past.

A direct protest to Persia by the British Government and the temporary occupation by the Royal Navy of the Persian island of Karak had caused this dramatic face-about. It changed the whole situation. No need existed now for an army to do all over again what words and one minor aggressive act had achieved. Persia, notwithstanding her Russian ally, had openly acknowledged British power and faced thereby both humiliation among nations and the heavy loss of a nine months' fruitless campaign.

Following this, a certain amount of trust—about as much

as can exist between checkmated diplomats—was restored between Lord Palmerston, British Foreign Secretary, and Count Nesselrode, for Russia. In response to a British note, Nesselrode had assured Palmerston that Russia had no offensive plans in the areas bordering on India's north-west frontier and that he believed Britain's and Russia's interests there were identical—to preserve peace and to confine themselves to commercial rather than political rivalry. For what it was worth, Palmerston had accepted this contention.

The expectation now was that the Governor-General would breathe a deep sigh of relief, countermand the military orders, let peace prevail and India prosper.

Not so, Auckland announced on 8 November 1838 both the raising of the siege and the continuance of the invasion 'with the view to the substitution of a friendly for a hostile power in the Eastern province of Afghanistan, and to the establishment of a permanent barrier against schemes of aggression upon our north-west frontier'.

Ham-handed in his attempts at statesmanship, Auckland had blundered hopelessly. First, he had made the fatal mistake of trying to play king-maker to a warlike and turbulent race, instead of coming to terms with their ruler. Secondly, ignoring the terms of his treaty with Shah Shuja, and Ranjit Singh, the Sikh ruler, he had committed British forces, instead of Sikhs to the invasion. Thirdly, he had disregarded the prudent warnings of his own commander-in-chief.

But Auckland and his advisers were living in a dream world. They genuinely believed that this invasion of the wild and mountainous home of a military race would be a grand tour in uniform accompanied by an eastern monarch and his court.

Auckland informed the Commander-in-Chief that Shah Shuja would lead this grandiloquently named Army of the Indus into Afghanistan, followed by the British forces, and that both would receive a 'welcome with general gladness' by the people there. How different it was all to be.

The organisation of the army went ahead. Planned to be

25,000 strong, it was composed of 14,000 of the Bengal army's best troops, 5,600 from the Bombay army and 6,000 irregulars recruited for Shah Shuja's own force—raw recruits mostly, trained and officered by the British. The Bengal contingent was assembled at Ferozepore in north-western India, under the command of Sir Harry Fane, who by now had serious misgivings about the entire adventure. General Nott and General Duncan were the two divisional commanders.

But the raising of the siege of Herat had reduced the army's objective to putting on the throne a puppet king, under the direction of William Macnaghten. Auckland decided that a smaller army was now adequate. Its strength was therefore reduced by one division, General Duncan's 4,500 men, and at this point Sir Harry Fane could stand no more. 'I do not think that for *this* my service is needed,' he wrote with some sarcasm to Lord Auckland, 'and I consider Sir Willoughby Cotton is quite competent to command. . . .'

Cotton was a cheerful old soldier of the Queen's army who had once been aide-de-camp to King George IV, but whose long service in India had made a little dull. 'I don't think Cotton has a mind which carries away much of verbal instructions,' Fane had caustically noted of him. Supreme command of the army was given to General Keane, with the Bombay force. Burnes, now Sir Alexander, in recognition of his co-operation, was appointed political assistant to Macnaghten, soon to become Sir William, on account of his having been appointed Envoy to the court of the monarch-to-be Shah Shuja.

Unusual was the power over the army given to Macnaghten and the political officers under his command—a group of ambitious young men seconded from their regiments to administer Afghanistan until the Shah had formed his own government.

The army, by directions of the Governor-General would first rely upon the political officers for its food, its camel and its horse transport and its fodder for them, in contrast to the normal method of supply by the military commissariat department.

But worse still, military operations in Afghanistan would be largely in the hands of the political officers, too—most of them inexperienced or incompetent.

The best troops would have deteriorated under this divided leadership. In time it was to become one of the main causes of the misfortunes of the Army of the Indus.

Chapter Five

The Army of the Indus now began moving towards its destiny in a cumbersome way. The 4,500 troops of the Bombay division were packed like sardines into the hellish nineteenth-century troopships at Bombay and shipped 500 miles north-west up the tropical Arabian Sea to Karachi, then a small fishing village. After a brisk naval bombardment to raze coastal forts that challenged right of entry—the area was then foreign territory, ruled by the Amirs of Sind—the force landed at Hajamro Creek near by on 3 December 1838.

Commanded by Major-General Willshire, under the overall command of General Keane, the army's commander-in-chief, the force was to march 300 miles north-east up the River Indus to meet at Shikapore the 9,500 men of the Bengal division, who would have marched 600 miles south-west from their depot at Ferozepore, which was barely 400 miles south-east of Kabul.

Thus, the Bengal army was to march 600 miles in the opposite direction to its main objective, Kabul, Afghanistan's capital, and then together with the Bombay army, march back another 600 miles north west up through Afghanistan, via Ghazni and Kandahar to Kabul again, a mode of operations which would have been splendid today, in a Marx brothers war film.

The original reason for this merry-go-round was that the southern entry into Afghanistan offered the quickest route to Herat, in the west, which had to be relieved soon, but when the Persians withdrew from this town the plans were unchanged because entry by the northern route directly to Kabul would have involved a march across Sikh territory—a move its ruler would oppose.

With the Shah's 5,000 ill-equipped and untrained troops included, the army now amounted to some 20,000, separated by about 800 miles of unfriendly territory.

When about to begin his march northwards, General Keane was shocked to discover, that the political officers had failed to build up provisions dumps, or secure camels and boats for carriage of his supplies and ammunition up the River Indus. For three weeks he was delayed, waiting; and for similar reasons the army at Ferozepore was delayed as well.

Sir Harry Fane, Commander-in-Chief India, who though not in command had remained to watch the course of events, was furious. 'Even an hour's delay is serious,' he protested to Auckland, 'and it is a great evil to the army to be delayed for want of common foresight.' And later: 'Supposing a reverse? What is to be the army's line of retreat? Magazines should be collected beside it. The safety of the army should be placed beyond doubt.'

But Auckland could only say lamely that he was concerned too, and that he had authorised General Cotton's troops, instead of the political officers, to requisition supplies by force in case of real necessity. With this minor concession to the cause of military efficiency the Bengal army at last set out on 10 December 1838 on its 1,200 mile journey to Kabul from Ferozepore—Shah Shuja and his ragged troops leading the splendidly equipped British force, so that he would appear to be in command.

These two armies were to be followed by a grand total of 40,000 camels and 60,000 camp-followers, that would stretch for 30 to 40 miles across country. For by custom no less than five camp-followers followed every Bengal army soldier and three those of the Bombay army.

They included doolie (stretcher) bearers, cooks, carpenters, personal servants, grass-cutters, camel-doctors and drivers, leather-workers, grooms, milk-girls, bellows-boys, saddlers, fiddlers, nautch-girls, blacksmiths, tailors, cobblers, and of course their wives and children. When a crisis came they would gravely handicap the army.

To carry the grain to feed 8,000 horses for one month 6,000 camels were required, but there were thousands more camels carrying ammunition and food for the troops and still more thousands carrying personal baggage.

'What a sea of camels! What a forest of camels' heads and humps and grain bags!' cheerfully wrote Lieutenant-Colonel Burlton, Commissary-General of the Indian army at this time. 'What plaintive moanings . . . ! What shouts of men! What resounding of sticks as the vast mass is driven slowly along, browsing as they go and leaving not one green leaf behind them.'

To describe this vast procession as vulnerable and un-manageable would be a truism. The system was a night-mare even for the most sybaritic commanding officer, and a few had protested vigorously, but uselessly against it. The whole system was, bag and baggage, part of the age-old scheme of things that the British had inherited in India.

'And so marched the Army of the Indus,' remarked the contemporary historian Sir John Kaye, 'accompanied by thousands upon thousands of baggage-laden camels and other beasts of burden, spreading themselves for miles over the country, and making up with their multitudinous followers of the camp one of those immense moving cities which can only be seen when an Indian army takes the field and streams into an enemy's country.'

The well-mounted 16th Lancers led the Bengal army, in tight short tunics of light blue, the sun glinting on the silver lace facings and silver buttons, the troopers' necks chafing in the constricting red collars. Captain Grant's troops of the Bengal Horse Artillery followed, with four horses to each of the four rattling cast-iron 6-pounder guns and shell wagons. Then came the lumbering camel-drawn howitzers, the long columns of red-coated infantry, more artillery, cavalry again and the long procession of lurching camels.

Sir Harry Fane had requested the officers to travel light, but General Keane had a personal baggage-train of 100 camels and Brigadier Arnold one of 60. Status apart from that of rank, was conferred by an officer's baggage-train. Dr.

Richard Kennedy, chief of the Bombay army medical staff, was accused of false modesty because he had only five personal camels.

'The officers,' noted J. H. Stocqueler, then editor of the *Bombay Times*, who camped at one time with the force, 'regarded the expedition as little else than an extensive pleasure promenade—an enormous picnic.'

They equipped themselves suitably with large field tents, carpets, complex camping equipment, books; wines, brandies and liquers by the crate; jams, pickles, cheroots, hermetically sealed meats; silver plate, crystal glass, crockery, candles, table-linen and mahogany furniture. One officer circulated an advertisement for a sideboard he wished to buy from among the furniture carried by his comrades.

The quantities of these good things were beyond belief. Stocqueler offered to leave a few boxes of cigars as a gift for the officers' mess in which he had stayed. He was politely advised that they would scarcely be valued. 'Our mess has two camel-loads of the best Manilas,' his informant said.

Stocqueler noted: 'Many young officers would as soon have thought of leaving behind them their swords and double-barrelled pistols as march without their dressing-cases, perfumes, Windsor soap and eau-de-cologne.'

General Fane, trying to reduce a camel train that stretched more than from London to Brighton, and having scant success with the officers, had ordered the infantry to carry their own packs instead of following the custom, in the killing heat, of clubbing together to hire baggage camels. But the exhaustion and sickness caused by this misguided order far outweighed the small savings on transport.

Beyond belief were the privations of the ordinary British soldier in India and of those who marched with the Army of the Indus to Afghanistan. They certainly contributed to the army's downfall. The soldier's pay was 7s. 6d. a week, less 1s. 10d. a week for his maintenenace, laundry, his 'necessaries' and 4s. for his food. The remaining 1s. 8d. was doled out to him in daily instalments.

His uniform might have been designed to hinder and

oppress him. In the stifling heat he wore a stiff, black leather stock round his neck to keep his head erect and his gaze ahead, a swallow-tailed coatee of heavy red serge with a tight collar and a hard black leather shako, or hat, tied firmly on by a tight chin strap.

Over his right shoulder hung a wide leather belt decorated with a regimental plaque and whitened with the same pipe clay with which he plastered his white trousers. From this belt, hung his bayonet, 16 inches of fluted steel. A cartridge belt attached on his right side to a waist-belt contained normally sixty 10-ounce balls for his Brown Bess musket, each ball wrapped in stiff black paper holding $4\frac{1}{2}$ drams of black gunpowder. In action, he tore the paper open with his teeth, primed the musket-pan with the powder rammed home the ball, fired and reloaded.

He carried in the grey canvas haversack which General Fane ordered him to carry across Afghanistan's scorching deserts a towel, soap, razor, a pair of boots, two leather neck stocks, two shirts, two pairs of marching socks, a pair of trousers, boot blacking, pipe clay, cooking utensils and enough bread when available to last him for a day or two. Compared with today's infantryman a light load, but only rarely is he unfortunate enough to have to march to the battle-front.

The British troops were mostly barely literate young country-men, preferred because they were stronger and more docile than urchins from the industrial slums. Their daily rations abroad was one pound of bread and three-quarters of a pound of meat—generally beef, but occasionally mutton or salt pork—an unhealthy diet. Through drinking infected water and eating the unwashed fruit they bought to supplement the monotonous boiled beef, they frequently suffered and died from dysentery, cholera and other diseases.

The War Office provided regimental canteens where the soldier could drink himself half crazy on raw alcoholic drinks like arrack—distilled from the coco-palm—sold at prices that brought a profit of more than £50,000 a year, but instead of being spent on the soldier's welfare this useful sum was seized by a greedy Treasury.

Discipline was harsh, often cruel and inhuman. Flogging with the cat-o'-nine tails was commonplace—nine cords 18 inches long, each about a sixteenth of an inch in diameter and each knotted at precise intervals with nine knots. Spread-eagled naked on the crossed halberds, a soldier was flogged for entering the barrack-yard drunk, even though drunkenness was unavoidable on the fiery liquor sold in the canteen; he was flogged for the insubordination that boredom and drunkenness caused—for being absent without leave, for selling his equipment and for untidy equipment. He even could be flogged for marrying without his C.O.'s permission.

Most officers disliked inflicting this punishment, but Queen's Regulations laid down when it was to be administered, as well as the number of lashes. If a soldier fainted or was said by the medical officer to be unfit for more, he was taken to the punishment cells and when he had improved, two or three days later, he was given the remainder.

Frederick, Duke of York, Commander-in-Chief in England, had in 1812 ordered regimental courts-martial not to award more than 300 lashes under any circumstances. Yet District and General Courts Martial were still free to award more than this—it could be as few as 25 or as many as 500, 1,000 or even the maximum of 3,000. Occasionally the victims died, but most recovered, became hardened to it, and proudly boasted of their endurance. One drummer claimed to have received 4,000 lashes in twelve months and a total of 26,000 in fourteen years service, which his officers confirmed.

The penalty for striking an officer, or for cowardice, or for refusing to carry out an order in face of the enemy was to be shot by a firing party of the soldier's own comrades. And though by no means as commonplace as flogging, this punishment was not at all rare.

Discipline then, was based on punishment for misbehaviour; and not until well into the nineteenth century was the system of good conduct badges and medals gradually introduced to encourage good behaviour and confer status. But it brought no more pay to the soldier as a reward and an inducement. A social outcast at home and abroad his life demanded rare fortitude to be endurable.

Why, then, was his morale so high in battle? What made him fight so doggedly? Iron discipline and very often the sheer love of fighting—for the soldier was a primitive man— but strangely enough patriotism as well. He had a pride in being British, in showing what he was worth, often a persistent obsessive belief that the enemy were a set of rascals who deserved punishment.

Officers in those days purchased their commissions, the cost depending upon the rank. It was established that after deducting the interest at five per cent a year upon what it cost to buy the commission, as well as regimental expenses, and income tax, an infantry ensign's annual pay came to £73; a lieutenant's to £85; a captain's to £108; a major's to £93 (despite his seniority) and a Lieutenant-Colonel's to £114. An ensign had at once to spend almost his entire first year's salary upon his uniforms and equipment.

Mostly officers were younger sons of country landowners, serving officers and clergymen, who generally, though not always, had some small private income. Without powerful friends or the money to purchase a high rank, promotion was tediously slow.

Should a senior captain, for example, die or be killed, the next in order of seniority moved up one, or sold the vacancy to someone else, and stayed put. In the artillery, where promotion depended upon seniority alone, the average time taken to reach captain's rank was forty years. The artillery officer in supreme command of the guns at Waterloo was still only a major twenty years later.

These, then, were the men and the conditions under which they served in the Army of the Indus. Troops of the Queen's army, they were taking their turn of service abroad in the empire. Their comrades-in-arms, the locally recruited sepoys, or Indian troops, both Moslem and Hindu, were by contrast all East India Company troops, organised in regiments commanded by the Company's British officers.

Hindu troops, it was agreed, should not be set beyond the borders of India, or over the sea, since this entailed for them loss of caste; nor should they be given beef as part of their rations—not even when it was called 'red mutton'. And in the 1830s Lord Bentinck, then Governor-General, had ruled that the sepoys were henceforward not to be flogged, though their British comrades could be—a ruling which caused furious resentment.

Normally, by respecting each other's attitudes and beliefs, the British and sepoy troops got on remarkably well together. It was usual to have mixed forces—the sepoys were believed to fight better alongside British troops, though this was a matter of argument.

Both races, however, being men of little education, depended on good leadership. Without officers who were skilled, brave and determined, their courage failed. The destiny of the army of mixed British and sepoy troops which invaded Afghanistan in December 1838 was to be ruled by this last need above all; for the power of the political officers over the military soon became apparent.

The columns moved slowly south-west across fine open country, presumably happy to have escaped the grim barrack rooms for a war which promised light-hearted adventure and loot. There were minor problems—some camels died through eating tamarisk leaves—the grain dumps were always short—some of the camel drivers vanished overnight with their baggage. But General Cotton finally reached the town of Rori where he intended to cross the River Indus during the third week of January with the force in good shape.

But for two weeks he was delayed while the rulers of this territory, the Amirs of Sind, were intimidated into agreeing to a treaty that squeezed huge sums from them by way of tribute to the puppet Shah Shuja and at the same time guaranteed they wouldn't harry the army's lines of communications.

Cotton set his columns moving again in mid-February, now facing the crossing of the swift-flowing Indus, some 500 yards wide at the point he chose. There seems in this force to have been an odd mixture of grave administrative incompetence and remarkable practical ability. No arrangements of any kind had been made in advance to get it across this challenging river. It arrived before the banks with no single thing except the drive of its junior engineer officers to help it across, the General seemingly being unaware of the vast problems of supply and transport.

The engineer officers, starting from nothing, organised the felling of timber and the weaving of rope for the construction of seventy-four large bridge boats, hundreds of wood platforms and anchors to hold the contraption in place across 500 yards of swirling water. Several times it was nearly swept away by a sudden rise in the river, sometimes the cables snapped, but finally some 38,000 troops and camp-followers, 30,000 camels, several thousand horses and cattle, the artillery and a long train of bullock carts crossed without loss of life. Captain Thomson, the chief engineer, 'was justly praised', as well he should have been.

The Bombay troops, marching north were delayed by similar lack of military foresight, lacking both reliable maps of the region—they did not exist—and knowledge of the terrain ahead through reconnaissance. They advanced and hoped for the best, and consequently were often delayed when the track had to be made passable for heavy guns. But eventually Keane reached Larkhana on 2 March and spent nine days resting. It was at Shikapore, a town of 6,000 mud houses and 30,000 people 40 miles north-east that General Cotton was to wait until Keane arrived to take command of the whole army.

Keane had become anxious about supplies and as early as 22 January had written to Auckland suggesting that Burnes and the political officers having failed to build up dumps of grain and forage and arrange water supplies, the advance from Shikapore to Quetta should be delayed until this had been done, but his wish was to be frustrated.

In the regions beyond Shikapore, known as the Pat, there was no water and no grass, not even the cicada singing in the infrequent dry scrub, only the barren salt-packed sand glittering in the hot sun like hoar frost, leading on to the dead mountains of the Bolan pass.

It was into this region, that General Cotton, disregarding his instructions, was now to launch his army and camp-followers—with barely enough food for the journey, no organised water supplies and practically no reserves of forage for his transport animals.

Chapter Six

Cavalry covering the rear of the Bengal force walked at a
snail's pace behind the rattling black-barrelled guns and
camped, on 20 February outside the unromantic town of
Shikapore. Here it was that the Bengal force was to await
the arrival of General Keane and the Bombay force, so that
the army could finally be united.

But these plans went by the board. Sir William Macnaghten produced a bombshell—he had just received the
news that the 'friendly' Afghans were about to occupy the
Bolan Pass, which dominated the route ahead to Kandahar,
and ambush the British. He urged General Cotton to march
at once across the intervening desert to frustrate this action.

Major Parsons, the Deputy Commissary-General, warned
of the food and forage shortage and pleaded with General
Cotton to keep the force at Shikapore for at least twenty
days, living as best it could off local provisions, while water
supplies and forage dumps were built up ahead.

One infantry brigade and a few guns could have held the
Pass against the Afghans with little difficulty while the main
force waited at Shikapore, but Cotton seems to have overlooked this.

He hastily issued orders for the force to divide into eight
columns and march two days later, on 22 February, at the
rate of one column each day, entering Afghanistan during
the 171-mile journey to Dadar, and thence onward another
86 miles through the blistering heat to Quetta.

The destiny of this expedition might well have seemed to
be pre-ordained among many of its God-fearing Victorian
critics. For error followed upon error, the generals seemingly
bent upon bringing it to disaster.

Macnaghten, having frightened General Cotton into an

advance that endangered his entire force and its transport now announced that he, Shah Shuja and that monarch's troops would after all wait and go forward through the Bolan Pass with General Keane and the Bombay army.

General Cotton marched with provisions for six weeks, leaving the same quantity stored at Shikapore for Keane's troops. Local chiefs had promised ten days' food at Dadar, at the head of the Bolan Pass, and twenty days' more at Quetta, on the far side of it, but these promises could not be relied on. And there were almost no reserves of food and fodder for the 3,000 horses and 30,000 camels. As Lieutenant Henry Durand, an engineer officer with the force remarked —'They were marched into this tract of country as if possessed of miraculous powers of abstinence.'

In a temperature of 100 degrees Fahrenheit hundreds of horses, camels and cattle died soon from hunger and thirst. The Afghans launched night attacks on the camp-followers and the baggage train—every camel lost deprived the force of a day's food for 160 men.

Cotton had fallen in with the wish of the politicals that his men should merely defend themselves, not counter-attack the raiders, frustrating as this was. But when the tribesmen grew bolder and attacked a hospital wagon, killing and wounding sick men, Cotton at last woke up and ordered the escorting troops to shoot the raiders on sight. In a protest symptomatic of the axiom of the politicals—that they were in friendly country—Burnes called this order 'bloodthirsty, and calculated to bring on a blood feud'—an outburst that Cotton was wise enough to ignore.

General Keane, when the Bombay force, too, endured these murderous attacks, would complain later to Lord Auckland: 'The political officers led me—and I suppose you —to believe that we should find the country friendly from Shikapore to Kandahar. . . . There was no hint that it was full of robbers, plunderers and murderers, brought up to it from their youth.'

Over the barren desert Cotton's force struggled forward, the host of half-starved camp-followers with the baggage-

train now in hopeless confusion. The advance guard reached
Sadar sixteen days later, on 10 March, but instead of ten
days' supplies there was hardly enough for one day.

The food situation had become really worrying, but now
near to the mouth of the 60-mile-long Bolan Pass, General
Cotton was obliged to order five days' rest to revive the
weakened animals enough to tackle the cruel march ahead
—for without capable transport animals the force would have
been immobilised, like a modern army lacking petrol for its
vehicles.

The passage of the Pass was costly. Hundreds of camels
dropped and died of starvation in the narrow track, or fell
in the wayside stream, tainting the water for those following.
And all the time hostile tribesmen staged ferocious night
attacks on the baggage trains, reaping a golden harvest.
Finally, on 7 March, the first column camped in a plain
south of Quetta and waited for the rest of the force to join
them.

A final count showed the loss of over 2,000 camels, carrying rather more than a month's food—a serious loss, for
almost none of the twenty-days' provisions promised the
political officers by local Afghan chiefs were available at
Quetta, nor were there any for sale locally.

General Cotton was now gravely embarrassed, for
General Keane had peremptorily ordered him on no
account to march beyond Quetta until he himself arrived—
and the cause of his embarrassment—Macnaghten's
warning of an ambush in the Bolan Pass—had proved false.
Yet instead of pushing on to Kandahar, where there was
more likelihood of obtaining provisions, he had now to wait
in enforced idleness for Keane, with his army eating its
remaining provisions.

On 28 March, nine days later, he was faced with the
stark fact that there were only ten days' rations in the camp
and almost no hope of obtaining any more. He had already
sent Major Craigie, Adjutant-General, to Keane—still
several days on the far side of Dadar—to tell him of the
danger in which his orders to wait at Quetta had put the

force. He probably hoped that Keane would undertake a series of forced marches so as to reach Quetta in a few days. But he was disappointed.

Keane wrote to say there was no object in leaving Quetta until Shah Shuja—whose column he had joined the day before, a day's march from the head of the Bolan Pass— arrived to lead the force into Kandahar. To have the Shah at the head of the force was now vital.

The route up into Kandahar led over the Khojuk mountain range—10,000 feet high and crossed by three passes. Cotton had many energetic officers who during these days of enforced waiting could thoroughly have reconnoitred them and returned before Keane arrived, with information about the most practicable one to enter. But Cotton neither took such action himself, nor assigned his officers to it. And the force paid for this inactivity.

With less than nine days' food in camp Cotton now had no alternative but to give his men short rations, but this he drew back from doing. He was, he said, 'frightened of causing discontent'. Captain Thomson the engineer officer, very alarmed now, went to the General and insisted that this was the only thing that would save them all from starvation.

And so the General carried out the captain's wishes, putting the troops on to half- and the wretched camp-followers on to quarter-rations.

Trying to keep alive upon things of such doubtful food value as fried sheep's skin mixed with a few grains of flour, the followers risked entering nearby Afghan villages with their pockets full of money to try to buy food. It was too tempting. Lieutenant Henry Durand noted: 'The inhabitants of the surrounding villages . . . became exasperated at the prospect of everything being eaten up by the halting multitude of troops, camp-followers and cattle; and finding the opportunity favourable for plunder, they deserted their villages and sought to indemnify themselves for any losses . . . by carrying off camels and by stripping and murdering camp-followers, who, though wanting food, were constantly found to have a good deal of money on their persons.'

The Bombay force meanwhile, in command of Keane, and reduced for various reasons to 7,000 British and Indian troops, about 500 of Shah Shuja's troops and several thousand of the inevitable camp-followers, struggled through the Bolan Pass in its turn, hindered by both the attacks of tribesmen and the rotting carcasses of camels, cattle and horses left by the Bengal force. Ten young tribesmen were caught and summarily executed by command of Keane on 19 March, the officer ordered to superintend this unpleasant task insisting upon written orders from Keane.

'The poor wretches had their elbows secured,' relates Dr. Kennedy, 'and were made to sit on the ground. Some resisted and, to keep them quiet, the execution party fastened their heads together by their long luxuriant hair, which served to secure them for their destruction. Two young lads seemed horrified to bewilderment by their fears and implored for mercy, seizing the feet and knees of the superintending officer, but they were made to sit down. Ere the fatal volley exploded they were endeavouring to embrace, leaning their heads against each other, weeping bitterly their last farewell. This was sad work and did no good: we were robbed and our camels stolen at every stage.'

A rough, short-tempered man, Keane was not much troubled about the methods he used to maintain security. It was war.

He rode ahead of the Bombay force at last and entered General Cotton's camp at Quetta on 6 April to find pinched and sullen faces.

He took over command and issued a surprising order of the day thanking General Cotton for the 'able and judicious manner in which he had led the Bengal force in highly creditable order into Afghanistan'.

But by pinning Cotton down at Quetta, Keane had seriously weakened the force on the threshold of an enemy country. In return he had gained the hollow triumph of Shah Shuja's being able to enter Kandahar at the head of the force. Perhaps he was guided by the words of Lord

Auckland's Simla Manifesto: 'His Majesty Shah Shuja-ool-Mulk will enter Afghanistan surrounded by his own troops and will be supported against foreign interference . . . by a British army.'

Auckland and Macnaghten had forecast a general welcome in Afghanistan for the force, yet not a single Afghan chief of any importance had come forward with his followers to join Shah Shuja. 'On the contrary,' says G. R. Gleig, the force's chaplain, 'the few whom consideration of policy had induced to seek his presence while yet at Shikapre, he had so disgusted by his coldness that they returned to their homes, and spread abroad tidings every way unfavourable.'

Keane now reorganised his divisional commands, putting General Cotton in command of the Bengal divisional infantry, known as the 1st Division, which up till then had been very efficiently commanded by General Nott; and General Willshire in command of the Bombay divisional infantry. General Nott, he planned to leave behind at Quetta with a mere brigade.

Nott, an able and experienced East India Company officer, was senior to both Generals Cotton and Willshire, who, like Keane himself, were Queen's officers. Now, in what he saw as a 'deadly hit' against Company officers, Nott found himself pushed aside to make room for them.

Hardly the man to accept such treatment willingly, he sought an interview with Keane, who told him that the Governor-General had ordered that command of the 1st Division must be given to Cotton—which Nott had good reason to know for a lie.

This rather comical interview then took a course which shows to what a disastrous peak of bitterness feelings between senior Indian and Queen's officers in this army had risen. Nott wrote it down afterwards.

'Your conduct is very extraordinary in an officer of your rank,' Keane began.

'Your Excellency is aware that I hold the Queen's commission of Major-General?' Nott responded.

'Yes.'

'I am therefore entitiled to the command of a division in preference to local Generals Thackwell and Willshire, and yet you have placed General Willshire in command of a division.'

'If you think yourself aggrieved, you can appeal to the Court of Directors, General Nott. I see clearly that nothing I can say will convince you.'

'No, Your Excellency, nothing that you *have* said on this subject can convince me.'

'You insult my authority.' Keane was bristling.

'I am not aware that I have; what I have said is my deliberate judgement, which nothing can change.'

Nott rose to go with the words: 'Well, Your Excellency, I trust I have left no ill impression upon your mind. I see the whole affair; I am to be sacrificed because I happen to be senior to the Queen's officers.'

'Ill impression, Sir! I will *never* forget your conduct as long as I live!' Keane shouted.

'Oh! Your Excellency, since that is the case, I have only to wish you a very good evening,' Nott responded.

The outcome of this interview seems like another stroke of fate. Nott, the ablest soldier in the army, was stupidly kept behind in the south with some 3,000 troops to guard the lines of communication, too far from Kabul to be of any use when the storm finally broke.

Keane's objectives now were an advance farther into Afghanistan to occupy the city-fortresses of Kandahar, Ghazni and Kabul and place Shuja on the throne. But Cotton having failed to procure him any information about which of the three passes he should choose over the Khojuk mountains ahead, Keane did possibly the only thing he could have done under the circumstances—he chose the one reported to have most water, marched on 7 April 1839, and blundered badly.

Chapter Seven

The advance began in the cool of the early morning when no hostile tribesmen were to be seen, but shortly after leaving camp the troops were alerted by repeated firing. It was the shooting of sixty cavalry horses, which were too weak from lack of food to march—an inauspicious start.

The Pass itself was reached a few days later and General Keane got out of his palanquin to ride ahead and reconnoitre this challenging 11-mile-long defile—a death-trap only 80 or 90 feet wide, rising from 6,800 feet to a summit of nearly 7,500 feet. The stony track, the rarefied air, the weakness of men and animals, all made the task of dragging through the 60-hundredweight 18-pounder guns and ammunition wagons practically impossible.

A long steep ascent with a sudden sharp left turn and at once a steeper hairpin turn to the right was followed by a long hard climb to the summit. Here there was worse—a dizzy one-in-three fall for 800 yards over a surface of loose broken rock with an occasional, sudden precipice. Captain Thomson's engineers had cleverly cut and blasted three separate paths—a narrow one for camels, another for men and horses and a wider one for the guns. Keane ordered the infantry and a camel-drawn battery of howitzers to march at 3 a.m. 13 April, then the camel baggage-train, cavalry and artillery.

Troops were to be told off to help drag the artillery across. Keane's order said: 'Only one camel can pass up at a time and H. E. impresses upon officers the necessity of having their own animals as well as those of the men as lightly laden as circumstances will admit. This will be the only mode of preserving their baggage as every camel that falls must be removed with his load out of the path. . . .'

But soon the underfed camels, grotesquely overladen, would fall, and die where they fell—the crystal glass and the silver plate would adorn the Afghan chiefs' bare mud forts and the tribesmen's hovels.

At 3 a.m. the bugles sounded—the long lines of Colonel Sale's red-coated 1st Infantry Brigade marched off, followed an hour later by the artillery and at six o'clock when the sun's rays were already hot, by Generals Keane and Willshire, the headquarters staff, their cavalry escort, retinues of Indian servants and the interminable baggage-train. Soon, the climb was so steep and the struggle upward so hard in the thin air that the baggage-train slowed to a snail's pace.

A 9-pounder gun then slipped over the edge of the road, rolling men and horses with it down a small precipice. By the time the gunners had replaced a wheel and man-handled the gun back a long queue had formed behind. Three or four miles to the rear, Brigadier Arnold, leading the cavalry, now floundered upon the tail of the baggage-train.

A dense mass of cursing men and bellowing animals soon blocked four or five miles of the Pass. Many of the camels dropped through sheer weakness, were shot where they fell —cavalry troopers then heaved them off the track and left them.

Bugles blew the halt to try to stop the confusion worsening. But by late afternoon it was clear that this horde of men and animals would be jammed together there for the rest of the day, a superb target for Afghan marksmen. Three companies of infantry were now ordered back to guard the supplies and ammunition still in the camp.

Through the press of guns, horses, troopers and camels, the infantrymen struggled and cursed their way, finally completing a chaos unmatched since armies first trod the arid mountains of Asia.

Far ahead, towards the summit, infantry working parties piled their arms and, stripped to the waist, grappled with the back-breaking task of manhandling the unwieldy guns on long drag-ropes up to the summit. Quite apart from their lack of weight and strength compared with oxen and horses, men were not made for tractive work. Four legs, it would seem, are essential, on a steep ascent especially, for a man must push forwards and upwards with one leg while he advances with the other. He falls easily and when one falls, many tend to fall with him.

Thus for the infantrymen bent at the drag-ropes and the wheels of the ponderous guns, blinded with sweat, slipping and scrambling upwards over the sharp shifting rock, panting in the mountain air, it was shattering labour.

They moved the guns forward inches at a time, then thrust stones behind the wheels to hold them. The sergeant shouted 'Heave!' and another foot was gained. After half an hour the exhausted men were replaced by another company of 100 men and the first breathless company fell out by the roadside to sip a little brackish water and lie flat on their backs.

On this first day only those of the infantry not needed at the guns, together with General Keane, the Headquarters officers, their several hundred servants and a fraction of the baggage came through the pass. They marched $2\frac{1}{2}$ miles the other side of it to the camp at Chaman Chokee, in a valley about 600 yards wide.

Commissariat animals loaded with supplies, the guns, the infantry, cavalry and 20,000 camp-followers spent the night jammed together in the Pass, testifying to the un-reality of General Keane's ideas about the mobility of his army.

The next day too, the infantry bent to their Herculean task, and despite the shortage of food and water, despite dust, heat and flies, their morale stayed high. As each gun and its ammunition wagon creaked to the summit, the gun crew attached brakeshoes to each wheel, reversed the ropes on the drag-links of the axle-hubs and manhandled one gun at a time down the dizzy slope from the summit and thence by degrees to the plain, where once more the horses took over.

But for all their sweat and muscle, the three or four

thousand infantrymen in small teams toiled for a week hauling 18-pounder guns, the 8-inch mortars and the 24-pounder howitzers over the Pass—not until 21 April were all the guns finally manhandled down into the plain.

Keane was lucky—one Afghan chief with a few hundred resolute marksmen could have brought the entire force to a standstill at this time by merely shooting down the camel transport. But Dost Mahommed was not loved by all; the flame of patriotism hardly burned as yet and the force was troubled only by the attacks of individual tribesmen.

Among the ammunition brought over for the army were 2,000 18-pounder shells, 10,000 rounds of smaller calibre artillery shell, more than $1\frac{1}{2}$ million musket rounds and no less than 425 100-lb. barrels of gunpowder.

An exact list of what was lost during the seven-day struggle was never made. Losses did include 27,000 musket rounds, 14 barrels of gunpowder—some of which were blown up to prevent the Afghans getting it—and about 3,000 camels who dropped over precipices, were shot when they fell down through exhaustion or were stolen.

Yet the crossing of the Khojuk Pass by the Army of the Indus ranks as one of the unsung triumphs of British military history—an epic of strength and determination and a tribute to the reputation of this army that subsequent disaster could not diminish. Henry Durand, an engineer-lieutenant with the force, rightly observed, more than 100 years ago: 'The patient endurance of the modern soldier in honourless labour merits praise as high as that bestowed upon the iron soldiery of Rome . . . and such praise was fairly won by the European regiments of the Bengal Army . . .'

Shuja and Macnaghten, having crossed the pass on 19 April had the Shah's brightly coloured pavilions and tents pitched a few hundred yards from the British camp. One evening, there was a sudden thunder of hooves. A dozen Afghan horsemen tore into the confused crowd of camp-followers, shot down twelve men, seized two women and flung them across their saddles then drove off two caparisoned elephants—the Shah's personal mount and one lent by him to Macnaghten to sustain the envoy's dignity. The raiders disappeared over the crest of the surrounding hills with their prize—and the Shah's troops had not the courage to give chase.

Only a few months earlier, Shaj Shuja had told the Indian Government in a letter: 'The Ghiljee, Dooranee and other tribes are ready with heart and soul to serve me.' And now, when he had only just set foot in the country, backed by a powerful army, they had murdered his followers, stolen his elephants and abducted women. It was hardly the welcome he had expected. He was depressed and nervous about the future.

He tried to reassure himself by an official tour of the British camp in his capacity as monarch—'a rather stout man of middle height with a long thick neatly trimmed beard dyed black to hide the grey', noted Lieutenant Henry Havelock, who, twenty years later, as General Havelock, won fame in the Mutiny.

'He was borne on men's shoulders in a gilded litter fenced from the sun by a kind of circular dome, guarded by about sixty attendants in scarlet armed with javelins or drawn sabres, some carrying silver sticks, other shouting their master's titles and all running along at a fast pace. The long caps worn by his retinue were the most unusual—red cloth ornamented by long horns of black felt which made them look like Lucifer.

'His skin is darker than most Afghans and his features if not decidedly handsome are not unpleasing; but his expression suggests a mixture of the timidity and duplicity often found in men of the ruling circles in southern Asia. His manner towards the English is gently calm and dignified, without haughtiness; but his own subjects complain of him as cold and repulsive even to rudeness.'

This last remark is something of an understatement. Moolah Shikore, Shuja's aged and diseased Chief Minister, or Vizier, shuffled around minus his ears. The official had offended him some years before, so Shah Shuja had ordered them to be cut off.

So far none of the chiefs had allied themselves with Shuja but the next day, 20 April, a party of about 200 horsemen appeared over the hill crest some 500 yards away. When a few warning shots were fired by sentries the horsemen halted and one of them boldly rode ahead alone across the plain to Shah Shuja's camp.

He was Haji Khan, chief of a large independent Afghan clan and a man, noted Major Hough, Deputy Advocate-General to the army, 'of considerable note in the country, having distinguished himself in the field and counsel. . . . Dost Mahommed is known to have said that the only mistake he committed in regard to this man was not having taken his life.'

Haji Khan was notorious even among Afghans for his intrigue and faithlessness. Hearing of the size of the British army, he had deserted his Afghan brethren and hastened to be the first to pay homage to Shah Shuja. Armed to the teeth with a pair of brass-buttoned flint-lock pistols, an Afghan knife and a *tulwar* with long curved blade, he prostrated himself before the delighted Shuja, the gold fringe of his turban touching the ground, his baggy cotton trousers slipping up at the ankles to show his fine leather half-boots.

The submission of this chief, notorious though he was, delighted the Shah, who ordered that his followers should be allowed to approach and pitch their tents in the Shah's camp.

Haji Khan, says Hough, told the Shah about the plans of the Kandahar chiefs. He said they were going to make a night attack yesterday on the British camp, but that he told them that *they* might expect to be attacked themselves; '"You have carried off two of their elephants; the English are not the people to allow this to be done with impunity. They will march with a large force and guns against you and you are unequal to a contest with such troops. Stay where you are and I will go and see if I can find out from what direction they are coming." I got them to retire, I then moved off with my party and so got rid of them. And I have now come to join your Majesty!'

Such an open confession of treachery was hardly attractive, but Shuja had to be content with whatever allies he could get. Later this day two lesser chiefs with a few hundred more cavalry rode in, paid homage to the Shah and pledged military aid.

These defections to the Shah appear to have unsettled the ruling chiefs of Kandahar, Kohan Dil Khan and his brothers, who were all brothers of Dost Mahommed. They waited for two days, uncertain whether to attack or not, then deciding against it, retreated inland towards Ghirisk, a fort 75 miles away on the other side of the Helmund River, rather than join Shuja against Dost Mahommed. Haji Khan, a doubtful ally at best, had at least saved the British a battle when weakened cavalry and artillery horses could easily have paralysed these arms and led to defeat.

A stretch of waterless desert now lay ahead. Keane had no alternative but to advance and make the best of it. He set the army moving again at daybreak on 21 April. The temperature rose to 120 degrees, the wells found along the route contained only undrinkable muddy saline water.

'At 3 p.m. no water in camp,' Major Hough noted. 'Thermometer in the tent at 3 p.m. 102 degrees; in the sun 130 degrees. Great suffering among the soldiers, European and native, and the cattle. . . . The artillery horses beginning to knock up; no grain and very scanty forage.'

Next day, before sunrise, the force marched over a mountain pass of broken stony ground. 'The country after quitting the pass had such great ascents and deep descents, that it represented a sea of rocks and stones,' Hough noted. 'As you ascended you lost sight of the troops descending and when at the top of the ascent, you could not see those in the descent, to the front or rear, unless close on the brow towards it; thus we could only see the troops near us; the rest were lost to our view.'

The cavalry suffered worst, and in the blazing heat of the afternoon Brigadier Arnold marched ahead to find water, his horses having been without any the whole day and little the day before.

The heat bounced back off the stony waste and after five or six miles the horses could barely walk. The troopers dismounted, led them by the bridle, even goaded them with lances to prevent them lying down to die in the heat, but several dropped dead.

At last a patch of green came into view and soon the cool gleam of the River Dori. Scenting the water, the horses stampeded weakly towards it—and now occurred a desperate race between animals and men, for the troopers were frightened that the water might be scarce and the horses would drink it all.

But there was plenty of water—too much. Some of the animals toppled weakly down the banks, fell into it and drowned through sheer weakness. That night the army camped beside the river, expecting the next day to make a formal entry into Kandahar with the Shah at their head.

But Macnaghten and Shuja, determined to show a bold front, led the Shah's troops in a night march on the city without even the courtesy of a message to General Keane. A salute of guns in honour of the Shah's entry at daybreak was the first the surprised Keane heard of the event. Fuming, he wrote an immediate protest to Auckland about an act which endangered the Shah's life and the success of the entire enterprise.

Fortunately, the Afghans were avoiding resistance at this stage. 'The king was surrounded by his loving subjects and his ragamuffin soldiers,' Lieutenant Henry Fane wrote, in a sarcastic letter to a friend, 'but by very few men of rank or consequence.'

The mob cheered the ruler they knew to be a British puppet imposed upon them by British bayonets, yet when the price of grain and other food soared as a result of the approaching armies, their smiles changed to open indifference and secret hostility.

By 4 May the gardens outside the walled city of Kandahar were gay with the white tents and fluttering pennants of the entire force of 15,000 troops, as well as the small brown tents and stalls of nearly 50,000 camp-followers, while 10,000 camels and 3,000 horses as well were tethered near by.

But Keane's army was a sorry reflection of the proud force it had been at its Indian bases, for since 29 March it had been that unlikely body, an army on half-rations with its horses on half-rations, or less, too. The Bengal contingent had marched 1,005 miles in 137 days in following the plans of Lord Auckland's armchair strategists in India.

But at least the force had occupied Kandahar peacefully and had gained the first of its objectives—a reliable base in Afghanistan. Keane was now well placed to carry out his remaining ones, which were: the capture of the ex-chiefs of Kandahar, who were likely to become a focus of future resistance to Shuja; the defeat of Dost Mahommed, and the capture of the fortresses of Ghazni and Kabul; the enthronement of Shuja and the destruction of any other resistance to him.

Shuja was duly proclaimed Shah a day or so later during a grandiose display staged to impress the indifferent Afghans with British military power.

But the army—so far engaged only in fighting the climate, the terrain and a few tribesmen—was soon to have to prove itself in action against troops traditionally known for their zeal in battle. And worst of all, the errors of the past had made Keane desperately short of food.

Chapter Eight

Three urgent needs faced General Keane, camping in the fierce heat with his army outside the ancient city of Kandahar. These were: to build up the strength of men and animals by rest and plenty of food; to lay in reserve stocks of grain and store cattle and to buy horses and camels to replenish transport.

All of these needs presented problems. The wheat was not ripe; the little left in the granaries at Kandahar had become enormously dear. Moreover, a convoy of 2,000 camels expected from Shikapore with 300 tons of it had arrived with only 60 tons.

Keane was forced to keep his troops on half-rations when he wished to strengthen them by giving them all the food he could. In face of their meagre diet the troops stuffed themselves with the fruit which could be bought so cheaply in Kandahar—plums, pears, pineapples, apricots, nectarines. Many of them as a result were hit by a mild form of dysentery, so their health instead of improving tended to get worse.

At the same time no less than £300,000 was spent in the first ten days in Kandahar buying camels, horses and a few store cattle. Soon the money chests were all but empty and local bankers were refusing to negotiate loans—though there was no question but that they would be honoured.

Then reliable Afghan secret agents brought reports that, unlike his brothers, the rulers of Kandahar, Dost Mahommed intended to fight the British and was then deploying a large army in the field between Ghazni and Kabul. This army was said to be daily strengthened and made ready for action.

For want of proper food supplies Keane's force was unable

to march on and attack while the enemy was still vulnerable. He was thus reaping the first bitter fruits of marching his army more than 1,000 miles into hostile territory without making solid, sure and certain arrangements to feed it. Lord Auckland's faith in the assurances of his political advisers—that friendly chiefs would supply food to the invaders—had made the army a hostage to fortune.

On 11 May Keane sent a force under Brigadier Sale to attack the hostile Kandahar chiefs in their fortress at Ghirisk. So bad was the army's health that he had to find fit men—1,700 infantry, artillerymen and cavalry—from seven different units. He was then forced to send them on a journey of 160 miles there and back with a likely battle on arrival on half-rations for only twenty days. Sale's orders were to slaughter the chiefs and the garrison should they resist.

Meantime, the so-called friendship of the Kandahar people to the force had given way to open hostility. Camp-followers and camel-men were frequently murdered. Thieves stole camels and horses, then sold them back again to the army. When the thieves—who often killed as well—were caught and ordered by Keane to be hung, Macnaghten, on Shah Shuja's behalf, countermanded the executions—it would antagonise the people.

Wrathfully, Keane protested in a latter to Lord Auckland: 'The country round Kandahar is as full of robbers as Kuch Gandava; and the King's name goes for nothing outside the palace gates unless backed by an overwhelming force. Robberies and murders go on daily and nightly, and, as my correspondence with Mr. Macnaghten will show, I am precluded from doing justice to those who look to me to protect them and the property of the government.'

Macnaghten insisted that these forays were the work of individual tribesmen and in no way reflected the genuine feelings of the people, which, he continued to insist, were friendly. But towards the end of May two officers, Lieutenants Inverarity and Wilmer, were returning from a fishing expedition, upon which they had gone unarmed, contrary to orders, when they were attacked by a party of Afghan swordsmen. Wilmer beat off his attackers with a stick, but Inverarity was so badly wounded by sword cuts that he died before sunset.

Keane's fears for his security in obviously hostile country must now have increased tenfold. Impatiently, he sat in his spacious tent in the beautiful old garden blooming luxuriantly below the walls of Kandahar, wrote angry letters to Auckland and waited for news of the arrival of the expected food and money he needed to be able to move again.

A camel convoy carrying 750 tons of grains and another with 10 lakhs of rupees (£100,000) were now both overdue. Keane feared that they might have fallen into the hands of Afghan raiders or have been intercepted by detachments sent out by Dost Mahommed. Early in June he sent a small but powerful force of cavalry, artillery and infantry to find and protect them.

Brigadier Sale had meantime returned from his expedition to Ghirisk at the end of May. He had crossed the River Helmund on rafts made of empty rum casks, only to find that the fort was deserted and that the hostile Kandahar chiefs had fled and taken refuge—it later turned out—in Persia.

Macnaghten, anxious for an advance into the country and an end to the campaign, urged Keane to march at once with the Bengal division only, leaving the Bombay division at Kandahar to follow on with the rations and treasure when these arrived.

Macnaghten assured Keane that there would be no danger in advancing with a smaller force, because he would personally stake his credit that not a single shot would be fired against the King on his march to Kabul.

It was stupid advice but Keane, equally tired of waiting, at first agreed, but before issuing orders to the troops, whom he had placed in readiness to march on 1 June, consulted his confidant Captain Thomson, the engineer officer. Thomson bluntly reminded him of one simple fact—that he, not Macnaghten, was responsible for the army's success or

failure, and he advised Keane 'to consider whether he had
found the information hitherto given by the political department in any single instance correct'.

Keane's hair must have stood on end when Thomson
thus revealed the possible danger into whom he had nearly
let the plausible Macnaghten lead him. He immediately
warned Macnaghten that he had changed his mind and that
the entire force would march together when the rations
arrived.

A day or two later, on 10 June, he also told Macnaghten
in a letter that he intended to form his own intelligence
department, because at present he was practically without
one. 'I have never seen the like in any army,' he protested.
'The Indian government differs from others, and tries to do
more by policy and negotiation than by the sword. You have
given me every assistance, but, after I leave this, I feel it will
be proper for me to have my own intelligence department.'

Keane, who already had won back procurement of supplies from the political department to his own military
commissariat, thus took one more step in his efforts to free
the army from the paralysing control of the political
officers.

On 1 June he issued the order of march to Kabul, placing
the troops in a state of readiness, but, of all things, ordering
the four 18-pounder siege guns to be left behind at Kandahar. These guns were designed for battering down strong
fortifications.

At the time, Keane's reasons for this were based on Macnaghten's positive assurances that the army would not be
opposed at Ghazni; and in the unlikely event of opposition,
upon an assurance from Captain Thomson that the walls at
Ghazni—though regarded by Asians as unassailable—did
not need such powerful guns as the 18-pounders to breach
them; and, finally, by a plea from Brigadier Stevenson, the
artillery commander, that his transport animals were still
not equal to the task of hauling these heavy guns. Keane is
reported to have agreed in a flash of temper.

Later, having decided that he was unable to rely upon

Macnaghten's military intelligence he made no reassessment but accepted Thomson's second-hand information about the walls of Ghazni—even when reports came through that Dost Mahommed had sent his own son to organise and strengthen the defence.

Brigadier Stevenson's plea that it would be hard to get the guns there, he could have brushed aside—bearing in mind the tremendous efforts over much harder terrain to haul them to Kandahar. The only question remaining was—should he gamble on the normally reliable Thomson's information—even though, if the gamble were to fail, his force would face destruction?

A simple analysis, but Keane either failed to make it or too readily accepted the opinion of his subordinates, and having once done so failed later to countermand his orders. And so the big 18-pounder guns were to be left behind at Kandahar.

Meantime, the situation improved with the safe arrival on 8 June of a convoy with 10 lakhs of rupees (£100,000). But later, the detachment he had sent out to protect the food convoy returned without even finding it. Keane impatiently sent out another—a body of irregular Afghan cavalry in the command of a freebooting chief named Uzeem Khan.

The vast food convoy of 3,000 camels toiling through the scorching mountains and deserts of southern Asia had in fact become a vital target for Dost Mahommed, who knew well enough that without it the British army might starve.

He determined to stop it reaching them, but instead of attacking Surwar Khan, the leader, and his followers, who had contracted to bring to to Kandahar, he sent agents to persuade them to come over to him with the camels and their loads.

Disguised as camel-men these agents quietly and persistently spoke of the great rewards that would follow were they to desert the British and join Dost Mahommed. Then Uzeem Khan with his 200 swordsmen arrived on the scene. More than half Surwar Khan's men had already opted for

Dost Mahommed, and the leader himself was wavering.

Uzeem Khan swore that he and his men would oppose this treachery with their lives. They won the day. All Dost Mahommed's agents but one fled, and this man Uzeem Khan made prisoner.

Thus, by great firmness and a vigilance which kept his men night and day on the alert, he defeated Dost Mahommed's emissaries in their efforts to divert the convoy. On 23 June, the 3,000 camels laboured at last into Kandahar under Uzeem Khan's watchful eye.

Keane, aware of the zeal and bravery the Afghan had shown, had him brought to his tent, warmly thanked the bearded, turbaned warrior and presented him with a handsome pair of English matchlock pistols together with his price for the job. The affair was a notable instance of Afghans fighting willingly and ably for the British against their own countrymen—probably an outcome of the hostility of the different tribes towards each other, and of the lack of a devoloped and constant national feeling among them.

Believing now that at last he had enough grain to march with full bread rations all the 190 miles to Kabul, Keane joyfully issued marching orders for two days' time, 27 June. But to his utter fury, the camel-men flatly refused to go a step farther—their wives and families, they pleaded, were in Dost Mahommed's power and would certainly be harmed were they themselves known to have accompanied the invading army.

Vainly, Keane stormed and threatened. The most that Surwar Khan, their leader, would do was to sell his camels to them, but without drivers the camels were useless. Keane was now faced with a choice of either buying the camels and then waiting until enough drivers could somehow be found while the army waited eating its rations in idleness and the enemy grew stronger; or, pushing on and hoping for the best and this, in an apparent fury of impatience he did, deciding to march as he had planned on 27 June, leaving the grain for which he had waited so long in

store at Kandahar, together with the 18-pounder guns. A
force of 2,000 he left as a garrison.

His army was now in desperate straits for food—there
was barely enough to march the 190 miles to Kabul at 10
miles a day and the fortress of Ghazni lay some 100 miles
ahead with Dost Mahommed's army beyond it.

Keane's actions and letters all confirm that he was an
impetuous, quick-tempered man who embarked on a
course of action after only the most superficial consideration. But once having made up his mind he stopped worrying and hoped for the best.

Thus he let himself be convinced that he could deal with
Ghazni with light artillery. As for grain—well, it was
harvest time up in the Afghan highlands and doubtless it
would be possible to buy or requisition some. He issued an
order, headed *Supplies on the March*: 'Every encouragement
must be given to the people of the country . . . to bring in
grain and other supplies and officers Commanding Regiments will assign some spot in the vicinity of their standard
. . . for the people to sell their goods in. A steady N.C.O.
must be present with them, throughout the day, to see that
they are not maltreated . . .' It will be seen how little disposed were the villagers to sell, however.

The moon was favourable, so the *assembly* was sounded
soon after midnight on 27 June and the men of the first
column of the Bengal force—the headquarters, the cavalry,
three batteries of artillery and a brigade of infantry, about
3,000 men altogether—poured from their tents, to begin the
first stage of the march to the fortress, about 100 miles
north-east in the highlands.

A long column of light blue, the cavalry brigade under
Brigadier Arnold led the way, made up of the 2nd and 3rd
Regiments of Light Cavalry, both Indian, stiffened by Her
Majesty's 16th Lancers. Headquarters, with the three
Generals, Keane, Cotton and Willshire, came next, in the
first column, followed by the infantry in their thick, red
broadcloth swallow-tail coatees, high black leather shakos
with brass-covered chin straps and white duck trousers

stiff with pipe clay—probably still wet from last night's application. After them rumbled the batteries of artillery, 6-pounders, 9-pounders, 24-pounder, howitzers and mortars—forty guns in all, with their attendant carriages and ammunition wagons.

The Ghilzye tribe inhabited the country through which Keane now marched. They were hostile—two weeks earlier Shah Shuja had sent them 10,000 rupees (£1,000) and a Koran, the traditional way among the Afghans of seeking allegiance. The money was for 'shooing the horses', or to enable them to prepare for the march.

Had they sworn allegiance on the sacred book, and had kept it, together with the money, he would know that they supported him. But they kept the money and contemptuously returned the Koran.

So it was no surprise when on either side of the column detachments of Ghilzye cavalry appeared, waiting for the right time and place to attack. Keane ordered cavalry detachments at the front and rear and on the flanks of the column to be strengthened and to march with increased vigilance.

But despite other rumours that a large-scale attack by Dost Mahommed was imminent, the tremendous heat was the worst enemy, taking the bigger toll of men and animals than the *jezails* of hostile tribesmen.

On the eighth day the army marched at 2 a.m., when the temperature was already 76 degrees and a gale of hot wind scorched the men's nostrils, dried the sweat on their faces and drove hot dust into their eyes.

By 1 p.m. it had reached 120 degrees, a blaze of heat in which the stony landscape shimmered and the hovering vultures were the only sign of life. Soldiers went purple in the face, saw their comrades and the landscape dissolve into a flickering kaleidoscope and fell vomiting with heatstroke. They were picked up by the *dhoolie* bearers, but lacking shade few survived the over-mastering heat.

Keane ordered the two columns behind to close up by forced marches and on 20 July the entire army encamped at Nani, only a day's march away from Ghazni.

Meanwhile, Dost Mahommed was doing his best for the defence of his throne and country. One of his sons, Hyder Ali Khan, he had sent to Ghazni with orders to build up the four gateways in the great 70-foot walls of the city, clear the deep moat surrounding them, strengthen the fortifications and lay in enough food for the 3,000 fighting-men and the citizens to sustain a six-months' siege.

His other son, Akbar Khan, a ferocious young warrior who was later to show himself am implacable enemy of the British, he sent to the Khyber Pass to incite the tribes there against the force of Sikhs that Colonel Wade was about to march through from Peshawar against him.

Dost Mahommed, according to Henry Durand, calculated that Ghazni would hold up Keane long enough for him, aided by the Ghilzye tribes, to attack the besieging force with superior numbers and under favourable circumstances. The strategy was sound, except that it was based on the false assumption that Keane had all the provisions he needed.

In fact, when he reached Ghazni, Keane had only enough for two days—and no heavy artillery. Unless there was some way out in a desperate do-or-die attack, the army was doomed.

Chapter Nine

Among General Keane and his staff early on the morning of 21 July there can have been little devil-may-care ardour for battle—rather tension and anxiety marking the sweaty faces beneath the tall shakos as they rode out ahead of the army to reconnoitre Ghazni. And no sound but the creak of leather, the jingle of steel cavalry scabbards and the drumming of horses' hooves.

The time for words had passed weeks ago when Keane had taken the ill-considered decision whose results he was now frantic to see. At that moment, as he jolted uncomfortably in the saddle, Keane's responsibility for leaving behind his heavy artillery must have weighed heavily upon him.

In his younger days John Keane had been called 'the fortunate youth' because his career was generally believed to have been founded more upon good luck and influential friends than upon ability. In 1794, his father, M.P. for Bangor and Youghal, had bought him at the improbable age of thirteen a captaincy in a newly formed regiment. Promptly, the regiment was disbanded and lucky John was sent home for five years on half-pay.

With this valuable military experience behind him and still only seventeen, he was appointed captain in the 44th Foot then in Egypt, where he served as aide-de-camp to Lord Cavan, Commander-in-Chief of British forces there. Lacking any more military know-how than what he had learned in this office, Keane four years later was made a major in the 60th Royal Americans, but he continued to serve Lord Cavan in Egypt and Malta for the next two years, after which he was able to purchase a lieutant-colonelcy in the 13th Foot. He served with this regiment for several years in Ireland and later commanded it at the capture of Martinique from the French in 1809—his first taste of real soldiering.

Thereafter, his military ability was tested and found wanting, but good fortune and promotion still attended him. In 1813 he joined Wellington's army as a brevet-colonel and commanded a brigade in the Peninsular War. But never once did that great commander deign to mention Keane's name in his dispatches.

Two years later, in January 1815, commanding a British brigade in the American War (begun in 1812), he led a much criticised, unsuccessful attack on New Orleans, where he was wounded. He was appointed later that year to command a British infantry brigade of the army of occupation in France after the defeat of Napoleon—an appointment, lacking any stern tests, in which Keane should have done well, yet in 1817 Wellington was obliged to remove him.

For six years, until 1823, Keane languished at home on half-pay, but in 1823 good fortune and helpful friends once more intervened and he was posted off to Jamaica to command British troops there for seven years.

From this command he was raised at the ripe age of fifty-three to the prized post of Commander-in-Chief Bombay—a total stranger to command in India, with its racial, religious and military problems that many officers had learned to understand only after years of service there. Over the heads of officers like General Nott, who had spent their lives soldiering in India with success, Keane's influential friends or his good luck won him this prized appointment.

And now six years later, nearly sixty, he found himself leading this grim campaign in Afghanistan. Would his good luck, he must have wondered, hold out? Or would the grave and serious military errors he had committed shatter it and explode for ever the reputation of a dashing and capable commander which he had tried to foster in India?

The aim of Afghan marksmen in the gardens surrounding the great fortress drew closer and their rounds whistled nearer. Keane and his party turned about and retreated out of range to wait for the army's advance columns. Keane knew all he needed to know for the moment—the fortress was formidable and it would be defended.

Soon was heard the rumble of the artillery on the road, the drumming of the cavalry horses on the right and the steady tramp of the infantry on the stony ground to the left. The clouds of dust would have signalled to the Ghazni garrison the approach of a powerful army.

'Keane,' noted Henry Durand, an engineer-lieutenant with the General's party, 'saluted with occasional shots from the Afghan skirmishers, had not to wait long before the heads of columns came into sight.'

The General now ordered two companies of infantry to drive the Afghan marksmen from the gardens while the artillery placed a few guns where they could hit the fortress to draw Afghan fire and see how well it was defended.

Captain Graves and Lieutenant Van Homrig each led a company of sepoys in an attack on the Afghan skirmishers in the outer gardens. The Afghans retired into a small stone building outside the main fortifications from which they began a brisk exchange of fire with the two companies.

Twenty 9-pounders of the Horse Artillery and the Camel Battery were quickly ranged in line upon a plateau 700 yards from the fort with cavalry and infantry to guard them from sudden attack. The blue-coated gunners crouched with lighted port-fires—the quick-burning match that, applied to the vent at the end of the barrel exploded the powder charge.

'Fire!' A sudden metallic roar—the wheels rushed back with the recoil, the gunners thrust wet mops deep into the smoking black barrels to extinguished dangerous sparks, ready for the next powder charge.

'Powder!' The 2-lb. charge was thrust down the barrel. 'Load!' The 9-lb. shrapnel shell, invented in 1794 by Lieutenant Henry Shrapnell, was rammed home—a hollow shell containing a score of shot an inch in diameter surrounding a powder charge fused to burst as needed.

'Fire!' The shell whistled over the Afghan ramparts and exploded with deadly effect over the defenders' heads.

Now the canonade crashed from side to side as the Afghans fired back solid shot. 'There were some casualties arising from the fire,' Major Hough noted. 'They had got the range pretty accurately and could they have sufficiently depressed their guns would have killed and wounded many. The shots struck close to the Regiment of Infantry, posted between a village and the angle of the fort and many struck the ground close to the Horse Artillery, some shot passing under the horses' bellies and some reaching to the cavalry.'

One of the enemy mounted up on the parapets, waved his flag and called out to the British to come on. A 9-pounder shot knocked off his head and down went his flag; the rest became more cautious. It was afterwards ascertained that the artillery had committed great havoc in the fort, killing and wounding many men and horses.

Keane now ordered the guns to cease fire and the troops to withdraw—Captain Graves had been badly and Lieutenant Van Homrig slightly wounded; two sepoys were killed and six wounded.

But Keane now knew without doubt that the Afghans would defend their fortress and that they were well supplied with the means of doing it.

It must have been a depressing moment. What in heaven's name could he do? Desperately, as a last hope, he sent Captain Thomson—the engineer officer who had told him about Ghazni's 'tumbledown walls'—with an escort of infantry to reconnoitre the fortress closely on all sides, including the gates, and to report as to whether there was anywhere weak enough to attack with any chance of success.

A 'hot and well-directed fire' Thomson relates, was aimed at him and his party from the walls, and the infantry escort drove off a squadron of Afghan horsemen who charged down at them from the neighbouring hills.

'The fortifications,' he soon reported, 'were found equally strong all round, the only tangible point observed was the Kabul gateway, which offered the following advantages for a *coup-de-main*; the road up to the gate was clear; the bridge over the ditch was unbroken; there were good positions for the artillery within 350 yards of the walls on both sides of the road; and we had information that the gateway was not built up, a reinforcement from Kabul being expected.'

Thomson therefore reported that the only feasible mode of attack, the only one which held the slightest prospect of success, was a dash at the Kabul gateway, blowing the gate open by bags of gunpowder.

This report was supported by one Abdool Rusheed, a nephew of Dost Mahommed's, who believing himself out of favour, had deserted to the cause of the Shah and had given Keane's engineers precise information about the fortifications—only the Kabul gate, of all four, he reported, had not been filled in with masonry, a story again confirmed by the sight of an Afghan soldier entering it.

Thomson knew well enough the risks of such an operation, and that even if successful it could mean severe losses. According to Durand, he said as much to Keane. As a safer alternative he suggested that instead of attacking Ghazni, the army should march to attack Dost Mahommed in the field—reported to be only five or six days' march away—and after his defeat, which was certain, the defenders of Ghazni would surely surrender without a fight.

Keane, says Durand, replied that it was not in his power 'to adopt the safer alternative, as the army had only two, or at the utmost three days' provisions, and could not therefore march against Dost Mahommed'.

The die was cast and Keane chose the most dangerous but the only possible course, staking all upon immediate success in one desperate gambler's throw.

What if he failed? What if the explosion party were shot down before they were able to reach the gate? Or, if the gate were to be blown, what if the Afghans massed at the entrance and held it, while from the ramparts above their bullets cut down the British massed outside?

After retiring with the probable loss of two or three thousand of his best men, Keane would be faced with two alternatives, both of which promised a fair chance of destruction. First, he could press on with his weakened army and face attack by Dost Mahommed's force *en route* from Kabul, plus the three or four thousand cavalry that would pour out from Ghazni behind him. In this way he would go down fighting.

Secondly, he could ignominiously accept total defeat, sue for terms and try to extricate his army from Afghanistan as best he could. But the trap that Dost Mahommed had set in letting the British force penetrate the mountain passes more or less unmolested would then be sprung. The Afghan ruler's whole strength would be thrown against the British in terrain that favoured the attacker.

Even if a rescue force were to be sent it would affect the outcome little because all its energies would be needed in self-defence. Keane's entire army would be wiped out either by starvation or the Afghan sword and bullet.

Whichever of the three courses he chose, Keane and his army faced impossible odds, but a violent blow against the enemy's weakest point—the Kabul gate—offered a tiny chance of success.

So Keane decided on this and assembled his staff to plan the assault. Macnaghten now sent the alarming news from the Shah's camp that Dost Mahommed had marched from Kabul five days ago, on 16 July—his army was expected to be barely a day's march from Ghazni by tomorrow, the 22nd.

Every minute was now valuable—the attack must be won —or lost—at once. Keane ordered the army—encamped on the southern side of the fortress—to march in two columns, right and left of it, and take up positions on the Kabul instead of the Kandahar side. At 4 p.m. the march began.

Darkness fell. Eerie blue lights, dropped around the fortress walls, were answered similarly by Afghan troops on the surrounding hills. Making a wide detour to keep out of range of the Afghan *jezail* fire, the British force stumbled along over the rough ground in the darkness, alert for a possible attack at any moment.

While the march went on, Keane received information which must have led him to fear that his army would surely be attacked in this vulnerable situation. An engineer officer reported that Ensign Nicholson, of the Shah's force, had told him that the intended assault on the fortress was widely known in the Shah's camp, from whence inevitably, Dost Mahommed's secret agents would swiftly have carried the news to Hyder Ali, the fortress commander.

Keane had felt obliged to let Macnaghten know of the army's peril and the projected do-or-die attack, so that he would be prepared for whatever was the outcome—'never anticipating that Macnaghten would divulge the scheme of attack, success in which mainly depended on secrecy and surprise', Durand noted.

But Macnaghten, 'ignorant or heedless of the possible consequences' made no secret of it in the Shah's camp and it later transpired that when the news became known in the fortress Hyder Ali had expected an attack that very night. He must surely have considered then a night sortie or *chupao* in force against the British to anticipate their move.

But presumably believing the fortress impregnable he sat tight, Keane's luck held good and the straggling serpentine procession, several miles long in each direction, reached its destination unhindered except for the occasional spent round from a long-range *jezail*. The troops, tired and hungry, finally encamped just before midnight, but the miles and miles of baggage and supply columns were still lumbering in until late next morning.

The army was now well placed. It could deploy for the attack on the Kabul gate; it could prevent Hyder Ali trying to escape to join his father Dost Mahommed; and it could stop any reinforcements reaching him from Kabul.

At first light Sir John Keane reconnoitred the northern face of the fortress; the gateway, and the road leading up to it from the hills above. He approved the details of the plan and chose as the place where the troops would await to advance, some flat ground half a mile from the fortress near the stone pillars commemorating Mahmoud of Ghazni, a former ruling prince, and son of Ahmed Shah, the founder of the Afghan Empire.

At the same time the dark-blue-clad artillery officers, led by Brigadier Stevenson, moved nearer to the fortress and under sharp enemy fire chose the exact position from which the gunners could best give the infantry supporting fire. Keane and his staff then returned to their tents to work out the precise details. All their lives depended upon its success.

Just before noon, trumpets sounded the alarm. A large force of Afghans with banners, about 4,000 men in all, had appeared on the crest of the hills to the east of the camp and were advancing in a great disorganised host to attack the Shah's camp below.

A force of the Shah's cavalry reinforced by infantry and two British 9-pounder guns at once moved out to repulse them—perhaps even too quickly, before the attackers could fully commit themselves in the plain below. A few rounds of shrapnel killed or wounded numbers of the attackers. A cavalry charge led by Ensign Nicholson, seventeen years old, made them lose courage, turn about and scramble back up the rocky hill.

Durand noted that a severe example might have been made had they been allowed to descend into the plain, but, however, Captain Outram with a party of infantrymen chased them up the hillside in face of heavy *jezail* fire to within fifty paces of their headquarters—marked by a standard-bearer holding a green-and-white banner, a sacred emblem later found to have been consecrated by the priests, to confer invincibility.

A British marksman shot down the standard-bearer and the enemy fled. The standard and a batch of prisoners, were captured and taken back down the hillside in triumph.

This first small clash was important, because it confirmed the British forces in their belief that when it came to open conflict in the field their organisation, disciplined attack and artillery gave them marked superiority over the Afghans.

The prisoners were taken before the Shah, who questioned them about what he termed their rebellion and treason. Sir Alexander Burnes, who was present, says that one of them shouted that he would glory in taking the Shah's life, because he was an infidel and he had brought into the country a whole army of infidels. To show that he was a man of his word, he drew a dagger and plunged it into the heart of one of the Shah's attendants.

The Shah's cruel and vengeful nature now asserted itself and he ordered all but two of the forty-six prisoners—these two he pardoned—to be beheaded. They were dragged away.

According to a British officer present, they were first tortured. 'I was walking in the camp,' he relates, 'and came upon the King's tents, at the rear of which I saw a fearfully bloody sight. There were forty or fifty men, young and old. Many were dead, others at their last gasp; others with their hands tied behind them; some sitting, others standing, awaiting their doom; and the King's executioners and other servants amusing themselves (for actually they were laughing and joking and seemed to look upon the work as good fun) with hacking and maiming the poor wretches indiscriminately with their long swords and knives. I was so horrified at coming so suddenly upon such a scene of blood, that I was, for the instant, as it were spellbound. On inquiry I ascertained that the King had ordered this wholesale murder....'

Keane, no doubt desperate with anxiety, was meantime at work in his tent on the details of the orders for the storming of Ghazni in the early hours of the next day. They were completed and made known to no one but the few senior officers in command later that evening.

The entire army was now aware of its danger—and that the lives of all of them depended upon their being able somehow to burst into the great grey fortress towering above them on its rocky base and overcome the garrison. One can imagine how forlorn a hope it must have seemed to the English soldier, awaiting this battle which could have no other end for them but victory—or death.

To young Lieutenant Tom Holdsworth, of the Queen's Royals, about to go into battle for the first time, the tension of the last hours of 22 July was by no means pleasant. 'That day I shall never forget,' he wrote to his father at home in Camberley. 'It was a dismal one. . . . There was a nervous irritability and excitement about us the whole day; constantly looking at the place through spy-glasses, etc.; and then fellows began to make their wills and tell each other what they wished to have done in case they fell; altogether it was not very pleasant and many longed most heartily for the morrow and to have it over. I felt as I used to do when I was a child and knew I must take a black dose or have a tooth drawn the next morning.

'We were to be formed ready for the attack at 2 a.m., close to a high pillar, about half a mile from the fort. We were to advance under cover of the artillery, who were to fire over and clear the walls for us.

'I laid down in my cloak directly after mess and being dreadfully tired never slept more soundly than I did the night before the storming of Ghazni.'

Throughout the whole army, waiting that windy night within gunshot of the great fortress, there must have been tension, anxiety and dread. Had they not tempted fortune too far? Was their fate not now beyond recall?

Chapter Ten

The assault on Ghazni on 23 July 1839 hardly ranks as a textbook example of a classic storming attack. The outcome depended solely upon success in blowing up the Kabul gateway—a tactical move that normally would have been one of perhaps several others upon which victory depended.

But in terms of daring, of courage, of single-minded determination to do or die, it ranks high. It is unique too in that all was over in so short a space of time—the outcome was decided almost at once.

Pictorially, the scene could not have been bettered. The fighting was concentrated in one small area. On the hills over-looking the fortress or peering through one of the narrow windows of the citadel itself, high above the walls, an observer could see it all and tell by the rattle of musketry, the crash of steel, the shrieks of men locked in close and bloody combat how the assault progressed.

For the British, all hung upon the courage and luck of the explosion party in reaching the gate under heavy fire—upon their skill in blasting it open, and upon the determination of Colonel Dennie's storming party, which was to burst through the smoke and debris and clear the defenders for the main body of troops.

The night of 22/23 July was dark and windy, favourable for screening the movements of the attackers. The artillery, some forty guns in all, moved off at midnight to take up as silently as possible chosen positions within 300 yards of the Kabul gate in a line facing the north-eastern walls. At the same time a regiment of Indian cavalry and three companies of sepoys marched round to the southern walls. There, under Captain Hay, they were to make a feint attack to draw away the defenders.

During these movements, according to Lieutenant Henry Havelock, the wind blew strongly in gusts from the east, and occasionally loudly enough to muffle the tramp of the infantry columns and the rattle of artillery wheels. Led by Colonel Dennie, a tough and experienced fighting soldier who could be relied upon never to give in, 240 picked men of the Queen's, the 17th, the 102nd and the 13th Foot assembled at the point of rendezvous half a mile from the fortress in readiness for their vital role as storming party.

Behind them waited the remainder of the Queen's Regiment and the 102nd Foot, all nominally at least, under the command of Brigadier-General Sale. A party of marksmen from the 13th and 17th Foot had already by 12.30 a.m. hidden themselves upon both sides of the gate, ready to give covering fire to the explosion party.

Finally, Colonel Stalker with the Bombay 19th Native Infantry made ready to ward off any possible attack by Dost Mahommed's army from the direction of Kabul.

Orders were that these first movements should be carried out in dead silence, but the jingle of harness, the rattle of artillery wheels and the tread of the infantry were heard above the roaring wind. Yet the Afghans took no action, seemingly lulled into a false sense of security by the British failure to attack the night before.

Earlier, the explosion party had essembled a few hundred yards from the moat bridge. They were Captain Peat, Lieutenants Durand and Macleod, and three sergeants, followed by eighteen Indian sappers carrying between them a 72-foot-long fuse and twelve sandbags, each of which held 25 lb. of gunpowder—300 lb. in all, a massive charge, enough not just to blow down the gate, but to shatter it and the surrounding wall too.

A minute after three o'clock, says Durand, 'the morning star was high in the heavens and the first red streak of dawn had appeared', when Captain Peat led his men in a steady walk through the twilight towards the bridge over the moat and the towering silent ramparts. At first all went well.

Then fifty yards away a hoarse challenge rang out from the ramparts and a few seconds later came a shot. Brilliant blue lights flared, a volley of *jezail* fire crashed from the loopholes and the crackle of muskets from Captain Hay's feint attack echoed distantly. Angrily, the artillery opened up with a roar that reverberated between the fortress and the surrounding hills like a number of great metal doors slamming. Ghazni was under attack.

Bullets ricocheted off the bridge as the explosion party crossed. Every loophole flashed fire, yet no shots came from the stone outer-works beside the bridge; the party crossed unharmed. Peat and a few infantrymen occupied a sally-port ready to repel any sortie from within.

Amid the whine of musket rounds, Durand coolly edged along the foot of the fortress wall and set the first powder-bag with its attached fuse firmly at the foot of the gate. Through the gaps in the wood as he bent down he saw the Afghan guard sitting smoking, *jezails* in hand in fancied security.

But the defenders above had left their loopholes for the ramparts to take better aim and hurl down huge pieces of masonry at the sepoys below hurriedly staking the bags under Macleod's watchful eye. They received only glancing blows and the entire 300 lb. of gunpowder were piled against the huge gate.

Durand and Robertson had meanwhile carefully uncoiled the fuse across the bridge. By another stroke of good luck it reached precisely to the sheltering sally-port there. Durand skipped into it and tried to light the fuse, blowing hard at the slow-match but failing to ignite it—had the fuse been even a yard shorter he would have been a certain target crouching in the open, with the light in his hands.

When the fuse finally blazed, it went out as soon as he put it on the ground. In the partial shelter of the sally-port, Durand drew his pistol ready to flash the fuse, but first held it against the slow-match and once more blew hard. This time it burned steadily and after watching the flame creep over the bridge towards the gate Durand and Robertson ran back for cover towards their own lines.

Confusion now followed. Durand shouted for Peat, to say that all was well and that his bugler could sound the advance to Dennie's storming party. But Peat somehow missed him and fearing that both Durand and Robertson had been shot down, he crossed the bridge to find out what had happened just as the 300 lb. of gunpowder flashed with a deafening roar.

The blast threw him head over heels and stunned him. He came to a minute later and stumbled through the darkness up to the gateway to see whether there was a clear passage for the assault. He saw only Afghan swordsmen on the far side of a pile of masonry and feared in his dazed state that the assault had failed.

Durand, meanwhile, certain that the gate was down, looked for a bugler to sound the assault. But Peat's bugler was dead, shot through the head.

The fire from the battlements was heavy. Durand ran to an officer with the nearest group of skirmishers and asked for a bugler to sound the advance. Stupidly, this officer told him not to draw down fire upon the men by speaking and to apply for the bugler through the normal channels.

Knowing that with every moment the element of surprise would be lost as the Afghans reinforced the breach, Durand did not stop to argue but turned and ran back desperately towards the troops' assembly point. On the way he met Broadfoot, another engineer officer, who took over and, says Durand, gave Sale the news.

But meanwhile, Dennie, who had followed closely behind the explosion party had saved the day. Without waiting for the signal he had led his men in a furious rush over the bridge into fierce hand-to-hand fighting with Afghan swordsmen in the ruined gateway. In the smoke and dark-blue gloom sword-blade clashed against bayonet, shouts and cries of struggling, wounded men rang out.

Led by Dennie, thrusting with his sword, the storming party won through to a wider, domed building leading from the gateway. Each section fired, then made way for the next one, all in turn pouring a deadly volley at the packed defenders. With a final bayonet charge they won through into an open square of the town and saw the stars twinkling above.

Hyder Ali, the Governor, was at this time hotly debating with his chiefs in a council of war up in the citadel, the vital issue of where the women should be hidden to protect them from possible violation. Suddenly they heard the explosion rumble and the boom of the artillery, but they still had no idea that the British were in until the volleys of Dennie's storming party crashed out in the streets below. Then there was panic among them.

Dennie, once inside, should by rights have occupied the ramparts on both sides of the gate, so as to secure command of it and leave the glory of exploiting his own initial victory to Sale. But disdaining such a static role and seeing no sign of Sale's men, he and the storming party with alternate volleys of musketry and bursts of cheering fought their way against the defenders up the steep winding streets into the town.

It was as well that they did, for confusion had beset Sale and the main force. Dennie related: 'Captain Thomson, commanding Engineers, who remained outside, under cover . . . perceiving that the advance had won the entrance, and hearing our cheers, followed by heavy firing, became anxious about the little band, apparently severely opposed, and sent Lieutenant Pigou to find Brigadier Sale and the main column.

'He went back all the way to the minar and there he found Sale's party—sitting down, and some fallen out. He communicated his message of our being in . . .'

Sale then marched his men towards the bridge. Tom Holdsworth noted the scene on the way—'Whilst we were marching down to the attack the fire on both sides was at its height. . . . I caught myself once or twice trying to make myself as small as I could.

'As we got nearer the gate it grew worse and the enemy, from their loopholes began to pepper us. They threw out blue lights . . . which looked beautiful and the flames of their and

our artillery, together with smaller flashes from the matchlock men . . . the roar of their big guns, the whizzing of their
cannon balls and ours, the sighings of the bullets . . . made
up as pretty a row as one would wish to hear.'

Not far from the bridge, at the head of his column, Sale
now met Peat, who, still half-concussed, called out—'Don't
go on—it's a failure!' Without even halting his men and
sending scouts ahead to see what had happened, Sale
ordered Bugler Wilson to sound the *retire* at once and his
column went right about and retraced their steps.

Dennie and the small storming party in the fortress were
now isolated. It was a critical situation. Once having recovered from their surprise, the Afghans could subdue them
by sheer weight of numbers.

But Captain Thomson, still waiting at the bridge for the
main column, grew desperate, finally ran back himself, over-
took Sale as he marched back the way he had come and
breathlessly assured him that Dennie was *in* and that for
some considerable time.

Bugler Wilson, described by one officer as 'the best bugler
I ever had' possessed a small, shrill Light Infantry brass
bugle that amid the greatest din was audible at some distance. Standing beside Sale he now piercingly sounded the
'advance double' without waiting for orders and so loudly
that despite the crash of gunfire the column heard it and at
once retraced their steps, finally crossing the bridge under
heavy fire.

At the gateway a violent rush of Afghan swordsmen drove
the foremost of them back. Among others, Lieutenant Stock
was knocked down. 'I felt myself sinking amongst heaps of
rubbish and broken timber,' he related. 'The first solid
support I met with was the face of a dead man. With this for
a *point d'appui* I contrived to rise and assisted in rallying the
men.

'To it we went again, under the inspiring influence of a
British cheer, and this time charged so rapidly that we . . .
contrived to get through all the cuttings, stabbing and shooting unscathed. . . . The leading and particularly the rear

companies were more roughly handled—some of the men *literally* cut to pieces.'

Brigadier Sale was leading his men in another charge over the shattered timbers when an Afghan swordsman wounded him in the face, knocked him down and sprang on him to finish him off. Captain Kershaw of the 13th Foot thrust his sword clean through the Afghan's body, 'but still the *desperado* continued to struggle with frantic violence'.

He wounded Sale again and the struggle ended only when Sale got his sword arm free and cleaved his attacker's skull to the eyebrows. 'Oh God!' the Afghan was said to have cried, and, not surprisingly 'never moved or spoke again'.

Dennie's four companies were now hard pressed. The Afghan garrison had made furious rallies, but the arrival of the main column and soon the reserve under Colonel Croker altered the balance. Through the narrow streets, pungent with the reek of gun smoke, the redcoats attacked mercilessly. The Afghans opened fire from balconies and windows—fifty of them died defending one tall building. Hundreds of frightened horses kicked and fought in the streets.

Among the defenders, 'there was horrible confusion and much carnage', Kaye relates. 'Some, in their frantic efforts to escape by the gateway, stumbled over the burning timbers, wounded and exhausted, and were slowly burnt to death. Some were bayoneted on the ground. Others were pursued and hunted into corners like mad dogs and shot down with the curse and the prayer on their lips.'

But the citadel above the town was undefended and by sunrise British colours fluttered from the battlements. Hyder Ali, the governor, was found hiding in a house with his women and given into the charge of Captain Burnes.

Within two hours Ghazni had fallen—the British army was saved.

More than 1,200 Afghan defenders were killed in this desperate assault, several hundred wounded, 1,600 unwounded made prisoner, while a few hundred escaped.

British losses were 17 men killed and 165, including 18 officers, wounded.

The capture of Ghazni was a brilliant but lucky achievement, for had the assault been launched even an hour later, it might well have been too late. Meer Ufzul Khan, the 'fighting son' of Dost Mahommed, was afterwards found to have been close on the British camp with 5,000 cavalry.

He heard the firing as he approached, just after dawn, and soon the British flag waving from the citadel showed him that he was too late. He turned and fled hurriedly to Kabul, leaving scores of elephants and tons of baggage behind him six miles from the camp; these were swiftly seized by the British the next day.

Moreover, an enormous amount of booty in Ghazni fell into British hands—about, 3,000 horses—for the Afghans had rather absurdly stationed a force of cavalry inside, instead of out in the country where it could attack; nine artillery guns of various calibres with more than 2,000 rounds; 22,000 lb. of gunpowder, hundreds of flintlock and matchlock guns and pistols; and, most important, 80,000 lb. of flour, 354,000 lb. of wheat, 74,000 lb. of barley, 3,500 lb. of peas and small quantities of salt and various other edibles. For the first time for weeks the army was put on full rations—one of the fruits of victory.

Keane was lucky in having engineer officers like Peat, Thomson and Durand, no less than fine fighting soldiers like Dennie and troops of the calibre of the storming party to save the day for him. But he took much of the credit for himself. And in a dispatch to the Governor-General magnified the exploit so much that it needed more words than Wellington's report on the Battle of Waterloo.

'I have the honour to acquaint your Lordship,' he began boastfully, 'that the army under my command has succeeded in performing one of the most brilliant acts it has ever been my lot to witness during my forty-five years in the four quarters of the globe in the capture by storm of the strong and important fortress and citadel of Ghazni yesterday.'

Glossing over the fact that he himself had endangered the army, Keane said that he 'did not hesitate a moment as to the manner in which our approach and attack upon the place should be made. . . . At daylight on the 22nd I reconnoitred Ghuznee in company with the chief Engineer . . . for the purpose of making all arrangements for carrying the place by storm. . . .'

Keane, who disliked Dennie—as he did all his best officers —went on to give the credit for entering Ghazni to Brigadier Sale, whose fumbling had in fact endangered the operation.

After this lie he went on to hand out congratulations and praise to all the other officers who took part in the operation except Dennie, merely in an off-handed way giving him his 'best acknowledgements' and thus effectively preventing the political and military authorities from knowing the truth. Such was the way of this hardly likeable general.

His report brought a protest from Dennie. In a letter to a friend that eventually was published in a Calcutta newspaper he modestly wrote: 'I am . . . more than usually stung at the ingratitude practised in this business, because I know good fortune or Providence did give me a great and important post on that day, upon which, perhaps, depended the safety and very existence of our army; who, had I failed, or even been checked as the rear column after me was, must all have met the common fate of certain destruction.

'The whole country was up and millions were at hand and all around us to cut off our baggage, food and every supply . . . who only waited . . . for the first symptom of disaster for their slaughter to commence.'

The victory was hailed as a great and extraordinary triumph both by the authorities in India and—to make an unpopular war more acceptable—by the Whig politicians in England. In a House of Commons eulogy Sir Robert Peel absurdly described it as 'the most brilliant achievement of our arms in Asia'.

Dost Mahommed, 90 miles away over the mountains in Kabul, heard the news of Ghazni's fall at five o'clock that day through swift horsemen stationed every eight miles

along the route. It had been thought impregnable. Shocked
and alarmed he assembled his chiefs, received from them
their not very reliable assurances of loyalty and then
sensibly sent his brother Nawab Jubbar Khan to try to
negotiate reasonable terms from Shah Shuja and the
British.

Chapter Eleven

The fall of the fortress of Ghazni was a turning-point for the British. Their army had been saved, the two chief cities of Afghanistan apart from Kabul, the capital, were in their hands and, as a result, many of the chiefs in Dost Mahommed's camp were bound to come over to them. The way ahead, which only a few days before had looked so desperate, now seemed all set for victory.

The Nawab Jubbar Khan, the emissary, brought an offer of surrender on condition that Dost Mahommed, as the brother of the murdered Futteh Khan, should be given the hereditary office of Vizier, or chief minister, held for so long in the past by his family.

It could possibly have been an acceptable way out of a costly campaign. Most of the chiefs would have agreed without more fighting; Dost Mahommed could have been bound to guarantee the loyalty of the tribes and thus reinforced Shah Shuja, where he was weakest, while the Dost's own powers could possibly have been limited, to keep him in check.

Moreover, having shown their strength, the British could have marched back to India with their basic aim accomplished. This would have been little more of a gamble than the alternative policy of unconditional surrender, repression of hostile tribesmen and an army of occupation dependent upon easily cut lines of communication.

But the pitfalls of thus putting Shuja in the Dost's hands were too obvious. Macnaghten rejected the terms, conceding nothing and offering the Amir only 'honourable asylum' in the British dominions, that is, exile and open captivity in India.

Jubbar Khan answered bluntly that Dost Mahommed

had no intention of surrendering his freedom and throwing himself on the bounty of the British Government. Indeed, he remarked, had the outlook for him been less hopeless that it was, he would sooner have thrown himself upon British bayonets.

Before riding away he asked Macnaghten: 'If Shah Shuja is really our king, what need has he of your army and name? You have brought him here with your money and arms. Well, leave him now with us Afghans and let him rule us if he can'.

He then rejoined Dost Mahommed with the news. Any chance of negotiations had now faded and Dost Mahommed sough to whip up the courage and loyalty of his wavering chiefs. Keane, instead of pushing on at once, rested for a week in Ghazni, then marched on 30 July 1839, leaving behind a garrison of about 1,200 men and 30 guns. Keane seems at this time to have tried to balance his lack of military judgement by over-enforcement of discipline. He now excelled himself in a characteristic order stating that any camp-follower 'found destroying grain or injuring cultivation . . . will be *hanged*. The Provost Marshal and his assistants are required to have at hand the means of giving effect to this order'—they were to travel armed with a hangman's rope.

Hearing from his brother the rejection of his offer, Dost Mahommed now marched his uncertain army from Kabul down towards Urgendeh, in the path of the invaders. He drew up his troops and his guns there on 1 August, intending however, to make a last stand at Maidan on the Kabul River near by, where the terrain would have been very much in his favour.

The Amir had won his kingdom, in the traditional Afghan way, by the sword, and ruled it after his own nature with severity tempered by justice. But time had so blurred the misfortunes of Shuja's reign of thirty years before, that many of the chiefs—especially now that the Shah had returned with a great and victorious army—thought of it in comparison as a golden age.

Dost Mahommed's authority began to fade like the

Afghan summer. Now that his son Akbar Khan had returned from the Khyber, his forces totalled 13,000 cavalry
and infantry and thirty guns, mainly 6- and 9-pounders, but
with insufficient reserves of ammunition for a set battle
with the British. Had this force been willing to fight a war of
hit-and-run tactics it might soon have worn down the far-
flung invaders into ultimate defeat. But the Dost evidently
believed that his only chance lay in an immediate clash with
them and now came the final misfortunes for this self-made
ruler. Having pledged loyalty to him the perfidious chiefs
refused to fight. Neutrality seemed the wiser course towards
the old king, Shuja, with the powerful army and the well-
filled treasure-chest.

Dost Mahommed made one last effort to restore his
authority, riding among them Koran in hand and harangu-
ing them in the name of the Prophet not to dishonour themselves by deserting him for the wicked former monarch who
had defiled the country by filling it with infidels. 'If,' he is
reported to have said, 'you are resolved to be traitors to me,
at least enable me to die with honour. Support the brother
of Futteh Khan in one last charge against these Feringee
dogs. In that charge he will fall. Then go and make your
terms with Shah Shuja.'

But this fervent appeal brought no response, and that
same evening Dost Mahommed, his family and 600 faithful
followers fled towards friendlier territory, leaving the guns
in position in the valley at Urgendeh. Keane, the next day,
3 August, at Shiekabad, where he had halted to concentrate
his forces, heard the news from the renegade chiefs who
arrived at the camp to pay homage to their new ruler.

An American military adventurer, the self-styled General
Harlan, who was in Dost Mahommed's camp at this time,
says that the Amir was not just deserted by his followers but
robbed as well. 'A crowd of noisy disorganised troops,' he
relates, 'insolently pressed close up to the royal pavilion—
the guard had disappeared—the groom holding the Prince's
horse was unceremoniously pushed to and fro—a servant
audaciously pulled away the pillow which sustained the

D

Prince's arm—another commenced cutting a piece of the splendid Persian carpet—the beautiful praying rug of the Prince was seized on by a third.... "Take all," said he, "that you find within, together with the tent."

'In an instant the unruly crowd rushed upon the pavilion —swords gleamed in the air and descended upon the tent— the canvas, the ropes, the carpets, pillows, screens, etc., were seized and dispersed among the plunderers.'

Harlan's report has the ring of truth and shows how little regard for anything but loot had these tribes whom the British hoped to convert into faithful allies.

Keane, after some hesitation, now decided to try to capture Dost Mahommed. Captain Outram volunteered and was given command of a force of 14 British officers, 100 cavalry and 2,000 of the Shah's Afghan cavalry, all under the guidance of Haji Khan, the chief who had deserted to Shah Shuja at Kandahar.

But only a few hundred of the Afghan troops arrived at the hour appointed, and when the small force finally started, Haji Khan delayed its advance by every possible trick. Eventually, Outram led the pursuers 15,000 feet up into the snowy mountains of the Hindu Kush, but Haji Khan—who had made working for both sides into a fine and subtle art—caused more delays and enabled Dost Mahommed to escape. He was arrested for his efforts when the pursuing party returned later to Kabul.

Keane himself marched on towards the capital, sending Major Cuerton and 200 Lancers on in advance to seize Dost Mahommed's artillery—found to be twenty-three guns mostly worn out, some even dangerous to fire, but loaded and sighted to front, rear and flanks. A quantity of powder and shot, with ammunition wagons, tumbrils and gun-bullocks were also captured.

Lieutenant Warburton, who listed this artillery, thought it useless. 'The shot is hammered iron,' he reported, 'and so uneven that unless weighed their weight could not be told. They are chiefly much under 6-pounder shot. . . . With regard to the other stores nothing was of the slightest service, except the old iron of the carriages, and the axle-trees, also good as old iron only, and to which purpose they have been appropriated.'

The army joyfully marched on, crossed the Kabul River on 6 August and camped three miles west of the city in the late afternoon.

Shah Shuja formally entered the next day as a British puppet king to take possession of the throne of his ancestors. It was a great occasion, An escort of Lancers, Dragoons, Artillery and Infantry were paraded in review order on the road leading to Kabul. A royal salute was fired as His Majesty approached the escort, and the squadrons saluted him as he passed, after which they wheeled up and followed in procession to the entrance to the town.

Wearing a coronet above his turban, a jewelled girdle and bracelets, with his long dark-black beard carefully combed and reaching to his waist, the new Shah rode a white charger whose harness glittered with gold and precious stones. William Macnaghten, in full diplomatic regalia, as the British Envoy accredited to the King, rode beside him, followed by General Sir John Keane, Sir Alexander Burnes and a vast procession of other officers. Sabres flashed at the head of the procession, artillery rumbled and bayonets glittered at the rear.

The return of Shah Shuja in August 1839 kindled no enthusiasm among the crowds who out of curiosity lined the narrow winding streets. The chiefs mostly stayed away and the citizens neither salaamed nor shouted acclaim, but merely rose to their feet to look hard and long at the monarch whom thirty years ago they had overthrown and who was now forced on them by the armed unbelievers.

When the steep slopes of the palace and fortress of the Bala Hissar had been ascended, the Shah led the way through the gardens, and with pathetic eagerness into the palace. He wept openly at the neglect and dilapidation that faced him, explaining to his sons and grandsons how fine it had all been when he was a young man, thirty years ago.

Such was the fateful home-coming of Shah Shuja; and

with it the Army of the Indus had after a march of 1,527 miles arrived at its final destination.

One of Macnaghten's first acts in Kabul was to persuade Shah Shuja to institute an order of the Durani Empire— which Afghanistan at the height of its power had been called—in three classes, like the Order of the Bath, to be presented to officers from the Commander-in-Chief and political agents downwards. A splendid state durbar was held for the presentation. It turned out to be something of a farce, according to the chief surgeon, Dr. Kennedy.

The Shah sat in the ruined garden of a courtyard, his throne an old camp chair, and behind him stood two fat eunuchs, each holding a dish. 'Up to this extraordinary dumb show we marched,' says Kennedy, 'and we were all ranged behind and on the right of the camp chair with the King in it.

'When all was ready . . . Sir John Keane stepped before the said camp chair with the King in it and gravely dropped on his knees before the Durani Emperor. One of the fat eunuchs waddled to the front and uncovered his dish in which was the decoration and ribbon of "the order of the Durani Empire".

'The Emperor with great difficulty stuck it on and Sir John's coat being too tight, it cost him some effort to wriggle into the ribbon: but the acorn in time becomes an oak and Sir John was at last adorned . . . A Knight Grand Cross of the Durani Empire. The decoration required eloquence; and Sir John, standing before the Emperor, delivered himself of a speech in which there was a great deal about "hurling a usurper from the throne"—at which my uncle Toby might perhaps have whistled his lillibullero.

'Mr. Macnaghten and General Cotton were next invested and Sir Alexander Burnes and Sir Martin Wade were told that they were created Knights Grand too, but that the goldsmith had not been able to make the decorations in time for them. . . . Lord Auckland was created a Knight Grand Cross also. How Colonel Pottinger escaped can only be explained by the wonderful good fortune that has attended that gentleman through life.

'The Grand Crosses being created, the Knights Commanders and Companions were to be invested, but the decorations had not been made; and it was clear that if there was to be a kneeling and kow-tow for each there would be no end of it, so an officer . . . shouted out the names of the "men whom the king delighted to honour".

'The decoration of the order is a Maltese cross, a bad imitation of the Guelphic order of Hanover; and it was the more absurd to give a Christian's most sacred religious badge . . . because the arabesque star of six points, which forms the ornament of the historic gates of the tomb of Mahmoud of Ghazni, would have been so peculiar and appropriate an emblem. . . . The ribbon, "party per pale vert and gules" is in good taste and when manufactured in England will no doubt be very ornamental.'

Meantime, in a letter to Lord Auckland, Governor-General, officially informing him that Shah Shuja had taken possession of the throne, General Keane remarked dryly: 'I trust we have thus accomplished all the objects which your Lordship had in contemplation, when you planned and formed the Army of the Indus, and the expedition into Afghanistan.'

In due course Lord Auckland published a General Order thanking Keane and the army: 'The plans of aggression by which the British empire in India was dangerously threatened, have, under Providence, been arrested. The Chiefs of Kabul and Kandahar, who had joined in hostile designs against us, have been deprived of power, and the territories which they ruled have been restored to a friendly monarch . . .'

How empty were these pretentious words events would soon prove.

Chapter Twelve

The invasion's object had been achieved. Shah Shuja was restored to the throne, the country was occupied as well as could be with garrisons in Kandahar and Ghazni, and an army at Kabul. The 'independence and integrity' of Afghanistan, to which Lord Auckland had referred in his manifesto justifying the campaign, seemed to be assured and according to its terms British troops should now be withdrawn.

But Dost Mahommed was still at large, a likely focus of rebellion should conditions favour the growth of one. And though the Shah sat on the throne of his ancestors once more, both he and Macnaghten never doubted that he could be kept there only by British bayonets. Even Lord Auckland had made the painful discovery that though a certain number of chiefs had declared allegiance to Shuja, most of the people were hostile.

He wrote to Macnaghten to say that he wanted to see the troops back in India and the cost of the campaign ended, but this must not be done while there was any risk of losing all that had been won by leaving before the Shah had a grip on the country. Macnaghten, who wanted a large army in Afghanistan, agreed; it was decided to return to India the smaller Bombay force and for the time being to keep most of the large Bengal one to support the Shah. A new Russian threat, potentially dangerous for India was to make this arrangement rather more permanent.

The next twelve months would be the decisive ones for the Shah—and for the British—since by their policies many of the Afghans who in the early autumn of 1839 were uncertain about their future allegiance could be won over or driven into hostility.

In theory the Shah was now an independent monarch, but from the very first days of the occupation Macnaghten became the real ruler, with ambitious young political officers—mostly inexperienced young army officers seconded for the purpose—appointed throughout the country and able to call upon the army to enforce Macnaghten's orders.

Of the whole field of government, Shah Shuja was allowed only the collection of revenue and taxes and the administration of civil and criminal law. He had no voice whatsoever in foreign policy or in internal security—that is, in the pacification of those turbulent tribes who at any time might rise and dispute his rule.

Nor, apart from his personal guard of several hundred, had he any power over his own armed forces. In September 1839 these amounted to 4,000 infantry, 2,000 cavalry and two troops of Bengal artillery—all commanded by British officers and under Macnaghten's sway. This army—except for the Shah's bodyguard—was, moreover, paid by the British, this presumably being the one sure way to see that the troops got their money.

Auckland's policy, which he had made clear to Macnaghten, was that the Shah should reform the abuses in government which he had inherited from Dost Mahommed; make his army efficient and reliable, and encourage trade so as to increase revenue from taxation to pay officials' salaries and troops' wages.

Auckland believed that this policy would enable all British soldiers to be withdrawn by the autumn of 1840—except for those officers who would stay for a time to run the Shah's army, And the Shah would thus be left to rule his dominions under the guidance of a British Envoy.

This policy was based on a clear directive of Sir John Hobhouse, President of the East India Company Board of Control in London, to whom the Governor-General was responsible. Hobhouse, as early as March 1839, when the army was crossing the Afghan frontier, had told Auckland: 'It is of the utmost importance not only so far as India, but as Europe is concerned, that there should be no appearance of any intention on your part to acquire any permanent possession beyond the frontier.'

He meant, of course, that there would be trouble with Russia should it appear that England sought permanent possessions beyond India's frontier. Again, in September, after the Shah entered Kabul, he stressed the point even more strongly. 'Above all remember,' he wrote to Auckland, 'that not only the Home Authorities but their Parliamentary critics look with the utmost apprehension, not to say jealousy, at any extension of the British power beyond the Indus,' The views of Sir John Hobhouse were in this matter largely those of Palmerston, who had tried carefully not to antagonise Russia.

But late in August 1839 Palmerston in London heard from Colonel Pottinger, British Envoy in Herat—the independent principality in western Afghanistan, near the the Persian border—the alarming news that a Russian army was marching on Khiva, on the River Oxus, in Turkestan (now one of the states of south-eastern U.S.S.R.). Pottinger expressed the opinion that if successful, a Russian advance towards Herat might follow, with Persian assistance—a clear potential danger for India.

The outcome was that Hobhouse, following agreement with Palmerston, urged upon Auckland in a letter dated 4 September 1839 what was termed 'a bolder policy' towards Herat. This, of course, meant possible occupation and keeping British troops in Afghanistan until the issue was settled.

Behind this new development was Palmerston's belief that diplomatic action in Teheran had failed to produce evidence of friendship between England and Persia. Afghanistan therefore replaced Persia in Palmerston's policies as the first line of defence of India against attack from the north-west. And this radical change implied for the time being a much more permanent British military presence in Afghanistan.

Macnaghten had learned in late August of the Russian march on Khiva and at once he used this information to try to persuade General Keane to agree to leave in Kabul a much large British force—for this was one of the things upon which Macnaghten, now practically Shah of Afghanistan, had set his heart. But Keane was by no means sure that Russia was capable of transporting her army across large tracts of central Asia to what Macnaghten called the banks of the Oxus. Jokingly he put off the Envoy with the remark that the only banks he now thought of were those of the Thames, for he had a house at Maidenhead.

But Macnaghten was not so easily put off. He seems to have been determined both to keep as much as he could of the army and also, it became clear, to embark upon some new military action that would increase his fame.

He therefore tried to embroil Keane in an absurd scheme that would serve his purpose. He showed the General a letter he said he was about to send to Auckland and asked for Keane's agreement on its contents. After referring to the proposed stay of most of the Bengal force in Kabul, the letter said that already—in view of the urgency, without waiting for the Governor-General's agreement—a force had been marched against distant Bokhara, to pursue Dost Mahommed, free the British Envoy, Colonel Stoddart, whom the ruler there had imprisoned; and march on north-west hundreds of miles to forestall Russia's troops at Khiva.

Keane managed somehow to control himself when he read of actions said to be occurring that he would never even have contemplated. Not trusting himself to write a reply, he showed his contempt by returning the letter to Macnaghten with a verbal message by an aide-de-camp— that he could not even consider joining in forwarding it to Auckland and the next day he bluntly told Macnaghten why such an expedition was an absurdity.

First, the mountain passes over which Macnaghten proposed to send the troops rose he said, to some 12,000 feet above sea-level. Snow was likely to start falling at that height within a few weeks. The troops would be isolated in the mountain town of Bamian for six or eight months. It would be impossible during winter to get supplies to them. Finally, he insisted, the Shah's troops, not the British, should undertake such a task; or, if British troops were absolutely essential, they should wait until the spring and then march in some force.

But Macnaghten was undismayed. Set upon his military adventure 'to drive Dost Mahommed beyond the Oxus' at once, despite all that Keane had told him he ordered Captain Hay to march west to Bamian next day, 11 September 1839, with one of the Shah's new Ghurka regiments, 200 cavalry, 3,000 Afghan irregulars and a troop of Bengal Horse Artillery—all from the Shah's forces.

On arrival there, Captain Hay, an experienced soldier, was to place himself under the orders of Dr. Lord, one of the medical staff, who had been seconded for political duties and who had no knowledge whatsoever of military matters. To one of the officers of the proposed force who wisely suggested waiting for two days until an engineer would be back with a report on the route over the mountains, Macnaghten replied sharply that he did not like difficulties being made and Captain Hay had no alternative but to march at once. He and his infantry toiled for a month on the 100-mile journey to Bamian, surmounting the towering passes with cumbersome guns and ammunition wagons, in order, as Henry Durand noted 'to lodge an excellent battery of horse artillery in a position where it could be of no use'.

Then, on the strength of an alarmist report from Dr. Lord that Dost Mahommed had assembled a large army and was marching to reconquer his kingdom—it turned out to be an Afghan invention—Macnaghten persuaded Keane to agree to leave the entire Bengal division of the Anglo-Indian army in Afghanistan when the General himself returned to India.

Shah Shuja was now saddled with a substantial foreign army in the country. There is no doubt that while Dost Mahommed was free to be a magnet for the discontented— a focus of rebellion—he was desperately anxious that the British should stay to do the fighting for which his own troops were still not reliable.

On the other hand, he hated the gleaming foreign

bayonets for the lie they gave to the fiction that he was king by popular consent.

Durand believed at this time that with a reliable and efficient force of his own occupying key points of the country Shuja would have been able to hold Kabul, Kandahar and Ghazni against all but an army with powerful artillery, which Dost Mahommed certainly would not command. With such domination of the country, reinforced by conciliation of the chiefs, for whose restless but petty ambitions he could have found outlets in the civil and military service of the State, Shuja could have braved any attempted return of Dost Mahommed.

And freed from the domineering presence of the Anglo-Indian army his popularity and his real power over the country would increase—always provided his financial measures proved fair.

The winter, whose extreme cold discouraged fighting in Afghanistan, would have enabled the king to have consolidated his power and to have raised a party of influential chiefs favourable to his reign.

But from the very outset these hopes were vain. First, the Shah's force showed no sign of becoming an effective fighting machine, even though it had been strengthened by increasing the number of British officers from two to five for each regiment. For the British hated their role, regarding it only as a stepping-stone to a lucrative political post.

Secondly, there was hardly a man among the chiefs whom the king could ask to join a government. They were all jealous of each other's power and in these feudal social conditions the King would never have found it possible to promote one at the possible expense of the other. As Vizier, or chief minister, he had appointed the worst man he could have chosen—Moolah Shikore, his companion in exile, whose faculties, Burnes says, were seriously impaired by age and disease. But he was not too old to be dangerous.

He appointed corrupt subordinates to collect taxes, while to satisfy Shah Shuja's demands as well as those of the collectors, the assessments had to be fixed at an exorbitant level. British forces were sent to aid in the revenue collection; often they were asked by the Shah's collector to attack the forts and villages of the obstinate.

Among so proud a race as the Afghans fierce resentment was aroused at what was seen as foreign oppression. In search of additional revenue, Moolah Shikore appointed corrupt judges who sold verdicts to the highest bidder. Law and justice were soon seen to be a sham.

But Moolah Shikore was stupid as well as corrupt. When the presence of the army caused a shortage of grain in Kabul and the surrounding districts, he seized the granaries and sold what remained at an inflated price fixed by himself—an act which caused much distress and spread discontent with the speed of a forest fire.

Later, wishing to placate Shah Shuja, he decided to replant the gardens of the royal palace and so conscripted a few hundred poor peasants to do it for nothing. Burnes tells how they were dragged into Kabul from their country hovels at seed time, when it was vital to sow their own lands, and forced to work planting flowers, without food or wages. Burnes warned Moolah Shikore that he would personally see to it that serious trouble would follow were they not paid. They were given a small pittance.

When those people who felt that they had been dealt with unjustly appealed to Macnaghten's officials the officials protested to Moolah Shikore, who thereupon punished the plaintiffs for daring to appeal.

The Shah contributed to this discontent as well. To those whom he wished to reward for services rendered, he conferred grants of land or houses owned by chiefs he believed were disloyal. The holders naturally resisted this confiscation, and Shah Shuja, lacking armed forces under his own command, turned to Macnaghten for enforcement.

Macnaghten, who had the sole power to order military action and who could not let the Shah lose face, sent troops to dispossess the land-holders—thus openly supporting injustice.

Dost Mahommed had ruled with severity, but on the whole fairly. Shah Shuja became known for tyranny and oppression from the earliest days of his return. The chances therefore of his ever being able to survive without the permanent support of a foreign army were small indeed.

Meantime, as winter approached, officers and men in Kabul settled down to enjoy the delights of any army of occupation in a strange land.

How did Kabul look then? Officers and men passing through the walls via the great gateways—always armed, though the people at first seemed friendly—found themselves in narrow winding alleys of flat-roofed houses of sunbaked mud round open courtyards, with here and there the taller house with its lofty tower, of a chief. Frequently they came up against great gateways of wood built across the streets which stopped all progress.

The Bala Hissar—the royal palace and fortress—was built into a rocky hill overlooking the city and consisted of three or four stories of brick and stone with the fortress at the top dominating the palace, the walled-in area below and the entire city. It was virtually impregnable.

Perhaps most interesting to the English soldiers of 1839 were the great bazaars, the chief of which was the Charchutta, which they found to be made up of four white stucco arcades—tall and wide passages crowded with horses, camels and even elephants, for sale.

Another of the arcades sold food—great doggets of mutton stuck on iron spikes, huge loaves of bread, fruit of every kind and trays of sweet cakes. In still another arcade were costly jewellery, silks, furs, carpets, embroidered skull caps and the baggy trousers, wide sashes and huge turbans worn by the Afghans. Fountains played into great stone basins at the intersections of the arcades.

In a street running from the Peshawar gate of the city to the bazaar, the British crowded the stalls of the sword and gunsmiths, the bookbinders, leather-workers and saddlers. Kabul bazaar at this time was a great mart for the produce and manufactures of all central Asia, a fabulous place for the young men from the quiet towns and villages of England to wander in.

And for young men with leisure, no worries and swords as their sides there were other diversions, too. Occasionally at they strolled through the crowded narrow streets, the windows of fine trellis and lattice-work that encased the balconies a few feet above would slide aside and sparkling eyes in a beautiful face framed in long dark hair looked down invitingly upon them.

The British assessed the situation with speed. Word went round that the Afghan ladies were willing and that affairs were possible. The facts of the situation probably came from Sir Alexander Burnes, who having spent some time in Kabul earlier, was well aware of local inclination and who, shortly after the arrival of the British there, had acquired several Afghan and Kashmiri girls and installed them in the house with which Shah Shuja had presented him.

The main reason for this laxity was that among the Kabulees many men were afflicted with homosexuality and apart from attending dutifully to the strict demands of procreation, they neglected the physical needs of their wives.

Within a month or two of their arrival, most young unmarried officers were involved with Kabul women; and this continued among many of the single men even after the arrival of the wives and daughters of English officers in 1840. Meetings with the Afghan women were mostly in secret, in houses many officers obtained from Shah Shuja for this purpose.

The men of Kabul, cuckolded by their conquerors, probably shrugged their shoulders and pretended not to know, but in time they grew to look upon the English as lascivious infidels and their early friendship turned to hate.

The army's moralising chaplain, the Reverend G. R. Gleig, grieved at these careless ways, noted later: 'Whatever errors they committed, the great mass of the garrison of Kabul atoned for them terribly; and the survivors, as years pass over them, will doubtless ... become convinced that the gratification of the moment is purchased at too high a price, if it occasion deep or permanent suffering to others.'

But this was, of course, only one small part of the

pursuits of the English in Kabul. Horse-racing and cricket were organised. Shah Shuja gave a valuable sword as a prize for riding, won by Major Daly of the 4th Light Dragoons. Soon the Afghans as well were taking part in flat racing and steeplechasing. Cricket they were prepared to watch, but they never took off their flowing robes and huge turbans to join in the energetic bowling, batting and fielding.

Both nations enjoyed wrestling, teams were formed and the Afghans, who prided themselves upon their skill in what was regarded as a national sport, were surprised to see their most noted wrestlers thrown time after time by the British champions. The British also attended the cock-fighting mains held among the Afghans, and betting, as was the custom, cheerfully lost their pay.

This fraternisation led the Afghan chiefs to invite senior British officers out to their forts for shooting and feasting, while in Kabul this hospitality was returned by the officers in regimental messes and in the houses they had acquired. A theatre was built, amateur theatricals were begun and light comedies were put on to amuse the Afghans; Burnes and others skilled in their dialects, translating the dialogue.

But the British were still looked upon by the Afghans as infidel invaders, blind to their feelings, customs and language. And it was in any case impossible for bitterness to fade when Macnaghten was known to be planning further war against them. And this, in a spirit of revenge he was about to begin.

Chapter Thirteen

The first targets of Macnaghten's desire for revenge were the chiefs of the Ghilzyes, who he recalled were hostile during the army's march between Kandahar and Ghazni; and the Khan of Khelat, Mehrab Khan. Though certainly not actively hostile—the Khan had even restrained the tribes in his domain during the passage of the army—he had yet failed to supply it with the grain he had promised. So it was forthwith decided on Burnes's recommendation to overthrow him and add his territories to those of Shah Shuja.

The formidable Captain Outram was on 7 September 1839 sent off with a force of 500 cavalry and infantry of the Shah's force and Captain Abbot's battery of 9-pounders to punish the Ghilzyes. Quickly and efficiently Outram destroyed their forts and scattered their troops, sowing anew seeds of hatred where conciliation and goodwill were needed. He then sent his force back to Kabul, marched across hostile country with only two guides and within forty-eight hours joined General Willshire, who had been assigned the task of dealing with Mehrab Khan while returning to India with the Bombay division.

The Khan had done all he could to come to terms with Macnaghten and Shuja, but nothing short of his surrender would satisfy Macnaghten. The Khan was to be deposed and sent into exile.

Mehrab Khan had good cause to hope for success in his negotiations with Shah Shuja and Macnaghten, having years before give the Shah shelter and protection when he was fleeing the country—hospitality that probably saved Shuka's life. Expecting therefore, some remembrance of his earlier service, even when he heard days before of the approach of Willshire's force he made no preparations for defence.

The day before Willshire's arrival, Captain Bean, the regional political agent, came to tell him Macnaghten's terms—unconditional surrender and exile for life with his wife and son. The Khan, who must have been shocked by this evidence of Shuja's ingratitude, replied that he would fight and die rather than surrender. Captain Bean rejoined Willshire, and the Khan sent his wife and son to hide in the mountains. He then called in a few hundred tribesmen from nearby villages and awaited the clash with the British.

General Willshire arrived early in the morning of 13 November 1839, on the plain before the fortress and walled town. The Khan's force of about 2,000 men and five guns were assembled on steeply rising hills about 300 yards north-east of the town wall. Willshire had 1,000 infantry and six 6-pounder guns. He saw that the Khan had little faith in his fortifications, to prefer to place his troops out on the hillside in the open.

The three red-coated infantry regiments advanced in column, while the British 6-pounders opened fire at 700 yards with shrapnel and case-shot. Mehrab Khan's guns answered seconds later, but their shot fell wide of the advancing British infantry, who continued at a steady march in face of sharp *jezail* fire.

The accurate case-shot and shrapnel from the British guns soon knocked down so many of the defenders that they lost courage and fled down the hillside back into the town, dragging their guns with them. The British charged to try to reach the gate first, but were just too late—the last of the defenders ran in and the great gates were slammed. The British sought cover near the walls while General Willshire brought up his artillery. A few shells blew down the gate and the infantry burst their way inside. Another column burst in through another gate and both grimly fought their way through the town to the citadel. Here, these gates were blown down by gunpowder and soon the British colours were fluttering from the topmost tower. The Afghans were finally subdued by late afternoon.

About 400 of them were killed, including the Khan himself, shot through the heart in reward for his stubborn bravery—he could have escaped with his wife and son and doubtless returned later to rule again.

Lieutenant Loveday, one of the political officers present, witnessed the Khan's funeral next day. 'There was one little hole in his breast,' he noted, 'which told of a musket-ball having passed through. He had no clothes on, except his silk pyjammas. One of his slaves whispered to me for a shawl; alas! I had nothing of the kind, but remembered a brocade bed-cover which I had bought in my days of folly and extravagance at Delhi. I called for it immediately and gave it to the Khan's servants, who were delighted with this last mark of respect and wrapping up the body in it placed their deceased master on a *charpoy* and carried him to the grave.'

But Loveday's respect failed to outweigh the hatred of Mehrab Khan's son for the men who had killed his father. He was not long after to undergo torture and death at the hands of the young prince.

Thirty-one British were killed in the attack and 107 wounded. Among the wounded at Kelat was Tom Holdsworth, who took part in the storming of Ghazni. 'As the man who fired at me was so very close,' he wrote home, 'the ball (10 oz.) went clean through and so saved me the unpleasant process of having it extracted by the doctors. I had my right flank exposed . . . and so the ball passed through my right arm into my right side and passing downwards to the rear came out at my back an inch from my backbone.'

Holdsworth yet recovered completely from this severe wound and was fighting again two months later. The ball was probably sterilised by the hot flame of the exploding powder.

The loot, which included the crown and zenana jewels was at first estimated to be worth about £60,000 but the jewels were eventually sold for much less than their true value and the total sum of prize money was no more than about £10,000.

Meantime, in September 1839, events which decided the future fate of the British garrison in Kabul had occurred. When it was decided to keep British troops there, the question of how they were to be lodged arose. Lieutenant Durand, the engineer then concerned, wanted possession of the Bala Hissar, which secured command of the entire capital. He pointed out this to Macnaghten, stressing that in it only 1,000 men and a few guns would be able to defy the whole of Afghanistan.

But Shah Shuja saw in the plan the risk of permanent British power. He therefore opposed it for various trivial reasons and Macnaghten yielded even while admitting that the objections were ridiculous.

General Sale expected to be in command in Kabul when Keane left for India in November 1839, and he too had a voice in the placing of troops for its defence. Durand relates how he took Sale over the different locations outside the city and over the Bala Hissar, telling him and Macnaghten that it was impossible before winter to build quarters for a brigade and its attached cavalry and guns outside the Bala Hissar. Inside, on the other hand, by utilising what was already there, it was possible to make good accommodation.

Sale agreed, and the Shah, informed that both the General and the Engineer had decided upon the Bala Hissar, reluctantly assented. Durand goes on to say that thinking the issue was decided, he immediately set the pioneers to work improving the defences and building cover within the walls for the troops, the stores and the ammunition. But the Shah no sooner learnt that the work had begun than he complained that the troops in the citadel above would overlook his royal palace and harem—that its occupation by the British would make him unpopular—and that he had already received strong protests.

Macnaghten, says Durand, with fatal weakness again yielded and peremptory orders were issued for the work to stop.

Durand therefore asked Macnaghten, who with the Shah was about to leave for the milder climate of Jellalabad for the winter, to allow the officers to occupy Dost Mahommed's two large houses, one at each end of a spacious garden in which Macnaghten was then living; and the men in the outbuildings near by, all of which were surrounded by a high wall at the foot of the Bala Hissar.

But Macnaghten for some reason rejected this proposal too. Durand tenaciously clinging to his objective of keeping troops in the Bala Hissar at all costs, then asked that the stables should be cleaned out for occupation by the sepoys and that H.M.'s 13th Regiment, then below strength, should be put in temporary huts close by.

This was agreed, and Durand seemed to have got what he wanted. Once in military occupation of the Bala Hissar, he thought, it was most unlikely that the troops would leave it and the occupation of the entire stronghold was in time likely to follow.

'But the Shah', relates Durand, 'as well as the Afghans, were averse to a measure which, so long as the British troops remained in Afghanistan, would keep Kabul subject to their efficient control. And Macnaghten, being in the false position of having to reconcile the declared intention of the Government to withdraw the army . . . with its present actual military occupation in force, wavered on the adoption of the necessary measures of precaution which might countenance the suspicion of a purpose . . . permanently to hold the country.'

Macnaghten accompanied the Shah on his winter stay in Jellalabad and the troops wintered fairly comfortably in the Bala Hissar, the British now convinced that they were there for good. But upon his return to Kabul in April 1840 the Shah objected, again Macnaghten foolishly yielded. Surprisingly, General Cotton, who on Keane's departure had returned to military command in Afghanistan, agreed.

The troops were marched out and their accommodation was taken over by the three or four hundred ladies of the Shah's harem.

And so in an arrangement that sounds like a sequence in a musical comedy was founded the fate of the British army. And now on a stretch of low swampy ground in an utterly defenceless position, commanded on all sides by hills, cantonments for the troops were built.

Afghan forts in the plain overlooked each of the circular bastions supposed to protect the new British cantonments and these forts were neither knocked down nor occupied. The cantonments, which were about $1\frac{1}{2}$ miles north-west of the Bala Hissar, and measured 1,000 by 600 yards, were made still harder to defend by crowding in upon Macnaghten's gardens and residences in which attackers could take shelter.

Having tamely quitted the Bala Hissar for, in the military sense, the worst possible position, the British Commander-in-Chief, General Cotton, now agreed to establishing his ammunition and weapons in an unfinished fort some 300 yards outside the fortified cantonments dominated by an Afghan fort some 400 yards eastwards. The stores of food and medicines upon which depended the army's very existence were placed, it is hard to believe, farther away in another fort.

Macnaghten seems to have insisted upon Cotton's acceptance of these gross military blunders. His object was to convince the Afghans that their conquerors had so little suspicion or fear of them that they did not even need to place their food and ammunition inside their own camp.

In the end, General Cotton had either to agree to this stupidity or ask to resign his command. He had evidently been given the command in preference to General Nott in Kandahar because that old campaigner had already made it clear that he would not tolerate interference from Macnaghten and his political officers.

When, however, General Cotton's command was confirmed, leaving General Nott in command at Kandahar, instructions to Macnaghten from the Governor-General stated that now Shah Shuja was established on the throne the new General's powers would be less than General Keane had enjoyed.

In the administration of good order and military discipline, General Cotton would have full control, but 'the disposal and employment of the force would be under political direction'. The military authorities would, of course, be *consulted* on both matters, and 'in the moving and cantonments of the troops both military and political considerations would be attended to'.

But the political officers would decide whether military operations should be undertaken and the Commander-in-Chief should merely give his opinion as to their practicability. The Envoy also would be in sole command of the Shah's force.

Thus the military had now been fully subordinated to the civil power in an occupied and unfriendly country. And of this the first outcome had been expulsion of the army from the Bala Hissar, their establishment in cantonments that could hardly be defended and the placing of their food and ammunition beyond their control outside their camp.

The Afghans could easily put the British at their mercy, were they to exploit this situation.

Shah Shuja's newly won empire was divided into two military commands at this time. The northern one had its headquarters in Kabul, the capital, and included also Ghazni, Jellalabad and the surrounding provinces, east as far as Peshawar, but excluding it. The southern one, commanded by General Nott, including Kandahar, Quetta, Khelat, Dadar, Gundava and the small but important fort of Ghirisk.

At the time of General Keane's departure for India in November 1839, H.M.'s 13th Light Infantry and the 35th Native Infantry with six field-guns besides the citadel guns were to garrison Kabul, supported by a regiment of the Shah's cavalry and some of his arillery, under the immediate command of Lieutenant-Colonel Dennie, the hero of Ghazni.

The 4th Brigade, including the 48th Native Infantry, the 2nd Light Cavalry, a troop of Skinner's Horse and six guns were to occupy Jellalabad.

Ghazni was to be held by the 16th Native Infantry, a troop of Skinner's Horse and whatever were available of the Shah's force. The 42nd and 43rd Native Infantry were to be stationed with some of the Shah's force and the heavy artillery under General Nott's command at Kandahar.

The total Anglo-Indian regiments left in Afghanistan were thus one British Regiment, the 13th Foot, seven of the Native Infantry, one of Native cavalry and one of artillery. The total number of fighting-men, British, sepoy, Afghan and Sikh amounted to about 20,000 with about 70 or 80 guns. Thirteen thousand of these were the Shah's force, leaving about 7,000 well-trained Anglo-Indian troops. But events were soon to show that these were not nearly enough.

Chapter Fourteen

Shah Shuja's only possible hope of getting the support of the chiefs and so reigning fairly peacefully was to try to emulate the rule by consent of Dost Mahommed. But it soon became only too plain that the Shah lacked the necessary capacity. By the late autumn of 1839 he had made himself hated even by the friendly chiefs who had called to pay homage to him.

His coldness, his lack of respect for them, his demand that they should throw themselves on their faces before him at the start of an audience—this, no less than flagrant injustice and misrule, made them hurry away, with the idea of rebellion growing in their minds.

Shah Shuja's failure marked a serious parting of the ways. If to rule the chiefs by guile, diplomacy and consent was beyond him, then, Macnaghten decided, they must be ruled in the only other way—by the destruction of their age-old power and influence. But to do so would demand a powerful army, ready and able to crush insurrection swiftly —a far bigger force than the British then had or could afford to keep in Afghanistan.

Macnaghten decided that the people must therefore be turned somehow against their chiefs—leaders to whom they were attached by strong ties of blood, social custom and economic interest. Despite having too few troops and those marked for eventual withdrawal, he adopted this dangerous policy.

He first set out to form regiments of tribesmen to enforce the Shah's rule over the chiefs, believing that since the troops were to be paid by the royal treasury and commanded by British officers they would be willing to act against their own leaders.

The chiefs saw what was afoot, forgot their own feuds and united in resentment against the Shah. The new regiments, on the other hand, showed dislike for the training and leadership of the infidel British and were never reliable.

The Khyber tribesmen were among those few who had eventually welcomed the Shah's return. In gratitude, without telling Macnaghten, he had promised them a huge subsidy for protecting traffic through the Pass—that is, for refraining from attacking it.

The tribesmen did not receive the promised money. They revolted. Troops were sent to attack them but meantime the political officer concerned, Captain Mackeson, had negotiated an annual subsidy of £8,000—four times more than Dost Mahommed had ever paid for similar restraint. The subsequent reduction of this sum was later to lash the tribesmen into a full-scale revolt.

Dr. Lord, meantime, at Bamian had launched various minor attacks against nearby rulers which, while in no way helping to consolidate the British position, caused resentment. Lord eventually wrote to Macnaghten for reinforcements on the grounds that he feared an attack soon by Dost Mahommed; and these were sent to him.

But the former king was then in no position to attack anyone. He had been living quietly in Kooloom, from where he had written to the Khan of Bokhara, trying to make an ally of him. The Khan, thinking it might do no harm were he to seize this enemy of the British, invited him for a friendly visit, then imprisoned him.

But Dr. Lord's skirmishings and advances had alarmed neighbouring rulers and one of them saw in the seizure of Dost Mahommed—the one ruler who had opposed the infidel invaders—a danger to them all.

This man, the Khan of Kokan, now warned his brother the Khan of Bokhara, against the imprisonment of Dost Mahommed and demanded that he be speedily released. To help the Khan make up his mind he deployed a force on his frontier.

Dost Mahommed was then allowed to escape and to

become once more a magnet for all the discontented chiefs in Afghanistan. Thus, Dr. Lord's futile playing at soldiers had brought the former ruler his freedom, which, in the strictly ethical sense was no doubt desirable, but politically, as regards the safety of Shah Shuja and the British, was one of the worst things that could have happened.

The spring of 1840 now heralded, as well, renewed rebellion by the Ghilzye tribe. Those fierce warriors saw a new power in the land that threatened their traditional supremacy, and the transit-dues which, apart from their flocks, brought them a living. They began to attack military messengers, the post and even convoys. General Nott sent a reconnaissance force of about 200 cavalry and found that the chiefs had assembled enough tribesmen to cut all the communications between Kabul, Kandahar and Jellalabad.

Macnaghten now realised with a shock that the Ghilzyes were actually in open rebellion and that his far-flung communications were at their mercy.

He requested General Cotton in Kabul to supply whatever troops were necessary to put them down. But meantime General Nott on 7 May 1840 had sent against them a battalion of 800 of the Shah's infantry with four siege guns of the horse artillery, the entire force in command of Captain Anderson. A sharp engagement followed that showed once again the supremacy of the British under good officers.

For thirty minutes the Ghilzyes withstood a blast of shot and shell, after which they swept from their positions and charged down upon the bayonets of Anderson's infantry, but these, commanded by three English officers, stood firm.

The Ghilzyes withdrew, reformed under the devastating shrapnel fire and charged again, only to be thrust back once more, when they retired leaving 200 dead on the field and more slain by the guns in their earlier position. 'The combat was a sharp one and very creditable to the courage of the Ghilzyes, who though superior in numbers were without artillery,' Durand noted.

General Nott learned afterwards that in two days' time 10,000 Ghilzyes would have gathered instead of 3,000 and, that if he had weakened his garrison at Kandahar in facing them, they would have stormed it in force and could have overwhelmed it. The Ghilzye rebellion had not been finally extinguished, however. The ashes of revolt still glowed.

Throughout the summer of 1840, hostile risings against Macnaghten's government of sentry boxes occurred from one end of the country to the other. In August a force of 500 infantry and three howitzers escorting a supplies convoy of 1,200 camels and 500 bullocks through the Bolan Pass was ambushed by Baluchi tribesmen. Major Glibborn, surrounded by the rocky sunbaked hills shimmering in the burning heat, tried hard to beat off the attacks while keeping control of the unwieldy convoy. Held down in a defensive position, his force ran out of water, suffered severely in a temperature nearing 100 degrees and finally was forced to retreat, losing 200 sepoys killed and many wounded, as well as more than 1,000 camels with their supplies, and all the bullocks.

In another of the passes a detachment of sepoys was cut to pieces.

Nusseer Khan, son of Mehrab Khan, the ruler who was killed in the fall of Kelat, then attacked Quetta, 300 miles south of Kabul. He was repulsed—only to assemble a force of some 12,000 men and attack his kingdom of Kelat, another 100 miles farther south. Held by Lieutenant Loveday and a garrison of 700 it soon fell. Loveday was captured, Nusseer Khan had him shackled and tortured. Some weeks later Loveday was found with his throat cut.

In late November General Nott marched to reoccupy Kelat, 300 miles south, which it was thought essential to keep in British hands. When he was within two days' march of it this veteran campaigner sent in proclamations assuring the inhabitants that if they remained quietly in their homes, they and their property would be protected and no violence would occur.

The city's dignitaries came to his camp the next night—'trembling and supplicating to know whether this could be true . . . I assured them,' he related in a letter to his family, 'told them that nothing could resist the force I had and said: "Go back to your city, and let me find the gates open on my arrival, and rest assured of complete protection."''

They believed him and thus Nott obtained possession of Kelat without firing a shot. This, he called 'military management'. He put guards on the gates with orders to let no one enter—'absolutely necessary to quiet the fears of the people'. One of Macnaghten's political officers was excluded—he protested rudely to Nott, who threatened him with arrest if he did not go at once to his tent.

'He said no more, but went to his tent; but I dare say he will write a long story to the Envoy, and he will inform the Governor General that he is horrified at my conduct . . . and I shall in due time hear *something very wise* from his Lordship, which I shall not care so much about, as my old grandmother would for a brass farthing. I have a sweet consolation—the devoted gratitude of an oppressed people.'

Leaving a strong garrison, the magnanimous Nott then marched back to Kandahar, uneasy and sad about the directions things were taking. 'All goes wrong here,' he wrote to a friend, 'we are become hated by the people and the English name and character, which two years ago stood so high and so fair, is become a bye-word.'

Whatever hopes for a respite Macnaghten may have had at this juncture were now destroyed with the sudden appearance of Dost Mahommed between Saighan and Bamian, where the political officer Dr. Lord was conducting his operations about 100 miles north-west of Kabul.

Alarmed at the reports of the large army that had flocked to the deposed ruler's standard, Lord wrote to Macnaghten pleading for the immediate dispatch of a brigade of troops, about 1,000 men.

Macnaghten had no wish to scatter his meagre army even more, but seeing danger in this possible attack from Dost Mahommed at his back he sent the able Lieutenant-Colonel Dennie, with cavalry, a battery of horse-artillery and the 35th Regiment of Native Infantry—all told about

1,200 men. Dennie arrived on 14 September 1840 and took command.

Four days later he heard report of the enemy. He rode out to meet them in a valley with 500 infantry supported by 300 cavalry and two 9-pounders. Overwhelming the enemy outposts, he rounded a bend—and came face to face with Dost Mahommed—at the head of a glittering army of several thousand.

Dennie attacked without hesitation. The guns boomed, cutting down scores of the assembled tribesmen, who turned and fled even before the Gurkha infantry could get to grips. The cavalry went after them with slashing sabres. Somehow the wily Dost Mahommed escaped in the confusion, but lost his tents, his horses and his personal equipment.

Joyful news for the worried Macnaghten and frightened Shah Shuja, was Dennie's victory and the peace it brought for the time being to this troubled region. It seemed that the main threat to the kingdom was overcome now that Dost Mahommed was again a fugitive without an army. But this elation alas, was short-lived, Macnaghten was soon fuming and Shah Shuja soon sighing again.

For Dost Mahommed reappeared in Kohistan, north of Kabul, where he was aware that the discontent that racked the country was most rife and where the chiefs most strongly opposed the Shah's persistent tax demands. Dost Mahommed's own rule had been weakest in Kohistan. He had executed rebellious chiefs and imposed heavy taxation himself there.

These self-same chiefs had as a result cautiously welcomed Shuja on his arrival fourteen months ago, but now the in-injustice of his rule, the presence of foreign troops to support it and the parsimony of his reward for their loyalty to him had made them so furious that they willingly supported their old oppressor.

Macnaghten next heard of plots by Dost Mahommed under his very nose in the city of Kabul. Alarmed, he recalled the stalwart Dennie with his artillery and infantry and at the same time summoned the Kohistan chiefs to

Kabul. Willingly enough the chiefs swore allegiance, and in a flurry of swollen turbans and ballooning cotton trousers made deep obeissance to the Shah, who hiding behind his dyed beard, stared at them with a curious mixture of fear and hauteur.

But Macnaghten, the astute orientalist, had not been taken in by their submissive assurance; nor perhaps had Shah Shuja. But neither guessed that the chiefs, observing how small was the garrison at Kabul, had returned to their mountain forts bound by solemn agreements to overthrow the Shah. These secret plans were now revealed in letters between them that Macnaghten intercepted.

Macnaghten decided then not to wait for precise news of Dost Mahommed's whereabouts and sent Sir Alexander Burnes with a force under the command of General Sale to attack the Kohistan chiefs in their own strongholds before the Amir could organise a large-scale rising.

For the next three weeks Sale marched his small force of infantry, cavalry and five guns from fort to fort in the parched and stony landscape, losing officers and men in frequent skirmishes, subjected to night attacks, but never managing to track down the Amir himself.

Dost Mahommed threaded defiles, descended gorges only to scale them again, hovered on the outskirts of various towns and came near enough to the British camp to put the troops on the alert for a battle. Having the entire region with him he successfully baffled every attempt at surprise and even had followers among the Shah's own troops.

But General Sale never relaxed his efforts and finally at the end of October ran the Amir to earth in a valley dotted with orchards and small forts. Dost Mahommed had again been warned and as the British cavalry rode up a party of two or three hundred Afghan horsemen led by the Amir rode away up the nearby hills. Captain Fraser led two squadrons of Bengal cavalry to head them off at the top of the valley. The Afghan horsemen now wheeled to face Fraser and his cavalry down in the valley below.

Dost Mahommed is reported then to have doffed his huge

turban—a religious act—pointed to his green-and-white banner, called on his men in the name of the Prophet to follow him against the unbelievers and led a charge down the hillside.

Fraser had formed up his troopers, but a distant bugle suddenly sounded the 'retire'. Instead, Fraser gave the word to charge and spurred his horse as the Afghans thundered down. The British officers all charged, but whether the bugle had confused the sepoy troops or the charging Afghans had unnerved them, was never known.

They broke and fled. Five British officers and Dr. Lord hurled themselves alone at the several hundred Afghans in a crazily brave but disastrous do-or-die attempt.

Lieutenants Broadfoot and Crispin and Dr. Lord were hacked to pieces within seconds. Lieutenant Ponsonby, wounded in the arm and slashed from forehead to chin, hardly able to see through his own blood, and with his reins cut, was miraculously carried out of the hurly-burly by his horse, whose ears were hacked off.

Wounded in the back, Fraser fought his way clear and, only half-conscious, with his right hand nearly cut off, rode back to Sale to tell of the disaster.

Dost Mahommed and his men escaped over the hills.

Burnes at once wrote to Macnaghten, without consulting General Sale, to say that there was no choice but to fall back on Kabul, where, he advised, all the troops in the northern command should be concentrated—an absurd decision, it turned out.

At Kabul meanwhile, Macnaghten, already aware that an uprising was only too likely, had mounted cannon on the Bala Hissar to frighten the city—and was even considering whether he ought not to concentrate all troops in the fortress, so gloomy were his expectations.

He is reported to have received Burnes's letter on 3 November, the day after the clash with Dost Mahommed, while taking his afternoon ride on the Kabul plain. There, not much more than a year before, he had seen himself as monarch supreme. Its contents must have sunk him into even deeper dejection.

But at that moment occurred a strange reversal of fortune. An Afghan horseman rode up to him and announced that the Amir was present.

'What Amir? asked Macnaghten.

'Dost Mahommed,' was the answer.

The Amir presented himself, dismounted before the astonished Macnaghten, presented his sword and said that he wished to surrender. Macnaghten, despite all his vilification of the Amir in the past, returned it to him and the two rode together into the cantonments.

The only explanation of Dost Mahommed's surrender—especially after a minor but encouraging victory—can be that after fifteen months he was weary of the life of a fugitive—that he had little confidence in the loyalty of the Afghans towards him—and that he wished to be reunited with his family, who were then under house arrest in Ghazni.

His voluntary surrender at once changed the outlook from a critical to a reasonably hopeful one. Shah Shuja's authority might be established fairly easily now that Dost Mahommed, the main encouragement to rebellion, would soon be exiled far off in India.

Macnaghten was overjoyed. Some weeks earlier he had written to Auckland: 'No mercy should be shown to the man who is the author of all the evils that are now distracting the country; but, should we be so fortunate as to secure the person of Dost Mahommed, I shall request his Majesty not to execute him until I can ascertain his Lordship's sentiments.'

A ruthless enough letter, beneath the obsequious phrases, but now Macnaghten wrote: 'I trust that the Dost will be treated with liberality. His case has been compared to that of Shah Shuja; and I have seen it argued that he should not be treated more handsomely than his Majesty was; but surely the cases are not parallel. The Shah had no claim on us. We had no hand in depriving him of his kingdom; whereas we ejected the Dost, who never offended us, in support of our policy of which he was the victim.'

Macnaghten was the chief of those who plotted to depose

Dost Mahommed on the grounds that he was a danger to British India. Now he admitted that the Amir had 'never offended us' and that he was the victim of our policy. Macnaghten's extraordinary vanity and ambition did much to blunt his capacities. But these handicaps could surely not have blinded him to the logic of his observations about Dost Mahommed as they affected the entire invasion. He could hardly have shut his eyes to the fact that with its ruinous cost in blood, reputation and treasure it was nothing more than a monstrous sham and should never have been launched.

The Amir's surrender brought a short lull—the restive chieftains may have paused to take stock of the new situation—but no real return to calm or to acceptance of the Shah and his British masters. And by the end of 1840 a new stage in the government of the country had arrived—Macnaghten had decided that interference in the internal affairs of the country—for example, in the control of revenue —had become vital for the establishment of tranquillity. Other realistic appraisals followed.

General Cotton resigned his command on the grounds of ill-health and his need to return to England, but before leaving he put on record his view that without the support of British troops the Shah had not the slightest chance of keeping his throne.

Then Sir Jasper Nichols, Command-in-Chief India, a wise and experienced old commander, argued, in a long analysis for the Governor-General, that Shah Shuja could neither survive alone, be replaced nor simply be withdrawn. The British would be obliged to continue to rule in his name and pay his personal, civil and military costs. Afghanistan could not be held with less than three British and ten native regiments. As this was likely to become permanent, in view of our other needs an increase in the army was necessary.

Auckland was shaken by the document. He put it aside for some weeks, then in January 1841 it was rejected by the Governor-General in Council. The army in India had already between 1838 and 1841 been increased by about 50,000 men.

The cost of Afghanistan was now officially estimated at the colossal sum of £8 million. In fact, it was even more, and the *Bombay Times*, using information from the Government Gazette and the Army List, accurately put it at a total of £12 million.

It had become a matter of the utmost gravity for India. Early in 1841 the Accountant-General wrote to Lord Auckland advising the unprecedented step of the total prohibition for the time being of all further cash remittances to England. The treasuries were bare. Yet the war began with a £10 million cash surplus in India.

In April 1841 Auckland was obliged to launch a loan at five per cent interest—it was a high rate, the British bank rate was only two and a half per cent—but the response was so poor that he had to increase the interest considerably to offset the lack of public confidence.

There were other repercussions. Taxation was increased to help meet the ceaseless demands for money. Measures to develop cotton production and plans for steam navigation in India were shelved indefinitely, through lack of funds. And all this was to retard the progress of the peoples of India upon which the more enlightened men in the government had set their hopes.

In England when these facts began to penetrate informed opinion, there was, to say the least, some disappointment. Even at the start of the war most of the East India Company Court of Directors were hostile to it. The Chairman, Sir John Hobhouse, was said not to have risked asking his colleagues for their approval.

But when Ghazni fell and Kabul was occupied the whole country was carried away by shouts of triumph. It was looked upon as the bitterest party rancour even slightly to criticise the campaign. Auckland was made an earl: Sir John Keane was raised to the peerage and a pension of £2,000 a year given to him and the next two generations of his descendants.

The general impression under these circumstances was of the acquisition of much territory and huge additions to the revenue. Hardly anyone expected that the laurels reaped had cost India £10 million and that England's new ally Shah Shuja could only be kept on this throne by 10,000 British bayonets and an expenditure of £3 million a year, and that the return for all this was less than nothing.

In parliament, the opposition were silenced both by the great victories and by deliberate deception, for while all Afghanistan simmered with plans for rebellion, Lord Palmerston, the Foreign Secretary, was assuring the nation that tranquillity and prosperity reigned and that our policy would soon prove to have been one of the miracles of modern statesmanship. A general election approached and Palmerston travelled the country saying that Englishmen could ride from one end of Afghanistan to the other unarmed and in perfect safety.

'The progress of British arms in Asia,' he assured the electorate in Tiverton, 'has been marked by a scrupulous reference to justice, an inviolable respect for property, an abstinence from anything which could tend to wound the feelings and prejudices of the people. . . .'

Palmerston must have had details of the reports from Lord Auckland to Sir John Hobhouse which showed on the contrary, that the initial invasion and the attempt at pacification had given way to a defensive war on the part of the British and that they were then engaged in no less than five separate military actions.

But in the deception of the British public over the war this was relatively nothing. The summit of deceit was reached with the publication of a government Blue Book allegedly reporting the early negotiations leading up to the war. In it Burnes's letters describing Dost Mahommed's wish for an alliance with the British were doctored—in effect forged— to give an opposite meaning. Letters which could not be fixed in this way were deliberately left out. The very opposite of the truth was thus foisted on the public in England. And Auckland made no protest whatsoever over what was then as wicked an example of political villainy as any in history. It saved his face, for the truth did not come out until years later.

In Afghanistan the military situation meantime continued to deteriorate. The health of the troops had been seriously affected by the unceasing marching, riding and fighting without rest or let-up. The *Bombay Times* in May 1841 reported an officially corrected list of thirty-three actions during the previous twelve months. The British had won only thirteen of them. At Kabul almost every battalion needed relief. Colonel Shelton had been ordered to lead a relief brigade through the Khyber Pass to Kabul, but it would take him at least four months.

Moreover, the domination of the military by the political officers was by the start of 1841 beginning to demoralise the army and about this General Cottom protested strongly before his departure for India: 'Some check must be imposed, or the whole system must be altered as regards young political officers sent to accompany regular troops. Much disgust has arisen from this and it is absurd that old experienced military men should be under the orders of lieutenants merely because they place after their names "Acting Assistant Political Agent".'

General Nott had a few weeks earlier used somewhat blunter language in a prophetic letter home: 'The conduct of the one thousand and one politicals has ruined our cause and bared the throat of every European in this country to the sword and knife of the revengeful Afghan . . . and unless several regiments be quickly sent not a man will be left to note the fall of his comrades. Nothing but force will ever make them submit to the hated Shah Shuja, who is most certainly as great a scoundrel as ever lived.'

Several of Shuja's sons of his numerous wives had been given official posts. With the possible exception of Prince Timour they were even less suited to responsibility than their father. One of them, Sufter Jung, made governor of Kandahar province with a salary of £140 a month, swiftly increased it to the very princely sum of £10,000 a month through the crudest extortion —the arrest of prosperous merchants and their torture until relatives paid £500 or more for their release.

He spent the money mostly on homosexual orgies, but turned to abduction for what money could not buy. The *Bombay Times* published a letter from his medical attendant on 21 October 1840 telling how he had enticed British soldiers into his residence, drugged them and performed homosexual acts upon them while they were unconscious. In his anxiety to back up Shah Shuja, Macnaghten prevented action against these and other criminal acts, so that among the Afghan population the British name began to stink no less than the King's and his sons.

By contrast, Dost Mahommed's sons were remembered for their manly and intelligent behaviour.

Yet the British were blind to the signs and warnings of approaching danger. The wives, daughters and young children of officers, noncommissioned officers and men had made the long perilous journey from India to Kabul and Kandahar to settle down in bungalows built there especially for them.

Lady Macnaghten, residing in the spacious house of the British mission, presided over the social activities of Kabul. She was challenged in her self-appointed role by Lady Sale —Florentia—a tall bony woman with plain features and a fearless disposition. Wife of the recently knighted General Sir Robert Sale, her daughter was married in Kabul to Lieutenant John Sturt who became the chief engineer officer at Kabul.

A bandstand was built in the middle of the large parade ground in the cantonments and there in the early evening officers in red or blue coatees, gold shoulder-scales, crimson sashes and sword belts competed with the highly paid political officers in formal black suits for the attentions of the young unmarried ladies in voluminous crinolines and extravagant hats.

Here, while the British bandsmen played military marches on trumpet and trombone, the off-duty troops and their womenfolk, a proud and glittering assembly, paraded as if Kabul would be their home for ever.

There were dinner parties and dances—a racecourse, cricket and sports events; there were engagements and marriages. Captain Warburton of the Bengal Artillery, fell in love with and married a niece of Dost Mahommed, Burnes and Macnaghten being witnesses (his son became Colonel Sir Robert Warburton, a famous administrator in India). Sergeant Dean married a beautiful Kabul girl.

But behind the facade of gaiety, entertainment and fraternisation in Kabul a note of danger was apparent and throughout 1841 the tempo of hostilities quickened as to the rhythm of a fanatical drumbeat.

Chapter Fifteen

General Sir Willoughby Cotton returned to India while the mountain passes in the south of Afghanistan echoed to the boom of British artillery and the sharp crack of the tribesmen's *jezails*.

Uktur Khan, a bold and impetuous Durani chief, angered by the ceaseless demands of the Shah's tax collectors, raised the standard of rebellion in Kandahar province and later routed Mahommed Allum Khan at the head of a primitive force of the Shah. General Nott sent Captain Farrington, leading 800 sepoys backed by cavalry and guns to cross the River Helmund in pursuit to defeat Uktur Khan's 1,500 tribesmen on 3 January 1841.

This quietened the Duranis temporarily, yet it merely proved all over again that without British arms the Shah's crown was worth no more to him than a box of sawdust. And despite the victory both General Nott, commanding the southern military region at Kandahar, and Major Rawlinson, the astute political agent there, knew the British position in the country to be extremely dangerous.

Nott looked to the efficiency of his troops and fulminated against the system of government, Rawlinson warned Macnaghten that there were signs that Shah Shuja had actually known of Uktur Khan's revolt, but had avoided telling the British because he wished to influence the chiefs in his own favour.

Macnaghten scoffed at these sinister accusations and informed the Shah, who became 'well-nigh frantic'. Declaring that such lies were the invention of the agents of Moolah Shikore—the former Vizier whom he had recently deposed—he threatened to seize them and 'having ripped up their bellies hang them up as food for the crows'.

Yet Macnaghten sympathised with the Shah and told Rawlinson in a sharply worded letter: 'I think you should sift these atrocious rumours to their head as diligently as possible. You have had a troublesome task lately and have been doubtless without leisure to weigh probabilities; but it may make the considerations of all questions more simple if you will hereafter take for granted that as regards us "*the king can do no wrong*".'

Rawlinson countered with the assertion that the only way to pacify and rule the province under the Shah's regime was by 'the forcible removal to India of at least fifty or sixty of the most powerful and turbulent of the Durani Khans'— a ruthless project that could have ended incessant fighting, but which Macnaghten turned down with the observation that 'Government would never tolerate for a moment the notion of such wholesale expatriation'.

Instead he and the Shah sought to pacify the region by recalling the corrupt agents of Moolah Shikore, inviting the chiefs to petition the Shah with their complaints and announcing his decision to visit them in Kandahar in the autumn of 1841.

It did little to help matters. The system of tax collection was perhaps the root cause of much of the trouble. Hordes of collectors billeted themselves on citizens, living well at their expense until they paid whatever tax was demanded —a system of blackmail that could be made as unpleasant as was necessary to reach a settlement.

In comparison, Dost Mahommed, formerly ruling largely by consent, had no need for a large and costly standing army. Moreover, his way of life being more modest he had taxed the people less. Shah Shuja had by now imported over 800 women for his harem, and scores of dancing girls. His officials, cronies from his exile, his many sons—all needed lucrative posts for which the citizens and peasantry must pay. His grinding taxes enraged the people and just as today redress for wrongs is sought in litigation the Afghans sought it with the sword and *jezail*.

Aware that the use of British troops in the last resort to

enforce payment added to the hostility with which the Afghans now regarded them, Macnaghten ordered Usman Khan, Shuja's new minister, to end the system of billeting tax collectors. But the needs of the Shah were enormous—he had been driven to borrow from the bankers to feed and clothe his regiment of women.

By early 1841 he and his government were bankrupt. There was a deficit of £100,000—even though the Shah's army was paid by India, and to introduce a fairer system of revenue collection while rebellion threatened on all sides was considered impossible. Things therefore went on more or less as they were, with hostility towards the British and the Shah growing stronger day by day and with Macnaghten still insisting on seeing the situation *'couleur de rose'*, as he put it in an optimistic letter to Major Rawlinson on 27 February 1841.

'All things considered, the present tranquillity of this country is to my mind perfectly miraculous,' he remarked. 'I look forward to the time when his Majesty will have an honest and efficient administration of his own, though the time must be far distant if ever it should arrive (certainly it cannot arrive during the present generation to whom anarchy is second nature) when we can dispense with our Hindustanee contingent. Here, we are gradually ferreting out abuses and placing matters on a firm and satisfactory basis.'

Macnaghten for good reason insisted on the tranquillity of the country, however loud grew the noise of conflict. He was expecting confirmation of his hopes for promotion to the dazzling heights of the governorship of Bombay—a princely appointment, the highest to which any civilian official in India could aspire.

It would crown his highly successful career and lead to a peerage; but since British policy in Afghanistan was almost entirely his creation there would be a black mark against him were he to leave the country in a state of chaos and insurrection—indeed, the Governor-General might even request him to postpone his departure until all was well; and

in Afghanistan that prospect was remote. So Macnaghten
minimised the risings and the hostility—everything was
tranquil—*couleur de rose*.

But only in his imagination. He had sent Brigadier
Shelton who was *en route* for Kabul with reinforcements, to
subdue a tribe of mountain warriors, the Sanga Khels,
who had taken to raiding conveys in the Khyber Pass.
Shelton, a tough, unpopular, one-armed martinet, scaled
the cliffs of the narrow defile at their lowest point, advanced
on the tribesmen from the rear, destroyed, one after the
other, all the 144 forts with which they dominated the
defiles, in a short but brilliant campaign in which he lost
only nine men.

At the same time, the Ghilzyes between Kandahar and
Ghazni had again turned hostile. Macnaghten decided to
occupy Kelat-i-Ghilzye, a fortress in the very heart of their
homeland, from which he would be able to crush risings
more easily and guard his communications through the
valley of the Turnak River.

Furious at this bold intrusion the Ghilzyes assembled to
prevent it and attacked a force of 700 infantry, cavalry and
artillery commanded by Colonel Wymer. But the British
artillery showered the Ghilzyes with grape-shot; the infantry
stood firm under repeated charges and with well-delivered
volleys and thrusting bayonets drove the Ghilzyes off.

And next, Uktur Khan, in the south, having gathered a
fresh force of some 6,000 men after his earlier defeat, took
up a strong position on the right bank of the River Helmund,
west of Kandahar, awaiting the opportunity to attack with
profit.

Such was the so-called tranquillity in early 1841—with
discontent, treachery and persistent insurrection in the
south and west threatening Kabul and the north too,
regions to which the surrender of Dost Mahommed had
brought a temporary lull.

Meantime, the question of a successor to Sir Willoughby
Cotton to command the troops in Afghanistan had caused
much speculation. Public opinion seized upon General Nott

because of his knowledge and experience of the Afghan scene no less than his fighting ability. But Nott, known for his contempt for the political officers, had already been passed over two years before in favour of Cotton. Even though Lord Auckland now realised he was best equipped for the post and wanted him, Macnaghten appears to have blocked his appointment.

And so while almost the whole army hoped for Nott's appointment, the General himself, as his biographer, Stocqueler, noted 'cherished no such expectations. He had had large experience of the jobbery of the Auckland administration; he knew that his plain speaking had made him unpalatable to the folks in power.' In one of his frequent letters to his daughters Maria, Letitia and Charlotte, Nott wrote at this time: 'I cannot alter my nature. . . . I cannot conceal my hatred and indignation at the oppression, cruelty and dishonourable conduct, and therefore, I am unfit for the scenes passing in this country. I cannot bend my spirit or bring my mind to their level, consequently I must suffer the injustice of those dressed in authority.'

Only two days after sending this letter the gallant Nott saw with surprise in orders the name of Major-General Elphinstone to command in Afghanistan, for he it was Auckland had chosen, thus at once upholding the sacred principle of seniority and assuring Magnaghten of a suitably pliant commander.

The most fateful step of all had now been taken.

Chapter Sixteen

Like Keane before him, Major-General William George Keith Elphinstone was a favourite of fortune. He had held a commission in the Guards and was said to be 'one of the most gentleman-like members of the Household Brigade'. Aged sixty, he had been commanding the Benares division of the Bengal army since arriving in India two years earlier in 1839, having returned to the active list only in 1837 after several years on half-pay.

He was a conscientious officer but had seen no active service since Waterloo, and very little before that. Nevertheless, his ability there in command of the 33rd Foot—or it could have been his aristocratic connections, for he was a grandson of the 10th Lord Elphinstone—had won him the orders of Commander of the Bath, of St. Anne of Austria and of William of Holland.

All that was twenty-six years ago, when he was in the prime of life. In 1841, by contrast, his crippling gout and rheumatism gave him unceasing pain and he was so lacking in mental and physical energy that it must surely have been clear that he had one foot in the grave when the command was offered him.

To be fair, Elphinstone himself had no ambitions at this time except to return home to England and die quietly in bed. Certainly he had no wish to command in Afghanistan, hundreds of miles away over the rugged mountains among a turbulent, rebellious nation, when he could hardly walk more than a few paces.

But Lord Auckland seemed to think that nothing more was needed of the general than to parade occasionally at the head of his troops, make obeisance to Shah Shuja and carry out the orders of the wise and far-seeing Macnaghten.

Knowing his own incapacity Elphinstone had at first turned down the Governor-General's offer, but Auckland had put considerable pressure upon him and finally he accepted, but only because he thought it wrong in a soldier not to go where he was ordered. It was a pathetic decision—the invalid general chivvied through his sense of duty into a command that could only end in tragedy.

General Keane was carried in a palanquin because he enjoyed it more than riding on horseback. Elphinstone rode in a palanquin because he was usually incapable of mounting a horse. And so, early in April 1841, he arrived in Kabul, exhausted after the long and tiring journey.

At the very start of his command the General's none too robust morale was undermined in a clash with Macnaghten. Brigadier Shelton's brigade, which should by now have been in Kabul to strengthen the garrison, had been marched up and down the country for weeks quelling minor risings at the behest of the political officers. Now Macnaghten asked the General to order it back 100 miles through the Khyber Pass to escort of all things, another convoy of women from Peshawar for the Shah's harem. Elphinstone protested, but Macnaghten got his way. It was the first setback for Elphinstone's authority.

Another, more significant setback followed. Sick though Elphinstone was, he saw at first glance that the British were in a hopeless position at Kabul. The cantonments stretched for more than half a mile across the plain and were 600 yards broad, yet protected only by a low rampart and a narrow ditch with circular blockhouses at the four corners.

Fenced gardens hemmed it in so that there was no clear line of fire; several small forts still held by the Afghans commanded it on three sides and the Behmaru Hills, from which Afghan 6-pounder guns could hit it, commanded the fourth or west side.

Three or four hundred yards from the south corner there was a village of mud huts surrounded by a low wall in which marksmen could hide. ' . . . The troops,' Lieutenant Vincent

Eyre of the Bengal Artillery, wrote later, 'could not move a dozen paces from either gate without being exposed to the fire of some neighbouring hostile fort garrisoned by marksmen who seldom missed their aim.'

Had Elphinstone been a younger, resolute general he would at once have defied political domination and insisted on taking over the impregnable Bala Hissar, the only place where his reserves of food, ammunition and medical stores could safely be kept. Indeed, in it he could have housed the entire garrison, for Lieutenant Sturt of the Engineers was then completing additional barracks there.

But Elphinstone was ill and so incapable of overriding Macnaghten's opposition. With fatal weakness he left the fortress in Shuja's hands.

Knowing, however, that something had to be done to improve the British defensive position, he urged upon Macnaghten the construction of a small fort near one corner of the cantonments, which could hold all the ammunition and much of the stores, yet be defended by about 200 men. Macnaghten agreed, the work was put in hand and the cost, a modest £2,400, was reported to Lord Auckland.

Some weeks later, on 28 June 1841, came a peremptory note from his secretary saying that the Government could not allow this expenditure. The mean refusal of this small sum of money caused the abandonment of work which could have given the garrison some real security.

Within a few weeks of assuming command Elphinstone had thus twice been overridden in issues which were strictly his business—once by Macnaghten and once by Auckland. Likely it is that the ailing old man shrugged his shoulders and decided to go with the stream.

Auckland, believing up to a point Macnaghten's contention that Afghanistan was tranquil, had good reason to oppose every pound of additional expenditure. In the spring he had again been under fire from the Board of Control, both about the military reversals the British had suffered and the cost of the entire campaign. And Sir John Hobhouse wrote arguing that the country must either be abandoned now to Shah Shuja or be held, and pacified at all costs with a much large force under open British rule.

In reply Auckland admitted that Dost Mahommed's exile in India and the Russian retreat from their threatening march to Khiva had disposed of two good reasons for the British staying on. Yet he pointed out that the British presence commanding the avenues of invasion gave a sense of security to India, which, he said, was of vital importance. He argued that there was no need for an immediate decision; the main cities should be held and for this the existing forces were enough.

The view of Sir Jasper Nicholls, Commander-in-Chief and military member of the Governor-General's council, about the advisability of a withdrawal from Afghanistan, had for some reason not been obtained. But Sir Jasper protested in his journal on 8 May 1841: 'We cannot afford the heavy, yet increasing drain upon us. Nine thousand troops between Quetta and Kurachee; at least 16,000 of our army and the Shah's to the north of Quetta. The King's expenses to bear in every part—28 political officers to pay, besides Macnaghten—Dost Mahommed's allowances—barracks—a fort or two to build—loss by exchange, etc. To me it is alarming.' And a few days later on 20 May: 'It will never do to have India drained of a million and a quarter annually for a rocky frontier requiring about 25,000 men and expensive establishments to hold it even by threats as at present.'

Mr. Prinsep, another member of the Governor-General's Council, put on record his view that it was intolerable that Sir William Macnaghten should support the Shah in extravagant spending of revenue regardless of the general welfare. Having conquered Afghanistan, he said, Britain had a duty to ensure that justice was done and the revenue was properly administered.

Auckland, now somewhat anxious about the trend of things, did, however, urge Macnaghten to tell the Shah bluntly that his expenses, especially those of his personal guard and his court must be cut. He said he failed to under-

stand why the Shah could not pay for his own government
when his revenue was greater than that of the former ruler,
Dost Mahommed, and while Britain paid for his army.

Macnaghten at first resisted these requests. 'His Majesty's
revenue is little more than 15 laks (£150,000) per annum,'
he wrote, 'hardly enough for the maintenance of his personal
state, and yet the government below are perpetually writing
to me that this charge and that charge is "to be defrayed
out of His Majesty's resources". God help the poor man and
his resources! !' he exploded.

But under pressure, Macnaghten was forced to change
his attitude. He now began in his turn to put pressure on the
Shah to economise. It led to a breach between them in the
middle of 1841 and Macnaghten, who earlier had nothing
but praise for the Shah was now writing that Shuja 'is an
old woman, not fit to rule these people'. And the political
officers took over more and more of the government of the
country.

Shah Shuja responded by complaining in a letter of 17
July 1841 to the Governor-General that the British took no
notice of his advice, followed unsound policies, left him with
little control over the country's administration and in
general were given to 'unlimited interference'. Thus while
doing what seemed the right thing, the British were alienat-
ing their only possible Afghan allies—Shuja's followers, few
as they were.

Earlier in the year Major Rawlinson had warned Macnaghten that south-west Afghanistan, where General Nott
was about to send a force to attack Uktur Khan's force of
6,000 men, had become a nest of rebellion. Despite their
traditional hostility for each other, some of the Durani
chiefs were even combining with the Ghilzyes, showing thus
the intensity of their dislike for the British.

Macnaghten answered then that he was taking 'an un-
warrantable gloomy view. . . . We have enough of difficulties and enough of croakers without adding to the number
needlessly.'

He went on: 'These idle statements may cause much mis-

chief, and repeated as they are, they neutralise my protest-
ations to the contrary. I know them to be utterly false as regards this part of the country and I have no reason to believe
them to be true as regards your portion of the kingdom,
merely . . . because Uktur Khan has a pack of ragamuffins
at his heels.'

He recommended that the Afghan mercenary cavalry,
the Janbaz, should join with the British force, make a forced
march by night, come in the rear 'seize the villain and hang
him as high as Haman and you will probably have no more
disturbances'. The Janbaz could remain out while revenue
collections in the region were going on, he recommended.
With his accustomed efficiency, General Nott again defeated Uktur Khan and the Ghilzyes.

Macnaghten now expected reinforcements to replace
General Sale's brigade, which was about to return to India.
Nott's defeat of the Duranis and Ghilzyes had also increased
his confidence; and by the end of August he knew officially
that he was soon to leave Kabul to take up in Bombay the
great position as Governor which meant to much to him.
Macnaghten began to feel he could leave the country in a
settled state, and with his head held high.

True, large forces of troops were still out in the west
pacifying Duranis who refused to submit; and Akrum Khan,
the chief who had joined in rebellion with Uktur Khan, was
still at liberty.

Macnaghten now decided to use unconventional methods
to seize him and bribed a tribesman to take Captain John
Connolly to his hiding-place. The informant's ankles were
tied beneath his horse's belly so that he could not escape, and
the party surprised the chief and carried him to Kandahar.
There he was handed over the Shuja's son, Prince Timour,
the Governor, who had him blown from the mouth of a gun
to settle matters for good.

Macnaghten joyfully made ready to leave now, and
Elphinstone, who had resigned his command already, because he felt himself too ill to bear it, prepared to go with
him.

Burnes had been concerned about the trend of events in Afghanistan for months past and even more worried about his own future. 'I am now a highly paid idler,' he had complained in a letter to his brother, 'having no less than 3,500 rupees a month as Resident at Kabul and being, as the lawyers call it, only counsel, and that, too, a dumb one—by which I mean that I give paper opinions, but I do not work them out.'

But now that Macnaghten's post seemed about to fall to him, Burnes saw better days approaching. There would be more worthwhile things than to write long memorandums which his chief ignored, and spend his days amusing himself with his Kashmiri girls. The day was coming when he would rule in Afghanistan. So dazzled must Burnes have been by this prospect that he forgot that many of the chiefs looked upon him as the man whose professions of friendship three years earlier had paved the way for the British invasion—a man therefore, whom they were bound to kill. So Burnes waited contentedly for Macnaghten's departure and what he saw as his own triumph.

Macnaghten, by the end of August, has decided that harsher policies were now needed towards the rebellious chiefs if he wanted to leave the country settled and quiet. A few months before he had called them 'perfect children', but now he spoke of them as 'without exception the most worthless and faithless wretches I ever knew'. To the political officer in the region of Helmund, Lieutenant Elliot, he wrote that execution and confiscation of lands were to be used against the turbulent Duranis. And on 29 August he told Rawlinson that 'the Durani chiefs who have been in rebellion must be effectively humbled. . . . We must never dream of conciliation. Terror is the only instrument which they respect. These fellows must be crushed . . .!'

In this mood, in mid-September, Macnaghten embarked upon a new policy towards the chiefs that served as a detonator for the dynamite to which their state of mind could be likened. Lord Auckland had urgently been pressing him to economise, including especially cuts in the big stipends paid to many chiefs. Macnaghten objected that these payments, amounting to £8,000 yearly for the Ghilzyes, were fair compensation for stopping their traditional privilege of robbing convoys and caravans along the mountain passes in their various regions and that 'we should be found in the end to have made a cheap bargain'.

But wishing, in the last week or two before leaving, to please the authorities in India and England, he summoned the Ghilzye chiefs to Kabul and told them that while they would still be held responsible for robbery within their lands, their monies would be drastically cut.

The chiefs objected, but vainly. Angrily, they fled Kabul, held secret meetings, took oaths upon the Koran to support each other in a confederation of rebellion and agreed upon a plan for war.

Chapter Seventeen

Now intent on war against the English, the Ghilzyes thronged the mountain passes between Kabul and Jellalabad and cut communication with India by the Khyber route.

At first, Macnaghten saw it as a small-scale rising which could be put down easily enough, but he confessed in a letter to Major Rawlinson on 3 October 1841 that he was 'suffering a little anxiety' about the Ghilzyes.

When more information about the extent of their rising reached him he grew more concerned and revealed to Rawlinson on 7 October: 'The eastern Ghilzyes are kicking up a row about deductions which have been made from their pay. The rascals have completely succeeded in cutting off our communications for the time being, which is very provoking to me at this juncture; but they will be well trounced for their pains. . . .'

The glittering prize of the Bombay governorship was dangling within Macnaghten's reach, but he was becoming worried that it might after all elude him. He told Rawlinson on 11 October: 'No sooner have we put down one rebellion that another starts up. The Eastern Ghilzyes are now in an uproar and our communications with Jellalabad are completely cut off. . . . Only imagine the impudence of the rascals in having taken up a position with four or five hundred men in the Khoord-Kabul Pass, not 15 miles from the capital. I hope they will be driven out today or tomorrow, but the Pass is an ugly one to force. This . . . is particularly provoking just as I am about to quit Afghanistan.'

It must have been, for warnings of gathering danger were widespread. Major Pottinger, then political officer in Kohistan, had come to Kabul especially to warn the Envoy that a rising there was inevitable; strong forces had been sent at once to crush it. Uktur Khan was again awaiting his chance at Bamian, joined now by Akbar Khan, the fiery son of Dost Mahommed, who, driven by implacable hatred of the English, had turned down offers of a big pension in exile for the life of a fugitive

In Kabul itself, officers and men were now openly attacked in the city. Dr. Metcalfe owed his escape from Afghan swordsmen to the speed of his horse, Captain Waller was wounded by a pistol shot, an infantryman was found with his throat cut and an Afghan stole up to a sentry post of the Horse Artillery in the night and shot dead a young trooper.

On 4 October, Captain Gray, returning to India with an escort of 400 loyal Afghans, was fiercely attacked in the Khoord-Kabul Pass. But Mahommed Uzeem Khan, chief of the escort, led Gray over the mountains by a little-known track and eluded the Ghilzyes.

Having done so, he frankly told him that all Afghanistan were determined to make one cause and to murder or drive out every Feringhee (*European*) in the country—the whole country, and Kabul itself was ready to break out.

Gray wrote Sir Alexander Burnes telling of the apparent volcano upon which the British were all too calmly sitting and Burnes wrote to Uzeem Khan a letter of acknowledgement and thanks. But despite this alarming revelation from a chief who had in the past proved his complete reliability, and despite other information in the hands of the British, the advance detachment of General Sir Robert Sale's brigade was to march for India on 9 October as though the country was indeed as peaceful as England.

This detachment, commanded by Colonel Monteith, consisted of some 800 men of the 35th Native Infantry, a squadron of 150 men of the 5th Cavalry, two 9-pounders under Captain Dawes and a detachment of Captain George Broadfoot's sappers. Broadfoot was one of three brothers, sons of a Scottish Presbyterian minister, one of whom, James, had already been killed in the cavalry charge against

Dost Mahommed's force at Purwandurrah. All three were to die fighting in Afghanistan. George, red-haired and, surprisingly, a wearer of thick pebble spectacles, had used a mixture of paternal benevolence and severe military discipline to hammer his 600 Indians, Ghurkas and Afghans into a force of accomplished light troops skilled in siege and entrenching methods.

Ordered to join Colonel Monteith's force with 100 of his sappers, the pedantic Broadfoot tried to obtain precise instructions as to the equipment his men would need.

The story of this attempt sheds a revealing light on the appalling disarray into which military organisation had already fallen between the fumbling hands of General Elphinstone and the all too dextrous ones of Macnaghten.

Broadfoot first sought information from Colonel Monteith, who said that he had not received any orders himself and could not therefore give any. He declined to apply to Macnaghten for instructions as he knew 'these people' too well and that it was not their habit to consult or instruct the commanders of expeditions.

Instead of using his own judgement, Broadfoot then went to General Elphinstone, whom he found ill in bed, but who nevertheless received him with 'his usual cheerful kindness'. He insisted on getting up, though he needed support to walk into his visiting room and was for half an hour so much exhausted by his efforts to attend to business that Broadfoot was sorry he had come at all.

The General said that all he knew was Macnaghten's instructions to send Monteith off with the given number of men. He had no information about the forts that might be encountered, or if any engineer was going as well. He left it to Broadfoot to decide what stores and tools to take with him, and he declined to refer to Macnaghten a military matter that should have been left entirely to he himself.

Broadfoot managed, however, to extract a note from Elphinstone to Macnaghten saying that what Broadfoot wanted to know was reasonable: whether there were to be hostilities or not, with whom, the strength and position of the enemy, and whether there would be forts to be taken and destroyed.

Macnaghten then quite fairly told the pedantic Broadfoot that being no prophet he could not tell whether there would be fighting, but that he would find out about the forts and would agree to whatever equipment the General felt was needed, and with this in a note he sent Broadfoot back to the General.

This very reasonable answer for some reason hurt the General who then complained bitterly of having been 'degraded from a general to the "Lord-Lieutenant's head constable".' He agreed, perhaps foolishly, that Broadfoot should see the Envoy again. This time, with the red-haired, meticulous Scot peering at him through his thick spectacles, Macnaghten declared that the General was fidgety, but Broadfoot insisted that until he knew what he would be expected to do he could make no preparations.

It was a stupid remark—Broadfoot too had caught the habit of the army and political officers of scoring off each other. Broadfoot should have been ready for anything in the disturbed conditions then prevailing, but Macnaghten patiently sent for his intelligence officers so that Broadfoot could try to find out what he wanted to know for himself.

Broadfoot then began to question the tactical plans and Macnaghten, who so far had endured it all patiently, at last lost his temper—he had given his orders and as to Broadfoot and his sappers, twenty men with pickaxes would do, for they were only wanted to pick stones from beneath the gun-wheels.

'Are those your orders?' Broadfoot demanded.

'No,' answered Macnaghten. 'It is only my opinion, given at the General's request and yours. The General is responsible and must decide as to the number of sappers and tools that must go.'

When Broadfoot, having left him, again returned from the General with still another protest in this futile but damaging row, Macnaghten rightly refused to listen any more and told Broadfoot that if he feared an attack, he

need not go—there were other officers. Broadfoot was
nothing if not brave and at this insult, he made a polite
bow and went. Macnaghten softened the blow by running
after him and shaking his hand.

Broadfoot still was not satisfied. He went again to the
General, whom he found, not surprisingly, 'lost and per-
plexed'. But at last even Elphinstone must have had enough.
He gave Broadfoot the order at last which either Colonel
Monteith or he should have given in the first place—to use
his own judgement.

And finally, the sick old man entreated: 'If anything
occurs, and in case you have to go out, for God's sake clear
the passes quickly, that I may get away. For, if anything
were to turn up, I am unfit for it, done up body and mind,
and I have told Lord Auckland so.'

In this revealing confession are the reasons for the whole
chapter of disastrous mistakes by which Elphinstone ulti-
mately was soon to bring the force to its knees before the
Afghans.

General Nott had at last been summoned from Kandahar
to assume command, but Elphinstone and Auckland between them had delayed this decision too long. And so incompetence lost to the British the one man who could have
saved them, for the tribes were now on the march.

Colonel Monteith left Kabul with the advance early on 9
October 1841—a force of some 100 troops encumbered with
the usual five or six thousand camp-followers and the long
string of baggage camels. He pitched his tent in the late
afternoon on open ground near the village of Bootkak, with
a range of hills that rose into mountains on his right and the
mouth of the pass through them about a mile off.

He was sharply attacked that night by the Ghilzyes. They
were beaten off, though not without some losses in men, and
camels with valuable loads. Many of the attackers turned
out to be armed retainers of chiefs living in Kabul in the
very shadow of the British headquarters. These armed men
had left Kabul and returned through Brigadier Shelton's
camp; but they had not been stopped or questioned.

Macnaghten, hearing of the attack early next day, ordered General Sale to march before dawn on the 11th, earlier than had been planned, to clear the passes with the 13th Light Infantry and some 300 irregular cavalry. But there was an acute shortage of transport animals and so, says Gleig, 'the men undertook cheerfully to carry their own knapsacks and the officers sacrificed without hesitation every article of private baggage which it might have been inconvenient to move.

'The men packed one spare shirt only, one pair of socks, one spare pair of boots and their blue trousers together with their soap, towel and cooking utensils and 40 rounds of ammunition instead of the usual 60, the balance being carted on company animals. Thus more lightly equipped than usual they swung along at so brisk a pace that they arrived at Monteith's camp in time for breakfast.'

Shortly after dawn next day General Sale's troops began to force the Pass. The Afghans let the column enter some distance into the long and dangerous defile and then opened a storm of fire from behind the sheltering rocks above. Here and there men began to fall. The British bugles blared, the leading infantrymen scaled the precipices and returned the fire as the column marched steadily forward. The Afghans retreated—soon the column was able to make its way through the rest of the Pass more or less unhindered, though casualties had been quite heavy at the start of the fighting.

Colonel Dennie praised 'the fearless manner in which the men of the 13th, chiefly young soldiers, ascended heights, nearly perpendicular, under the sharp fire of the insurgents'. Thus the Pass was cleared, the Afghans, afraid of being taken in the rear, quickly retreating towards Tezeen.

Colonel Monteith and his force were now left to camp in the Khoord-Kabul valley beyond the pass, while Sale and Dennie marched their contingent back again to await further reinforcements at Bootkak.

General Sale, awaiting reinforcements, kept his force divided in this way for several days, Monteith being isolated in a vulnerable position. Soon he was joined by Captain Macgregor, a political officer highly thought of by Macnaghten. Through Macgregor a party of 'friendly' Afghans now obtained permission to camp next to the British. On the night of 17 October, just when British sentries had reported the advance of a column of Ghilzyes, the friendly ones opened fire, killing Lieutenant Jenkins and thirty sepoys. Monteith was soon heavily engaged on all sides with the ferocious Ghilzyes. He eventually drove them off, though not without more casualties and the loss of 80 camels laden with 30,000 rounds of ammunition, some gunpowder and medical stores. For the Ghilzyes it was an encouraging encounter.

Macnaghten now decided to crush these rebels—they were delaying him. He strengthened Sale's force from the Kabul garrison with some 2,000 more fighting-men, two 9-pounders of the Horse Artillery under Lieutenant Walker; a battery of mountain artillery, 300 more of Broadfoot's sappers, a squadron of cavalry and a few hundred Afghan irregular troops.

On the morning of 20 October. Sale marched the column safely through the Khoord-Kabul Pass once more and joined Monteith in the valley beyond.

Macnaghten had now supplied Sale with a force which vigorously led could end the Ghilzye rebellion finally and make the links with India safe again. He could then have ridden triumphantly away to Bombay, for the reverberations of a decisive victory would have sobered the chiefs all over Afghanistan.

But now, Macnaghten's political subordinate Macgregor, upon whom he had put so much store, interfered at the decisive moment. Khoda Buxsh, the Ghilzye chief of Tezeen, had deployed his men in the valley, instead of above on the precipices. In doing so it seemed he had thrown away his most valuable advantage and exposed his men to the full power of the British artillery. But his force being the weaker, he knew what he was doing.

Early in the morning, Colonel Dennie formed up to

attack, the long column of red-coated infantry on either side of the black barrels of the artillery, the cavalry a mass of pale blue at the rear of each flank. Overwhelmingly superior in numbers, weapons and discipline, victory under Dennie's bold leadership was certain.

The bugles were ready to sound 'forward' at Dennie's command, the men were tense and impatient, when an Afghan rode furiously up to Macgregor's tent with a message from his master, Khoda Buxsh—a declaration of surrender and a request for negotiations.

Macgregor must at once have persuaded Sale to countermand the attack. Perhaps affected by a painful leg wound that still kept him on his back, Sale immediately agreed. Dennie was informed just in time. The bugles sounded the *retire* and the men, hot for battle, returned once more to their tents.

Negotiations now could gain the British nothing, lose them the chance of effectively crippling the Ghilzyes and enable Khoda Buxsh to avoid defeat. But Macgregor failed to realise this. Sale, too, made a fatal error in agreeing to talk when an easy victory was at hand—a victory which assuredly would have freed the British from the Ghilzye danger and calmed the entire country.

Macnaghten had left matters 'very much to your discretion' in his letter of 18 October to Macgregor. If the rebels 'were very humble' he did not wish to be too hard upon them. But he stipulated that 'the defences of Khoda Buxsh's fort must be demolished' and for the other chief Gool Mahommed, there was to be 'nothing but war'. He concluded: 'I should be sorry to hear of their bolting, probably to renew their depredations. . . .'

Macnaghten expected Sale to deal them a crushing blow.

But instead there were only negotiations, in which the pliant Macgregor was worsted at every point. It was agreed that Khoda Buxsh's fort should be left intact. The supplies in it and his other property, which rightly should have been seized as recompense for the robberies carried out by his tribesmen, were instead bought at a high price by the

British. The claim of the two chiefs that their annual pay-ments—recently cut by Macnaghten—should be restored to the former level, was also agreed.

To cap it all, Macgregor supplied them with 10,000 rupees on the understanding that the chiefs needed it to call out the tribes to keep the passes clear. Finally, there was to be no British garrison at Tezeen to prevent the Ghilzyes rising again and even massing against the British in Kabul.

The day before, while awaiting a report of the stern measures for which he had asked, Macnaghten had written impatiently to Major Rawlinson at Kandahar: 'I had hoped ere evening to have announced to you the capture or dis-persion of the Tezeen rebels; but of this there is no hope tomorrow. Our people in this quarter have a happy knack of *bitching* matters. However, let that pass. All's well that ends well. In the meantime it is very satisfactory to think that, notwithstanding we have rebellion at our very doors not a single tribe had joined the rebels. The interruption of our communications is very provoking, but the road will soon be opened. . . .'

Macnaghten had no doubt whatsoever that the rebellion would not last long. His letter went on: 'I do not think I can possibly get away from this before the 1st proximo. The storm will speedily subside; but there will be heaving of the billows for some time, and I should like to see everything right and tight before I quit the helm. Burnes is naturally in an agony of suspense about the succession to me. I think and hope he will get it. . . . And now that tranquillity is restored (or will be in a day or two) all that is required will be to preserve it.'

Macnaghten's policy at this time was sound. He assured everyone that there was little to worry over, and so tried to keep an optimistic spirit alive while at the same time furnishing the troops needed to put down rebellion. If Mac-gregor and Sale had done as he ordered, the Ghilzye rising would indeed have ended quickly.

Then came Macgregor's report, with all its implications of danger. Bitter indeed must have been Macnaghten's sorrow to learn that Macgregor had snatched away Dennie's sword when it was raised for the decisive blow—only to let himself be tricked by the guile of a wily Afghan chief.

Macnaghten put as good a face on it as possible, merely saying that he thought the terms far too favourable. Shah Shuja also was dissatisfied, but Macnaghten, true to his habit of making the best of a bad job, backed up his subordinate as well as he could. 'I do not entertain the smallest doubt of the policy of your proceedings or of the wisdom of your granting such favourable terms,' he wrote Macgregor on 27 October.

'I shall probably make a start on Monday morning, the 1st proximo, that is, if everything is quiet; but matters still have a threatening appearance in the direction of the Kohistan, and I dread to open the letters I receive from Pottinger. . . . I am a good deal bothered, as you may imagine, just now. Now that my departure is so near, every fellow is having at me.' On the same day he wrote bitterly of the Ghilzye treaty to Rawlinson: 'Nothing has annoyed me so much as the mode in which this settlement has been effected. . . .'

His worst fears were soon to be justified. Sale had marched onwards on 26 October, not in peace and safety as the treaty guaranteed, but with serious shooting between his rearguard and the enemy. Sale saw at once what he had lost by not fighting, and the danger that threatened him.

Ahead was the quaintly named Pass of the Fairy, a winding gorge with steep precipitous sides. Sale guessed there would be a mass attack in the close confines of the Pass, so he took instead the road south which by-passed it and led his column safely into the valley of Jugdulluk on the other side without opposition.

The Ghilzyes were, in fact, massed in thousands along the brink of the Pass of the Fairy, hoping to trap Sale where his artillery would be useless and their accurate *jezail* fire would tell. Sale now led his column on to Gundamuk, the next stage of the journey and camped there, on 30 October, among orchards and a sparkling stream. His rearguard and baggage-train were attacked on the way and 120 of his men killed.

In face of this breach of the treaty, Sale should now have launched a punishing attack on the treacherous Ghilzyes. Once he knew the facts, Macnaghten would no doubt have agreed—it was the only way of ensuring safe communications with India. Sale had in men, weapons and supplies ample resources, and in Dennie a fighting, capable leader.

But instead, Sale sat in camp among the orchards at Gundamuk awaiting further orders—passiveness that heralded among a primitive fighting race the belief that the British could be cheated without fear of retribution. The moollahs and the chiefs spread the fiction that Sale had purchased permission from the Ghilzyes to pass unharmed through their territory.

All this blew like a strong wind on the smouldering embers of rebellion in Kabul.

Rumours later began to drift in to Sale with friendly tribesmen that all was not well there. Some spoke of a rising. Sale might now have sent loyal Afghans as spies to find out the truth of this, so that, if necessary, he could march back to the rescue. But he sat there awaiting further orders.

Several days later, on 10 November, came an alarming letter to the political officer Macgregor, from Macnaghten. Dated 9 November, it read: 'My dear Macgregor, I have written you several letters, urging you in the strongest manner to come up with Sale's brigade to our relief, but I fear you may not have received them. Our situation is rather a desperate one unless you arrive, because we can neither retreat in any direction, nor leave the cantonments to go into the Bala Hissar; but if we had your force we should be able to hold the city, and thus preserve both the cantonment and Bala Hissar.'

What precisely had happened in Kabul?

Chapter Eighteen

Kabul at the end of October and the beginning of November was strangely calm and quiet, Neither General Elphinstone, who was packed and ready to leave; nor Macnaghten, who wanted to go, but was held there by ever more frequent risings, nor Burnes, who longed for the departure of his chief so that he could take over, suspected that the storm of rebellion that had been threatening them would soon break.

Lady Sale was now keeping a journal in which she noted down events, often hourly, intermingled with her comments upon them, but she neither saw nor heard anything significant at this time. Her husband had written from Tezeen that his wound was healing well and that the chiefs were very polite . . . she was to leave for India any day, together with Macnaghten and his wife and Elphinstone . . . she was happy to go, but she regretted having to say goodbye to the snug little house in the cantonments which Sale (this was how she always referred to her husband) had caused to be built to his own plan. She was sorry too at leaving the little kitchen garden—in which when not away chasing rebels her husband grew cauliflowers, artichokes, peas and potatoes—as well as the flower-beds which she herself had grown and which the Afghan gentlemen who came to visit admired so much. . . .

But General Sale was now encamped among the orchards near the village of Gundamuk with Colonel Monteith and a brigade of some 5,000 troops, separated from his wife and daughter by 70 miles of mountains held by rebellious and bloodthirsty tribes. General Nott was far south at Kandahar, and already the winter snows had blocked the high mountain passes between the two cities.

In the cantonments General Elphinstone waited anxiously to leave, too ill now to command his 5,000 troops effectively. Shah Shuja looked anxiously down at them from the impregnable heights of the Bala Hissar, with 3,000 troops of his own, not a very capable force. Macnaghten and his wife resided in lordly style in the British mission buildings next to the cantonments, while Burnes enjoyed himself in his mansion in the middle of the crowded, mob-ridden city.

But even Sir Alexander, who had the best intelligence service in Kabul, had decided that all was well at this time, having chosen to ignore warnings that his life was in danger.

Staying with him on 1 November were his brother, Lieutenant Charles Burnes, and Lieutenant William Broadfoot, brother to George Broadfoot, then in Gundamuk with General Sale. William Broadfoot had just arrived at Kabul to start work as military secretary to Burnes and the day was doubly meaningful for him—it was also the first anniversary of the death of his brother James in the forlorn cavalry charge against Dost Mahommed at Purwundurrah.

Burnes's mansion in the city's centre was built round a courtyard and with a gallery overlooking the street, and here Burnes lived well. For Dr. Kennedy, the Bombay force medical chief who had returned to India with General Keane, the dinners and the wine with which Burnes had plied him were one of the memorable events of his stay. On the evening of 1 November the three young men had doubtless dined equally well, on pheasant or quail, with two or three bottles of Burnes's fine claret, to celebrate Broadfoot's arrival.

But Burnes was anxious about his promotion to Envoy. Confirmation had not yet come from the Governor-General and his anxiety was reflected in his journal: 'What will this day bring forth?' he had written on 31 October, the day before. 'It will make or mar me, I suppose. Before the sun sets I shall know whether to go to Europe or suceed Macnaghten.'

But by the evening of 1 November he was still awaiting

Lord Auckland's fiat. Other men, however, not the Governor-General had decided his fate—and it was a grim one.

The same evening, not far off through Kabul's twisting alleys, several of the most fanatical among the rebellious chiefs had gathered in a large towered house—the home of Sydat Khan, chief of the Alekozye tribe. Most influential of those there was Abdoollah Khan, a chief whom Shah Shuja had dispossessed and kept as a hostage at the court. A proud and vindictive man, he had spread discontent and spurred on the other chiefs to rebellion. Burnes had learned about these dangerous intrigues and in an angry message had called him a dog, threatening—merely to frighten him—to advise Shah Shuja to cut off his ears.

At this, Abdoollah Kahn's ferocious nature asserted itself. Years earlier, he had got rid of an elder brother, the heir to the family inheritance, by burying him up to his neck, hitching to it a wild horse and driving the animal round in a circle. He looked for blood now. Supported by Aminoollah Khan, a wolf in sheep's clothing who hid hatred for Shah Shuja beneath professed friendship, he urged three immediate acts.

First, the use of the Shah's name as a rabble-rouser by washing the text from a document bearing Shuja's name and above it forging a letter to the chiefs ordering them to kill all infidels. The second act, dear especially to Abdoollah Khan, was the murder of Burnes, feared because of his intelligence service and hated because of his believed treachery in paving the way of the British into the country. The third act was an attack on and pillage of Captain Johnson's treasury, in his house opposite—he was the paymaster of the Shah's troops. The chiefs agreed to put the plans into effect that night—including the murder of Burnes.

But the conspiracy leaked before midnight. One of the first to hear of it was Mohan Lal, a British agent, who rushed off to tell Burnes, seemingly with little effect. Taj Mahommed, son of a Durani chief and a friend of Burnes's, also heard what was afoot, stealthily entered Burnes's house and warned him that the chiefs had marked him for death before daylight. But Burnes again refused to take the report seriously.

Next came Naib Sherrif, who enjoyed the same tastes as Burnes—together they had spent many convivial evenings. He told the same story and went as far as to offer to send his own son with 100 armed men to guard Burnes day and night till things calmed down. This could have saved Burnes's life and possibly fended off the major disaster that was to come, but Burnes stubbornly refused Naib Sherrif's offer.

Finally, came the fourth would-be samaritan, no less a person than Usmin Khan, the Shah's new Vizier, and even while a mob could be heard clamouring at the gate, he pleaded with Burnes to come with him and his escort to the safety of the Bala Hissar. Again Burnes refused; the Vizier said goodbye and went.

To all these warnings Burnes's attitude was that the Afghans had never received any injury from him, but on the contrary he had done much for them and he was quite sure they would never harm him.

So he scorned to run for it, but at about six o'clock in the morning when the mob was yelling outside he sent a messenger with an urgent note to Macnaghten asking for troops to be sent to guard him and suppress the uproar, for such it was at this time. Mohan Lal, watching from the roof of his own house saw shortly after six o'clock four horsemen, whom he recognised as Abdoollah Khan, Aminoollah Khan, Sikander and Abdul Salam, ride up to the mob before Burnes's house with a crowd of armed retainers.

Burnes, he says, sent out two servants to ask the chiefs why they had risen against him, and assuring them of his wish to restore their stipends and privileges. In reply, Sikander Khan drew his sword and struck off one servant's head. His fellow conspirators cut at the other man with their swords. Badly wounded he managed to escape into the house and covered in blood reported back to Burnes.

The conspirators now ordered their men to climb to the housetops and open fire into Burnes's house and garden.

Soon the crackle of musketry mingled with the howls of the mob. Shots crashed through the windows and ricocheted about the rooms. Burnes had ordered his sepoy guard of several men not to fire and now in a final effort at conciliation he faced and harangued the mob from the gallery above the street, promising a handsome reward, says Mohan Lal, if the chiefs would call off the violence. But in reply there were more shots and yells for blood.

Burnes ordered his sepoys to fire back. He, his brother and Broadfoot, determined to save themselves until the troops arrived, also fired at the mob. Almost at once Broadfoot fell with a wound in the heart. Burnes and his brother carried him dying to a downstairs room.

Some of Burnes's servants now offered to carry him away wrapped up in a tent, as if they were carrying plunder, like many other people in the street seemed to be, but this, too, Burnes refused—he said he could not leave Broadfoot and his brother. Mohan Lal saw flames leap up round the front of the house and the firing and the shouting grew louder.

The flames spread to the room where Burnes and his brother were waiting for British troops to save them. They went out into the garden to escape the flames. Broadfoot, presumably dead by now, was left in the room so that his body would be burnt and saved from multilation. A few Afghans now burst into the garden.

Charles Burnes killed six of them with his sword before he fell and was cut to pieces. Alexander Burnes seems to have believed his eloquence might yet prevail and began to address them, but on the death of his brother he abandoned all hope. Says Mohan Lal: 'He opened up his black neckcloth and tied it on his eyes that he should not see from whom the death blows struck him. Having done this he stepped out of the door and was cut to pieces by the furious mob.

Mohan Lal—employed by Macnaghten but much attached to Burnes—left his house when the blaze began, to seek help, but was seized and would have been killed but for the arrival of Prince Mohammed Zaman Khan, who rescued him, took him in and 'placed me among his ladies, who, having received some assistance from me some time before, brought me a sumptuous dish of pulav for my breakfast. To enjoy such hospitality from the hands of the Afghan fair on other occasions would have been an unexpected and highly valued nourishment, but at the present disastrous moment every grain of rice seemed to choak me in the throat and I refused to touch the dish.'

Later, on the roof of the Prince's house, he saw Burnes's mansion smouldering and the mob tearing baulks of timber from it. When the fire was out Naib Sherrif entered the garden. He found the limbs and torsoes of the two Burnes and buried them there.

The conspirators had worked quickly, for by now the mob had swollen from a few hundred to one or two thousands armed with swords and *jezails*, yelling for plunder and blood of infidels. The house of paymaster Captain Johnson—who luckily had slept that night in the cantonments—was a veritable gold mine and they fell on it like wolves on their prey.

'The insurgents gained possession of my treasury by undermining the wall,' Johnson related, 'and my house by setting fire to the gateway. They murdered the whole of the guard (one subardar and 28 sepoys, besides non-commissioned officers); all my servants (male, female and children); plundered my treasure to the amount of £17,000, burnt all my office records for the past three years, which comprise unadjusted accounts to nearly one million sterling and possessed themselves of all my private property, amounting to upwards of ten thousand rupees (£1,000).' It was about the worst that could happen to a paymaster's home.

Soon the whole city was in a tumult. Vigorous military action by the British could still have crushed the insurrection. The Kabulees were terrified of the redcoats and constantly expected the tramp of marching feet and the crash of disciplined volleys. 'They are coming—they are coming!' was heard on all sides, and they waited in terror.

Chapter Nineteen

Captain George Lawrence, military secretary to Sir William Macnaghten, was out walking at 7 a.m. on 2 November when he heard the sound of firing and was told in the cantonments that there had been a rising in the city. He sought out the Envoy, whom he found some time later arguing with General Elphinstone and his staff officers.

One of them handed Lawrence a note from Burnes begging for troops to be sent—no action had yet been taken though the note had arrived some time before. Lawrence's opinion was sought and he suggested that a regiment should be marched straight to the city to rescue Burnes, disperse the mob and seize the chiefs responsible.

Here was the first turning-point, for through such action, even if only out of mercy for Burnes, the British could have saved themselves untold suffering, but already among Elphinstone and his staff a kind of moral paralysis had set in. 'My proposal was at once set down as one of pure insanity and under the circumstances utterly unfeasible,' Lawrence says.

So the first of many fateful decisions to do nothing was taken, and Burnes was left to his miserable fate. Brigadier Shelton was merely ordered to have his force ready to move not into Kabul but into the Bala Hissar, if the Shah agreed to it. Lawrence was ordered to ride the two miles to the fortress to inform Shuja of this useless request and he galloped off with an escort of four troopers.

After twice being attacked on the way he reached the Bala Hissar safely and was ushered into the presence of the Shah, who was walking up and down before his throne in great agitation.

'Is it not just what I always told the Envoy would happen

if he would not follow my advice?' Shuja exclaimed, referring to his wish, refused long ago by the Envoy, that he
should be allowed to seize and execute the rebellious chiefs.

Lawrence then requested that Brigadier Shelton should
be allowed to occupy the Bala Hissar with his brigade. 'Wait
a minute,' the King replied, 'my son Futty Jung and the
prime minister, Mahomed Usmin Khan, have gone down
into the city with some of my troops. I have no doubt they
will supress the tumult. Sir Alexander Burnes, I am happy
to say, has escaped.'

Lawrence waited, as the King wished. He saw from reports that from time to time came in that Futty Jung's
efforts to restore order seemed at first successful, reflecting
that 'the gallantry of that young prince, with his undisciplined levies, was nearly accomplishing what *ere then we
should have effected ourselves*'.

Elphinstone, so far, had done nothing but talk, chiefly
about action he felt it was impossible to take—such as
taking up the gauntlet the insurgents had thrown down and
crushing the challenge to authority while it was still in an
early stage.

Brigadier Shelton was at last ordered to take his brigade
up to the Bala Hissar, but Elphinstone sent him a note
countermanding this. It was followed by another note
ordering him to march there immediately; he would receive
further orders there from Captain Lawrence, the Envoy's
military secretary.

He was marching off when Elphinstone again ordered
him to halt. In a fury of impatience Shelton now sent
Lieutenant Sturt, General Sale's son-in-law, to ride up to
the fortress and find out the reason for the delay.

In Kabul meantime, apparent immunity spurred on the
Afghans to fresh arson and plunder and only the Shah's
small force sought to check it. The tumult grew, the flames
spread—shops were gutted, houses burned, anyone, man,
woman or child suspected of friendship with the infidels was
slaughtered. But no British companies, skilled though they
were in street fighting, arrived to stop it, though only two

miles away in the cantonments more than 6,000 of them were ready.

'The state of supineness and fancied security of those in power in cantonments,' Lady Sale wrote angrily in her diary, 'is the result of deference to the opinions of Lord Auckland, whose sovereign will and pleasure it is that tranquillity do reign in Afghanistan. . . . Most dutifully do we appear to shut our eyes to our probable fate.'

Captain Sturt, Lady Sale's son-in-law, who on Brigadier Shelton's command had ridden off unescorted and had run the gauntlet of Afghan attacks, reached the gate of the hall of audience of the palace safely. He dismounted and was about to enter the palace when an Afghan leaped out of the crowd. stabbed him three times in the face and throat and fled. 'Sturt', says Lawrence, 'rushed into the court, sword in hand, bleeding profusely and crying out that he was being murdered. The King calling his Master of the Horse, desired him, on pain of losing his head, immediately to search out and arrest the assassin. I washed and staunched poor Sturt's wounds and he was sent back in one of the King's palanquins, under a strong escort to the camp.'

There his wife and his mother-in-law took him into their charge. His wounds were painful but not dangerous, and with the extraordinary vitality of the nineteenth-century soldier he was soon to recover.

The King's followers now urged him to recall his son and his Vizier from the city—their lives were too valuable to be lost. Asked his opinion, Lawrence answered: 'Let them stay where they are, they can do much good.' He silently lamented that our troops were not there as well, aiding them, as they should have been.

But the King, frightened for his son's life, sent a messenger recalling both the Prince and the prime minister, Usmin Khan. Lawrence related: 'The latter, a bold, uncompromising man came in panting from the fray and, greatly excited, said in an angry tone to the King—"By recalling us just in the moment of victory your troops will be defeated, and evil will fall on all."'

Usmin Khan had uttered an unerring prophecy, but no one there, not even Lawrence, comprehended the awful truth of his words.

The Shah and his courtiers argued and wrung their hands. The Prince and Usmin Khan swore and grew angry. Lawrence, desperate to see something done, and aware that Shelton was still waiting for the word to advance to the fortress, persuaded the Shah to send him with an escort to give the word, so that in the Bala Hissar Shelton would be well placed to attack the city.

The Shah agreed and Lawrence galloped the two miles to the Seeah Sung camp—north of the Bala Hissar and two miles east of the main cantonments on the other side of the Kabul River. 'I reached the Seeah Sung cantonment un-hurt,' he says, 'and Shelton, under my instructions, set out at once. . . . with a force consisting of a squadron of the 5th Light Cavalry, a company of the 44th Foot, a wing of the 54th Native Infantry, four Horse Artillery guns and the Shah's 6th Infantry.'

Lawrence returned now to Macnaghten, at the mission compound beside the cantonments. Elphinstone, still con-ferring with his staff, had decided against a full-scale attack on the city—the only move which could have saved the day. Lawrence obtained permission from Macnaghten to return to the Bala Hissar and Sir William agreed, directing Cap-tains Troup and Johnston with a strong escort to go with him.

They reached it about 3 p.m. and found the Shah still walking about the court surrounded by his officers, debating what should be done. Lawfence heard the thump of artil-lery and the crackle of *jezails* near by. He sought out Shelton —he was directing the fire on the city from two of his guns. 'Shelton, on my joining him,' Lawrence recalls, 'seemed almost beside himself, not knowing how to act and with incapacity stamped on every feature of his face.' Lawrence knew him as a strict disciplinarian, intelligent and person-ally brave, but apt to condemn all measures which he him-self hadn't intitiated.

He recalls that Shelton now asked what he should do. 'Enter the city at once,' Lawrence urged.

'My force is inadequate, and you don't appear to know what street firing is,' Shelton protested.

'You asked my opinion and I have given it. It is what I would do myself,' Lawrence said.

Rounds from the Afghan *jezails* whined past their ears, whisked Captain Macintosh's hat off his head, and in reply the iron 9-pounders belched red flame, rent the air, threw their shot targetless into the city.

Lawrence pleaded that two of the guns should be placed on a platform high up on the fortress so that they could fire with effect at the limited area of the revolt—an easier target from above. The Brigadier agreed and ordered Captain Nicholls to take up the guns, but Nicholls argued that the slope was too steep for horses.

Lawrence lost patience and turning to the Brigadier exclaimed: 'Really, sir, if you allow your officers to make objections instead of obeying, nothing can be done. We had better unyoke the horses and two companies of the Shah's own Native Infantry will soon put the guns in position.'

The Shah's troops manhandled the guns up the slope and soon they were again thumping shells into the city.

The Shah himself, who had witnessed all this, now sharply asked Lawrence why Shelton's troops did not act instead of standing around while every moment the rebellion grew stronger. Lawrence thought he was 'deeply annoyed'—remarkable restraint while his kingdom was going up in flames.

'Shelton well knew the King's anxiety that he should take active measures for quelling the disturbance, but he was in fact quite paralysed and would not act,' Lawrence says. Shelton, of course, had received no orders to attack from General Elphinstone.

Indeed, for the General the crunch had already come, earlier in the day. From so irrevocable and violent an act as a full-scale attack he had turned weakly away, preferring inaction and hope instead.

Shelton, though he fully understood how urgent it was to attack, was hardly likely in face of this to commit his troops in a dangerous role, knowing that heavy losses were inescapable and that with the bad feeling there was between him and the General he would be blamed if he were defeated and blamed too if he won.

So the artillery blasted the city, the infantry stood to arms and waited, the King continued annoyed and Lawrence took leave of him—'as it happened for the last time' —and returned to the cantonments escorted by the cavalry.

The sharp crackle of *jezail* fire down in the city grew louder. Shelton sent an officer to reconnoitre—the Shah's troops were retreating after heavy losses while under fire from roof-top marksmen. Shelton sent a company of sepoys to cover their retreat and the defeated force came safely into the fortress.

Oft criticised by the British, the Shah was yet the only person in authority who at this time made any attempt to crush the rising. He failed because his commander tried to force a way to the heart of the city through the narrow streets to where Burnes was under attack. Lawrence believed that had he entered by the wider main thoroughfare he would have arrived there with less opposition and probably have saved both Burnes and the Treasury, as well as putting down the revolt in the Shah's name and thus restoring his authority.

Meanwhile, all that Elphinstone had done down in the cantonments was to recall to Kabul the 37th Native Infantry left by Sale to guard the lines of communications and issue orders to strengthen the cantonments against attack. Lieutenant Vincent Eyre of the Bengal Artillery placed every available gun in position round the perimeter—some 3,200 yards in extent.

But Sale had taken most of the guns and four had gone up to the Bala Hissar with Shelton. Eyre found only a pathetic little arsenal left in the magazine—six 9-pounders, three 24-pounder howitzers, one 12-pounder howitzer and three $5\frac{1}{2}$-inch mortars, with which to defend a total of 3,200 yards.

And there were not enough artillerymen to man even these efficiently, only 80 Punjabis—'very insufficiently instructed and of doubtful fidelity', Eyre decided.

Late in the day while the looting and burning in the city still raged, Elphinstone sent a worried note to Sir William Macnaghten—who, with his wife had now moved into a tent in the cantonments so as to lessen the area to be defended. 'My dear Sir William,' Elphinstone wrote. 'Since you left me I have been considering what can be done tomorrow. Our dilemma is a difficult one. Shelton, if re-inforced tomorrow, might, no doubt, force in two columns on his way towards the Lahore gate, and we might from hence force that gate and meet them. But if this were accomplished what shall we gain? It can be done, but not without very great loss, as our people will be exposed to the fire from the houses the whole way. Where is the point you said they were to fortify near Burnes's house? If they could assemble there, that would be a point of attack; but to march into the town, it seems, we should only have to come back again; and as to setting the city on fire, I fear, from its construc-tion, that it is almost impossible. We must see what the morning brings and then think what can be done. . . .'

The old General's state of hopeless confusion stands out as clear as daylight in this worried note, in which he suggests what could be done only to find reasons for not doing it. His lack of urgency, his total failure to come to grips with the danger can only be called tragic. He had confessed his in-capacity—'done up, fit for nothing'—but self-esteem alone prevented him handing over to a younger, fitter man.

In the evening, news of the death of Burnes, his brother and William Broadfoot, and the looting of Johnson's treasure was confirmed. It left Elphinstone unmoved—not even sympathisers and friends like the artillery officer Vincent Eyre noted any feelings of regret or remorse. Still less did he resolve to crush this challenge to his authority at its outset.

And so the British allowed 2 November to pass in apathy and confusion while the Afghans gained confidence and determination. News of the rising was carried swiftly throughout the entire region. Hundreds of tribesmen seized *jezails*, rode from their villages into Kabul, assembled beneath the rebel banners and swore on the Koran to defeat the infidel invaders.

Chapter Twenty

Throughout the night of 2 November the sharp rattle of musketry heralded that two of the British forts were braving all the attacks the Afghans could muster. Captain Trevor, with his wife and seven children in one fort on the outskirts of the city, and Captain Mackenzie in another, fought on grimly, but no help was sent them. Like Burnes, they were disregarded.

At 3 a.m. a heavy burst of firing was heard from the Seeah Sung hills, about two miles east of the cantonments. Drums beat the alarm; scouts said a large force approached.

The whole garrison stood to arms and peered into the darkness, expecting that a powerful Afghan army would make a *chupao*, or night attack. Then came the cheering sound of British bugles and soon the welcome news that the force was the 37th Native Infantry, some 1,000 men under Major Griffiths.

Recalled only the day before from a post in the Khoord-Kabul Pass, they had for twelve hours successfully fought off the attacks of 3,000 Ghilzyes right up to Kabul. 'They had by their bold bearing and discipline utterly baffled their enemies,' noted George Lawrence, 'arriving in perfect order with their followers, tents and baggage, having had only two or three sepoys and one officer wounded.'

The conclusion to be drawn, that properly led his fighting-men were for sure more than a match for the Afghans, passed the General by; the accomplishment in no way rescued him from the passivity that bound him to defensive tactics when attack was vital. Needlessly, he decided now to contribute to the defence of the Bala Hissar—a move which would weaken still more the relatively small force in the cantonments. Accordingly, 400 infantry, two mountain guns, one 9-pounder, one 24-pounder howitzer, two $5\frac{1}{2}$-inch mortars and ammunition—this useful force moved on 3 November up to the Bala Hissar to reinforce the troops already there under Brigadier Shelton, the Second-in-Command.

What was Shelton to do there? 'Brigadier Shelton,' Eyre states, 'was ordered to maintain a sharp fire on the city from the howitzers and guns and to endeavour to fire the houses by means of shells . . . from the two mortars; should he find it practicable to send a force into the city he was to do so.'

Responsibility for any decision he might make to attack the city was thus put squarely on Shelton's own shoulders, for Elphinstone himself had already said he would not expose the troops to *jezail* fire in the narrow streets.

But though Elphinstone spared precious troops to assist in the defence of the Shah in the impregnable Bala Hissar, Trevor with his wife and family, and Mackenzie with troops and rations in a fort commanding the northern outskirts of the city he ignored, though they fought bravely.

Colin Mackenzie, a dark, aquiline Scot who had distinguished himself with the 48th Madras Infantry in India and was now one of Macnaghten's assistants in charge of the Shah's commissariat, lived in the fort of Nishan Khan on the outskirts of the city gardens. The fort held most of the provisions for the Shah's troops—he refused to have them in the Bala Hissar—with a guard of one havildar (sergeant) a few horsemen and twenty sepoys.

Mackenzie describes vividly his defence of this important fort at the beginning of the outbreak. Camped close by in a grove of mulberry trees were a force of loyal mercenary *jezailchis*, commanded by Lieutenant Hassan Khan, and sixty of George Broadfoot's sappers with wives and children. About 500 yards away to the east was the large tower in which lived Captain Trevor, his wife and seven children, with a small guard of sepoys.

Early on 2 November news of the riot in Kabul had been brought to Mackenzie and he had ordered the guard to stand to arms. Shortly after, he says, 'a naked man stood before me, covered with blood from two deep sabre-cuts in the head and five musket-shots in the arm and body. He proved to be a *sawar* (horseman) of Sir William Macnaghten, sent with a message to Captain Trevor, who had been intercepted by the insurgents.

'This being rather a strong hint as to how matters were going, I immediately ordered all the gates to be secured, and personally superintended the removal of the detachments . . . with their wives and families, into the fort.'

A force of several hundred Afghans attacked Mackenzie's fort almost before he had brought the mercenaries inside. 'The whole of the gardens,' Mackenzie relates, 'were then occupied by the Afghans, from which, in spite of repeated sallies during the day, we were unable to dislodge them; on the contrary, whenever we returned to the fort, they came so near as to be able, themselves unseen, to kill and wound my men through the loopholes of my own defences.'

Towards the afternoon of 2 November Mackenzie and the *jezailchis* had fired nearly all their ammunition but that in the soldiers' pouches. Determined not to give up the fort to the Afghans, Mackenzie sent an urgent request for reinforcements and ammunition.

Captain George Lawrence, the Envoy's military secretary, was present in the cantonments when Elphinstone received the message. 'I proposed to General Elphinstone,' he relates, 'to order out two companies immediately to reinforce Mackenzie, and throw fresh ammunition into his fort, volunteering to lead them. . . . My proposal was condemned by the staff as most imprudent, as they feared exposing their men to street firing.'

Thus, at once Elphinstone abandoned Mackenzie and Trevor and his family in these outposts to their fate. 'It was in vain that we strained our eyes looking for the glittering bayonets through the trees,' Mackenzie related wistfully. Attacks went on throughout the night; at dawn on 3 November the enemy were found to be mining the fort, so Mackenzie had a shaft dug down with four resolute men there ready to shoot the attackers as they appeared.

The women were howling over the dead and dying; at the same time 'whenever the *jezailchis* could snatch five minutes to refresh themselves with a pipe, one of them would twang a sort of rude guitar as an accompaniment to some martial song, which, mingling with the notes of war sounded very strangely'.

Captain Trevor had been holding out in his tower to the east of Mackenzie. Several Afghan chiefs from Kabul, including Osmin Khan, Taj Mahommed Khan and Abdool Rahim Khan had come to see him with offers to help. Nawab Zeman Khan even voluntarily sent one of his younger sons to Trevor as a hostage for his own loyalty—for none of this minority group of chiefs wished then to be involved in the anti-British rising. When the General sent no help, Trevor refused to keep the boy. The chiefs bade him farewell and went.

Despairing of aid, early next morning, 3 November, Trevor led his wife and seven children, most of whom were carried by his sepoys, out of the tower and by a roundabout route to the cantonments. But they were seen and attacked. 'On the road,' Mackenzie relates, a blow was aimed at Mrs. Trevor by an Afghan. A Hindustani trooper by her side saved her by stretching out his bare arm. The hand was cut off by the blow, yet he continued to walk by her with the blood flowing from the stump until they reached the cantonments—an act of true heroism.'

The Afghans now occupied the ramparts of Trevor's tower and with their long-range *jezails* maintained an accurate fire on the western face of Mackenzie's fort—so accurate that it was cleared of defenders. 'It was only by crawling on my hands and knees up a small flight of steps and whisking suddenly through the door that I could even visit the tower that had been undermined,' notes Mackenzie. 'On one of these visits the sentry told me that there was an Afghan taking aim from an opposite loophole. I looked through our loophole, but could not see him. As I moved my head the sentry clapped his eyes to the slit, and fell dead at my feet with a ball through his forehead.'

That afternoon the Afghans began hammering the ramparts of the fort with light artillery and this, together with the shortage of ammunition, began to lower Mackenzie's riflemen's hitherto undaunted spirits. The Afghans next began piling up stacks of firewood ready to burn down the fort door. The twenty horsemen in the fort mutinied and pulled down the interior barricade at one of the gates to try to escape by the speed of their horses, leaving Mackenzie and the rest of the defenders to their fate.

'This I quelled,' Mackenzie relates, 'by going down amongst them with a double-barrelled gun. I cocked it, and ordered them to shut the gate and build up the barricade, threatening to shoot the first man who should disobey. They saw that I was determined, for I had made up my mind to die, and they obeyed.'

Mackenzie and the riflemen had now been fighting for nearly forty hours without let-up. He himself had not eaten anything owing to weariness, excitement and the fact of his absence for five minutes disheartening the fighting-men. On top of this, the wounded were dying for want of medical aid. He had, he reflected, been left to certain death by his own countrymen, but the Afghan mercenary riflemen had remained loyal to him to the end, even though the enemy, under cover in the nearby gardens, shouted tempting offers to them to seize Mackenzie and come over to them.

Their leader, Hassan Khan 'more than once pretended to listen to the overtures of the enemy in order to lure them from under cover, and then sent his answer in the shape of a rifle ball'.

At last when there was hardly a round left, Hassan came and saluted Mackenzie: 'I think we have done our duty,' he said. 'If you consider it necessary that we should die here, we will die, but I think we have done enough.'

These words softened Mackenzie's heart. He had determined to die defending the fort, in face of his desertion by the General, but now he yielded and prepared for a retreat in the early part of the night, when—it being the Moslem fast of Ramzam—he knew the Afghans would be at their principal meal.

The *jezailchis* were ordered to lead the retreat and to answer appropriately all questions from Afghan sentries; the wounded and the women and children were placed on ponies, all personal baggage was to be left behind and Mackenzie made up the rearguard with a few regular troops. He recalled how a beautiful young Ghurka girl of about sixteen with fair complexion and dark eyes girded up her robe and stuck a sword into her waistband. She threw all she possessed on the ground and said to him—'Sahib, you are right, life is better than property.' Mackenzie never saw her again—she was killed or taken prisoner.

They rode out into the darkness. The rear, with Mackenzie, became separated from the *jezailchis* in front and Mackenzie found himself alone with two horsemen and a wailing crowd of women and children. One of the women, unable to carry both her child and her pots and pans, dropped the child and began to make off. Mackenzie drew his sword and thumped her soundly with the flat of it until he made her take up the child, so when a few seconds later he was suddenly attacked his sword was ready.

He first thought the Afghans who had surrounded him were his own *jezailchis*—until a shower of sword cuts were aimed at him. 'Spurring my horse violently, I wheeled around,' he related, 'cutting from right to left . . . and I was lucky enough to cut off the hand of my most outrageous assailant. My sword went clean through the man's arm, but just after I received such a tremendous blow on the back of the head that, although the sabre turned in my enemy's hand, it knocked me almost off my horse. The idea passed through my mind—"Well, this is the end of my career, and a miserable end it is, in a night skirmish with Afghans." But then came the thought that all was right. I commended my soul to God and became insensible, hanging on the saddle by only one foot, but I did not let go the bridle.'

Somehow Mackenzie rode through the attackers and two volleys of musketry, then hurled himself against another body of the enemy only to find that they were his own men. Eventually they reached the cantonments safely and the General, who had left him to his fate, sanctimoniously thanked him for holding out for so long.

Meantime, there had been much talk and no action among Elphinstone and his staff about the need to occupy two forts commanding the cantonments. Among several other forts on the plain Mahmoud Khan's fort stood 600 yards south of the southern wall of the cantonments—beside the Kabul River bridge, over which ran the road from the King's Garden (a small wooded park) up to the Bala Hissar. Mahomed Sheeref's fort stood only 150 yards south-west of the cantonments; both forts remained unoccupied by the Afghans on 3 November.

Like many Afghan forts they were about 80 feet square and about 40 feet high, with walls of sun-baked mud 6 to 8 feet thick at the base narrowing to 3 feet at the top with a higher tower at each corner, and pierced with numerous loopholes for wallpieces (2-pounder guns) and *jezailchis*. The British normally took such forts by means of artillery bombardment with 6- or 9-pounders, followed by infantry assault.

It will be remembered that General Cotton, at Macnaghten's insistence, to show British goodwill, had allowed the reserves of ammunition to be placed in a fort known as the magazine fort 150 yards south of the southern wall of the fortified cantonments and the huge reserves of food, drink, uniforms and medical supplies in a fort called the commissariat fort about 400 yards south of their south-western corner. Provisions for officers and men, their families and the camp-followers were drawn daily from the commissariat fort, only enough for a day or two being kept in reserve in the cantonment—a hazardous enough arrangement at the best of times.

But the 150 yards to the magazine fort and the 400 yards to the commissariat fort could both be swept by *jezail* fire from the intervening Mahomed Shereef's fort—the route to the commissariat fort indeed, passing barely 150 yards from it. So that, already, with a general rising seeming certain, it was vital to take this fort. Moreover, the store, upon which the lives of the entire force depended, was held only by a junior officer, Lieutenant Warren, and eighty sepoys unsupported by British troops—a force hardly strong enough to ward off attacks by a thousand or more Afghan marksmen.

Constant criticism of the British command may seem uncharitable. The General was ill and his subordinates were frightened of responsibility, but the fact remains that Lieutenant Warren, who held the key to British survival, was left to himself with a handful of Indian troops; and nothing at all was done to seize Mahmoud Khan's fort, and the even more important Mahomed Sheeref's fort. Confusion and indecision reigned when action was vital. .

Yet there were on 3 November—the insurrection in the city began early on 2 November—only enough provisions for three days in the cantonments, while in the commissariat fort there was a huge quantity—enough for three months.

Vincent's Eyre's account of the origin of this Alice-in-Wonderland arrangement is worth recalling: 'Captain Skinner, the chief commissariat officer, at the time this arrangement was made,' says Eyre, 'earnestly solicited from the authorities a place *within* the cantonment for his stores,' but received the topsy-turvy answer that 'no such place could be given him, as they were far too busy in erecting barracks for the men to think of commissariat stores'.

If the General was unconcerned, Lady Sale, that tireless recorder of hourly events, was not. Noting on 3 November with some alarm that there was only enough food for three days in the cantonments, she wrote: 'Should the commissariat fort be captured we shall not only lose all our provisions, but our communications with the city will be cut off. This fort—an old crazy one, undermined by rats—contains the whole of the Bengal commissariat stores. . . .'

But there was a safe alternative—the impregnable Bala Hissar. Into it the women, children, camp-followers and families, the troops and the artillery could have been moved during three or four nights, when it was too dark for the Afghan marksmen to see. At the same time, having first temporarily occupied Mahomed Shereef's fort, enough provisions and ammunition could at the same time have been transported from the commissariat fort to the Bala Hissar as well.

But this move, which was considered, would have involved stern military action of a kind that the General was then unable to initiate. Perhaps Elphinstone is no more to be blamed than his staff, who seemed to be taking all his decisions for him and were strongly against any such move. 'As a body,' Captain Lawrence noted, 'they were characterised by the most deplorable vacillation and absence of energy'—men, it would appear, recognised by Elphinstone as kindred spirits. But their reasons for not abandoning the cantonments for the Bala Hissar were, it is hard to believe, financial ones. They feared blame for the cost in pounds sterling of the loss.

The first hesitations in this developing tragi-comedy of errors were followed by a move of equal import. Having refused to attack Kabul with a force strong enough to make victory sure, the General now in futile fashion sent a force so weak as to make defeat certain. He ordered Major Swayne with a mere 200 sepoys and two 9-pounder guns to join Brigadier Shelton in an assault on the city's north-eastern gate, opposite the Bala Hissar.

But Elphinstone's staff gave Swayne the wrong orders, sending him to the Kohistan Gate, two miles to the west of the appointed Lahore Gate opposite the Bala Hissar. Swayne marched his tiny force there, came under heavy fire at once from the embattled marksmen and lost an officer and twenty men.

Under what cover he could find, he waited anxiously for Shelton's force—but it was two miles away, at the Bala Hissar, still waiting for him, Eventually. seeing no sign of its arrival, he did the only thing he could in this desperate situation—he ordered the bugles to blow the retire and took his men back to safety as fast as he could.

This, another British failure, lashed the Afghans into a frenzy of excitement. After Burnes's murder, and the rising, fear of a savage British attack had sent the conspirators into hiding and terrified the mob, who dreaded the crash of British artillery and the bayonets of the merciless redcoats in the city streets. What was their jubilation when instead of the expected bloody reprisal, a weak, incapable force marched up to a strongly defended gate, lost a number of men in an impossible attack and promptly ran away.

The conspirators seized their chance, came out of hiding and whipped up the fanatic temper of the mob—already drunk with blood and plunder. What was in Kabul at first only an isolated revolt now changed into full-scale rebellion.

Chapter Twenty-one

Just after sunrise on 4 November a force of some 400 Afghan marksmen occupied the Shah's Garden and Mahomed Shereef's fort, 150 yards from the south-west corner of the cantonments. This simple but decisive move now enabled them to cut off the British from their food reserves in the commissariat fort: to attack Warren and the sepoys there and to open fire on the cantonments from a sheltered position. They began at once to attack the commissariat fort from behind the walls of the Shah's Garden. These were the first grim results of the General's inaction.

During the afternoon Lieutenant Warren reported the danger of his position in his ramshackle fort—a blunt warning that his ammunition was nearly all gone, his sepoys were little disposed to fight, and that unless reinforced he might have to abandon. Ensign Gordon, aged nineteen, a friend of Warren's, volunteered to go to his aid and in broad daylight, against heavy *jezail* fire from Mahomed Shereef's fort, set out with eighty sepoys encumbered by eleven slow-moving camels laden with ammunition.

Almost at once Gordon was shot dead. The sepoys tried to go on, but after more than twenty of them had fallen, they turned the camels about and urged them back into cantonments. The first tribute of blood for the initial failure to occupy the fort had been paid.

Now came a sequence of errors and false moves that tolled doom like a bell. Without a word to Captain Boyd and Johnson his commissariat officers, Elphinstone ordered a party to be sent to escort Warren back and to abandon the fort and three months' food to the Afghans—a momentous decision. Bravely, Captain Swayne (not to be confused with Major Swayne) led the party of four officers and 100 men without any covering fire from artillery into the blanket of *jezail* fire.

The outcome reads like a roll of honour. Captains Swayne and Robinson and four men were killed at once; Lieutenants Hallahan, Evans, Fortye and sixteen men wounded in less than 50 yards. It now seemed to the officer upon whom the command fell, noted Vincent Eyre, 'impracticable to bring off Ensign Warren's party without risking the annihilation of his own; he therefore returned forthwith to cantonments'.

Elphinstone, it appears, did not believe in night attacks—they did not make them in the Peninsular War, twenty-five years before, and he turned down suggestions that further efforts should be postponed until dark. On his orders, a party of cavalry now galloped out into this withering fire, intending first to sabre the marksmen in the King's Garden, but they found the gate shut. They had already lost eight troopers killed and fourteen badly wounded so they, too, retreated into the cantonments.

One wonders at the mental state of Elphinstone in deciding to abandon the commissariat fort. Had he forgotten perhaps, that the food was there? Or is it possible that he didn't know? It must be remembered that logistics before the twentieth century were beneath many generals' notice—matters for less gentlemanly officers. A likely explanation was that Elphinstone—'the most gentleman-like officer in the Household Brigade'—had hardly bothered himself about the whereabouts of such mundane things as provisions.

Lady Sale seems to support this view. 'The General appears to be kept in a deporable state of ignorance,' she noted. 'Although reports are sent in daily, he scarcely knows what supplies are in store, or what is our real daily consumption.'

And Elphinstone was at this particular time more sick than usual. He had been helped on to his horse the day before, so that he could inspect and inspire the troops. The animal fell and rolled on him when he was already suffering the agonies of rheumatic gout, weakened by malaria and shattered mentally by the strain of his command. From that moment onwards he seems to have been incapable of taking a rational decision.

Captain Boyd learned that these sorties were not to reinforce the commissariat fort but to help in giving it up. Horrified, he hurried off to try to make the old man realise how disastrous it would be—the fort, he explained, held not only the reserves of wheat but also rum, wine, beer, medicine and hospital stores of all kinds—without which nothing could be done for the wounded—as well as all reserves of uniforms and boots.

General Elphinstone, who now for the first time understood why the fort must be held and that loss of these stores would mean starvation, promised to reinforce it and to send a letter ordering Warren to hold out at all costs. The message Warren later denied ever having received. Certainly no reinforcements were sent, and as night fell Captain Boyd to his bitter disappointment saw that there were no preparations to do this.

Together with Captain Johnson, he again went to see the General, where says Kaye 'the two officers, in emphatic language pointed out the terrible results of the sacrifice of our supplies'. The General listened and agreed and was ready to promise all that was asked. Then came another note from Warren saying that the enemy were mining below the walls while his sepoys were climbing over them and running away—that the enemy were also preparing to burn down the gate and that if reinforcements were not sent at once he would not be able to hold out. A messssage was sent that he would be reinforced by 2 a.m.

At midnight, Elphinstone, two of his staff—Major Thain and Captain Grant—together with the two commissariat officers, Boyd and Johnson, and Lieutenant Vincent Eyre, were still debating what to do, with Boyd, Johnson and Eyre all urging the General to reinforce the commissariat at once.

Macnaghten walked in and said bluntly that unless Mahomed Shereef's fort were taken that very night, we should 'lose the commissariat fort or at all events be unable to bring provisions out of it for the troops'. Macnaghten had no idea that Elphinstone had already decided to abandon it.

The General now answered that the disasters of the day made him unwilling to expose his men again. It was patiently explained to him that it would be hard for the Afghan marksmen to hit our men during darkness, and besides, they kept a poor watch at night.

A loyal tribesman employed by Captain Johnson was sent out to reconnoitre. 'He returned in a few minutes with the intelligence that about twenty men were seated outside the fort near the gate smoking and talking and from what he heard of their conversation he judged the garrison to be very small and unable to resist a sudden onset,' noted Johnson.

Another hour passed in useless debate, but still the General hesitated. A second spy was sent, whose report tallied with that of the first. Still vacillating crazily, Elphinstone now sent Lieutenant Eyre to get the opinion of another lieutenant—Sturt, the engineer officer, lying wounded in Lady Sale's house and hardly able to speak.

Sturt, says Eyre, 'at first expressed himself in favour of an immediate attack, but on hearing that some of the enemy were on watch at the gate, he judged it prudent to defer the assault till an early hour in the morning . . .'

And this young lieutenant's opinion finally, after hours of debate, enabled the General to make up his mind to attack at dawn. Orders were given for about 100 men to be ready at 4 a.m. Captain Bellew volunteered to blow open the gate of Mahomed Shereef's fort while another detachment marched to the relief of the commissariat fort. It was well after dawn, however, before the men were under arms, and then it was too late.

Lieutenant Warren, unable to hold out any longer, arrived with his garrison, having tunnelled beneath the fort's walls and escaped, leaving all the army's stores and provisions to the Afghans. The attack on Mahomed Shereef's fort was at once abandoned.

That day, 5 November, Captain Ponsonby, the Assistant Adjutant-General, ordered Warren in a public letter to state the reasons for abandoning his post. Warren responded to this attempt to brand him by coolly saying he was ready to do so before a court of inquiry, which he requested might be set up to investigate his conduct. But the abysmal story of the failure to reinforce him would have reflected upon the General and no inquiry was held.

Thus in three days only, Elphinstone's fatal leadership had lost the army its entire three months' reserves of food and medical supplies. Quite apart from the loss of the forts upon which the defence of the cantonments depended, the General had placed his men, the camp-followers and their women and children practically at the mercy of a ferocious and vengeful enemy. Only a miracle could save them now.

Chapter Twenty-two

That wintry morning, 5 November 1841, Captain Johnson reported in his *Journal*: 'Ere noon thousands and thousands had assembled from far and wide to participate in the booty of the English dogs, each man taking away with him as much as he could carry—and to this we were all eye-witnesses.'

The sight, barely 400 yards distant, of sacks of flour, barrels of beer, great stone jars of rum being manhandled away by the Afghans, caused 'a universal feeling of indignation to pervade the garrison' Vincent Eyre noted, and 'the impatience of the troops, but especially the native portion, to be led out for its recapture'—could not be ignored even by the defeatist commanders.

Eyre went to the General and 'strenuously urged' him to send a party to capture Mahomed Shereef's fort by blowing open the gate. Against any sudden advance of Afghan cavalry, he volunteered to hold the road with two 9-pounder guns, under cover of whose bombardment the storming party could advance, protected from the fire of the fort by a low wall.

Elphinstone agreed, but in a note to Macnaghten about it showed only confusion and worry about failure. 'After due consideration,' he wrote, 'we have determined on attacking the fort this morning with 50 men of the 44th and 200 Native Infantry. We will first try to breach the place and shell it as well as we can. . . . It seems the centre . . . is filled with buildings; therefore if we succeed in blowing open the gate, we should only be exposed to a destructive fire from the buildings, which . . . would no doubt be occupied in force, supported from the garden. Carrying powder-bags up under fire would have a chance of failure. Our men have been all night in the works, are tired and ill-fed; but we must hope for the best and securing our commissariat fort with the stores.'

Then followed the most cowardly suggestion of all: 'It behoves us to look to the consequences of failure: in this case I know not how we are to subsist, or, from want of provisions to retreat. You should therefore, consider what chance there is of making terms, if we are driven to this extremity.'

After three days' avoiding attacking the enemy, Elphinstone now talked of surrender. Some contemporary writers on this war, notably Vincent Eyre, shed tears for Elphinstone, when they might better have felt anger. The General clung jealously and needlessly to his command when it must have been clear, even to him, that he was no longer fit for it—when already by his incapacity he had sent many men to their deaths and was now edging the whole army to its doom.

One stroke of his pen under an order appointing either the most senior or the most capable officer in his place could have restored to the force its confidence and skill, so that before it was overcome by starvation, it could have met and defeated the Afghans—which past experience shows it could easily have done.

But the aristocratic self-esteem with which Elphinstone was saturated, tied his hands. He hung on—helped out of bed, across to his desk and back to bed again. His helplessness, his impotence, it will be seen, began to cripple his staff and his commanders and soon some of his junior officers and men.

At noon, the party ordered to storm Mahomed Shereef's fort under Major Swayne marched out of the western gate of the cantonments, led by Vincent Eyre with two guns of the Horse Artillery. Behind the partial cover of some trees Eyre briskly shelled the fort at 100 yards range. Major Swayne was to have charged forward under cover of the wall to assault the fort, but instead he kept his troops uselessly lying under cover for twenty minutes, while Eyre's shells screamed overhead.

The General, having limped as far as the rampart to watch, saw that the guns had only a few rounds left there and instead of ordering more he recalled the entire force into the cantonments before it could advance a single pace.

Thus, still another British failure encouraged the Afghans. They now readily believed the words of their *moollahs*—that into their hands the Prophet had put an enemy whom they could destroy at a blow and thereby reap great riches. The chiefs, on the assumption that the British were suddenly incapable of fighting called into Kabul every warrior in the region.

Macnaghten meantime, had arranged with the chief of the village of Behmaru, a short distance in rear of the cantonment, to sell them grain. The prospect of immediate starvation was thus avoided.

The supplies were necessarily bought at a very high price; and Khojah Mahomed, owner of the village, tried at the same time to be friendly with the insurgents as well. Moreover, the village and its fort, on the Behmaru hill, to the north-west of the cantonments, had only to be occupied by the Afghans to bring the British under *jezail* fire. It was unlikely therefore that Macnaghten's efforts would keep supplies flowing for long.

Artillery bombardment by both sides went on in fits and starts by day and night. 'The enemy saluted our house with six-pound shot,' Florentia Sale noted, 'which rattled about and passed us, and several struck the house; one was embedded in the wall under Mrs Sturt's window. At night we threw shell as usual into Mahmoud Khan's fort, and could plainly distinguish the sound of "Ullah ul Alla" as they burst'—here perhaps imagination carried away this normally accurate scribe.

Another attempt was at last made early on 6 November to occupy Mahomed Shereef's fort, the one which so effectively dominated the route to the commissariat fort; this the Afghans had still only half emptied of supplies. Lieutenant Sturt, the engineer officer, a realistic and capable one, staggered out of bed in his shirt and pyjamas and

—still not fully recovered from his wounds—went to superintend the bombardment of the fort with three 9-pounder
guns and two howitzers before an attack by about 200 men
under the command of Major Griffiths.

For two hours, the 9-pounders hit the fort's bastions at
short range while Lieutenant Warburton's howitzers
pounded the weaker parts of the walls. 'In the space of about
two hours,' says Eyre, 'a practicable breach was effected,
during which time a hot fire was poured upon the artillerymen by the enemy's sharp-shooters, stationed in a couple of
high towers which completely commanded the battery....'

Major Griffiths then led his men in a rush at the fort and
with few casualties speedily occupied it. Eyre now had a 6-
pounder gun dragged over to the Shah's garden opposite
and sent several rounds of grape shot whistling through the
trees. Colin Mackenzie attacked the enemy there with a few
of his *jezailchis*, but with no support he had to fall back.

Elphinstone, who had persuaded himself that he was
short of gunpowder and shell, had refused to follow up this
success with an immediate attack upon both the Shah's
Garden and the commissariat fort. And so this and its supplies unfortunately still remained in Afghan hands, even
though the British at last held Mahomed Shereef's fort.

Captains Boyd and Johnson, the commissariat officers,
had meantime also been successful in obtaining supplies
from surrounding villages. 'For the last four days,' Captain
Johnson wrote in his *Journal* on 8 November, 'I have been
busily purchasing grain from Deh Meru; I have established
a reasonable rate; and the villagers will sell willingly from
the stores which they had laid up for the winter.'

On 6 November Elphinstone wrote Macnaghten another
confused and worried letter persuading him to surrender:
'We have temporarily and I hope permanently got over the
difficulty of provisions. Our next consideration is ammunition; a very serious and indeed awful one. We have ex-
pended a great quantity; therefore it becomes worthy of
thought on your part, how desirable it is that our operations
should not be protracted. . . . Do not suppose from this I

wish to recommend or am advocating humiliating terms, or such as would reflect disgrace upon us,' he protested; 'but this fact of ammunition must not be lost sight of.' And in a postscript whose feebleness must have disgusted Macnaghten: 'Our case is not yet desperate: I do not mean to impress that; but it must be borne in mind that it goes fast.'

Elphinstone's conduct in seeking terms from the enemy—for capitulating—was dishonourable almost to the point of treason. There was no lack of ammunition or gunpowder. The army carried huge amounts from Kandahar; much more was captured at Ghazni and there had been ammunition convoys from India. Elphinstone clearly preferred to surrender rather than fight or to give up his command to an officer who would fight.

Macnaghten, who wished to retrieve the British position at all costs, sought a way out by two different moves.

The first was secretly to commission the British agent Mohan Lal, through Lieutenant John Conolly, to offer rewards for the heads of the Afghan leaders. 'I promise 10,000 rupees for the heads of each of the principal chiefs,' Conolly wrote Mohan Lal on 5 November. This scheme went forward while Macnaghten was at the same time trying to bribe the same chiefs to stop the rising. Macnaghten kept the tightest rein over his assistants; he must have planned the scheme himself. Like a boomerang it would swerve back at him with deadly effect.

A week of unbroken failure for the British had thus led to efforts by General Elphinstone to have Macnaghten negotiate with the Afghan leaders; and to Macnaghten offering blood money for their heads—a fantastic anomaly.

As his second move, Macnaghten now persuaded Elphinstone to return the tough, one-armed Brigadier Shelton from the Bala Hissar. Bringing with him only the Shah's 6th Infantry and a 6-pounder gun, as he had been ordered, Shelton set out.

'I left the Bala Hissar between six and seven and marched in broad daylight without the enemy attempting to dispute my passage,' he wrote. 'I was all prepared for opposition had any been made.'

The garrison—the troops and younger officers especially —received him almost as a deliverer. On his return, Shelton, a small man, called 'the little Brig' by his men, says he 'read anxiety in every countenance' and 'was sorry to find desponding conversations and remarks too generally indulged and was more grieved to find the troops dispirited'.

He strode round the cantonments and 'found them of frightful extent . . . with a rampart and ditch an Afghan could run over with the facility of a cat . . .'.

Able and courageous, yet lacking polish and social ease, Shelton clearly suffered from an outsize inferiority complex which he tried to hide behind military perfectionism and over-strict discipline. This discord led him on the one hand to high standards of bravery—he was said to have stood unmoved outside his tent in the Peninsular War while surgeons completed the amputation of an arm lost at the storm of St. Sebastian—and on the other to petulance, vindictiveness and quick anger.

Fortescue in his *History of the British Army*, suggests that incessant physical pain due to the rough surgery of those days may have been responsible, recalling that in India, General Napier's intellect was completely unbalanced by the pain of an old wound and that Lord Anglesey, though he never uttered a sound, would lock himself into his room and roll on the floor in agony.

Macnaghten had hoped Shelton would be able to co-operate with the General and tactfully give a lead in taking the fight to the Afghans. But it soon became clear that this was the last thing that would happen. Both men disliked each other from the very beginning. 'I was put in orders to command cantonments,' Shelton wrote later, 'and consequently in course of my inspections, gave such orders and instructions as appeared to me necessary. This, however, Elphinstone soon corrected, by reminding me that he commanded, not I.'

Shelton, the taciturn, not very likeable fighting soldier,

who by Elphinstone's standards was no gentleman, offended the General so deeply that he denounced him in a report to the Governor-General. Perhaps he also found in Shelton a convenient scapegoat.

'On the 9th, not finding myself equal to the duties,' he wrote later . . . 'I recalled Brigadier Shelton from the Bala Hissar, but I regret to be obliged to disclose that I did not receive from him that cordial co-operation and advice I had a right to expect; on the contrary his manner was most contumacious; from the day of his arrival he never gave me information or advice, but invariably found fault with all that was done, and canvassed and condemned all orders before officers, frequently preventing and delaying carrying them into effect . . .; he appeared to be actuated by an ill-feeling towards me. I did everything to remain on terms with him.

'I was also unlucky in not understanding the state of things and being wholly dependent upon the Envoy and others for information,' he concluded lamely. Yet much later he could not but praise Shelton's ability: 'I beg to be allowed to express my sense of the gallant manner in which the various detachments sent out were led by Brigadier Shelton,' he wrote, when his own death was near.

Thus, command of the force was now bedevilled by Elphinstone's and Shelton's quarrel.

Shelton, having made a thorough appreciation of the military situation, decided not to support risking the force in a large scale attack on Kabul; and despairing of being able to hold out the winter there, he vouched for an immediate fighting retreat to Jellalabad.

Macnaghten was disgusted. Faced now with a General who wished to negotiate and a second-in-command who wished to retreat, despairingly he looked about him and saw still only two chances to stay in Kabul and save the army and himself from the ignominy of a retreat. The first again, was his secret policy of blood money for the chief's heads.

The second hope was that General Nott, 290 miles away n Kandahar, and General Sale in Gundamuk, in answer to his letters, would march troops to the rescue. Lady Sale noted in her diary on 10 November that 'Nott may be here with his brigade in three weeks,' but he had not then received the letter and would not until 14 November.

Meantime, the Afghans, still on the offensive, occupied the three or four other forts dotted about the plain within range of the cantonments. From the Rikabashee fort, about 400 yards east of the cantonments, they poured a heavy fire at troops manning the defences—one or two of the infantry were hit and a gunner was shot through the head while in the act of loading.

These Afghan marksmen were not regular troops but, many of them, tradesmen of Kabul, and, according to Lady Sale the two best shots were a barber and a blacksmith, who had picked off many British troops. 'They completely commanded the loop-holes with their long rifles,' she wrote, 'and although the distance is probably 300 yards, yet they seldom fail to put a ball through the body or into the clothes of anyone passing them. It was sufficient for the loophole to be darkened to be fired at.'

Tireless in her self-appointed role as recorder of day-to-day events, Lady Sale never slept now till daylight but sat up, often on the roof—'to watch passing events, and give the alarm if need be, and have kept my nightly watch ever since the insurrection commenced. Our troops are as yet staunch; and if we are attacked, and succeed in repelling the enemy, we shall be able to keep our own until Sale's brigade arrives,' she commented hopefully.

Shelton was authorised by Elphinstone to occupy the Rikabashee fort, but he seemed to have lost his fighting spirit in the enervating atmosphere the old General created. Shelton would attend the many councils of war Elphinstone summoned, but would insultingly lie down on the floor and pretend to go to sleep, while beside his prone body the discussions, which decided nothing, went on.

While shot from the Rikabashee fort thudded into the cantonments, Shelton delayed attacking until Macnaghten insisted that Elphinstone should issue peremptory orders.

Elphinstone reluctantly did so and Shelton began to assemble a force of some 2,000 men, when Elphinstone had second thoughts. 'I was occupied,' says Shelton, 'in telling off the force about 10 a.m., when I heard Elphinstone say to his aide-de-camp, "I think we had better give it up"— which was done, and I returned, as you may conceive, disgusted with such vacillation.' Clearly, the bitter quarrel between the General and his second-in-command was affecting operations.

Shelton complained to Macnaghten, who managed to bring the General round again to the importance of occupying the fort—from which bullets still whined past the ears of those in the cantonments.

Captain Bellow volunteered to blow the gate open by gunpowder, but in the excitement of the moment he blew open a small wicket gate instead and when the storming party under Colonel Mackrell rushed forward only one at a time could get through. Mackrell and Lieutenant Bird forced their way in, many soldiers were shot down outside, Captain Westmacott fell with a round in his brain, Captain Macrae was sabred.

While the storming party milled about outside there was a cry of 'Cavalry!' The British troops wavered, then turned and fled. The one-armed Shelton now showed his courage, standing upright where the Afghan fire was hottest to rally his men. Under his example, the disorderly lines re-formed, but when Shelton called for an advance only a Scottish private named Stewart responded. The demoralised British gave way to the Afghan cavalry and once more the fearless Shelton's example inspired them. Finally, when shells from the 9-pounders in the cantonment began to bowl over the Afghans, Shelton was able to lead his men forward to capture the fort.

Of those who had forced their way in earlier there were only two survivors. Colonel Mackrell was found bloody and almost unrecognisable from his wounds and carried into the cantonment to die; several men had fallen to huge gashes from the Afghan *tulwars* (sabres). Lieutenant Bird and a sepoy had barricaded themselves into a stable with logs of wood from which they had shot down thirty Afghans who had tried to enter; the bodies lay in a heap before the door.

So the fort was occupied with an absurd and tragic cost in lives. One or two other small forts near by were also taken and the action kept the Afghans quiet for the next two or three days.

The ever-watchful Lady Sale after having watched this and other actions, noted that the Afghans had some advantages over the British troops. 'One consists in dropping their men fresh for combat,' she observed. 'Each horseman takes a foot soldier up behind him, and when he is arrived at the spot he is required to fire from, he is dropped without the fatigue of walking to his post. The horsemen have two or three matchlocks or *jezails* each, slung at their backs, and are very expert in firing at the gallop. Their *jezails* carry much farther than our muskets and, whilst they are out of our fire, theirs tells murderously on us. They fire from rests and then take excellent aim; and are capital riflemen, hiding behind any stone sufficiently large to cover their head, and quietly watching their opportunities to snipe off our people.'

The British troops were armed with the musket known as the Brown Bess, only slightly improved since first used in India nearly 100 years earlier in the time of Robert Clive. Made either in gun factories surrounding the Tower of London or in Birmingham, it weighed 11 lb. 2 oz., and had a barrel 46 inches long with a bore of 0.753 inches.

Against the hand-made Afghan *jezails* with barrels 60 and even 70 inches long, and greater accuracy, range and muzzle velocity, the unfortunate British infantrymen found the Brown Bess a very sorrowful weapon, for its effective range was little more than 300 yards. Beyond this range British artillery usually took over—6- and 9-pounders firing case- or grape-shot, only really effective against massed troops, just as was the controlled fire-power in repeated volleys of infantrymen armed with the Brown Bess.

Meantime, Mohan Lal, Macnaghten's secret agent, had advanced 9,000 rupees and promised another 12,000 directly the heads of two of the chief rebels, Abdullah Khan and Meer Musjidi, were brought to him. He chose these two chiefs as his first victims because they were most influential —the ringleaders in the attack on Burnes's house and Johnson's treasury.

Two tribesmen, Abdul Azeez and Mahomed Oolah, were his chosen assassins. Within a few days Mahomed Oolah broke into Meer Musjidi's house at night and strangled the chief while he slept.

It is hard to say what Macnaghten really hoped to gain by isolated assassination of this kind, for it was hardly possible for him to bribe assassins to kill all the ringleaders of the rising. But Macnaghten by now must have become desperate in his burning wish for effective action against the rebels. It must be remembered that this irritating rising of a humble race had occurred when he was about to step up to the very pinnacle of his career.

But assassination did little immediate good, for on 13 November things worsened. An Afghan force of several thousand assembled on the Behmaru ridge—which was about 600 yards west of the north-west corner of the cantonments—obviously to stop food going from there to the British and to attack the cantonments with *jezail* and cannon fire. No counter-action having been taken by noon, Macnaghten insisted that Elphinstone should order Shelton to counter-attack, but by mid-afternoon still not a shot had been fired. Macnaghten then sought out Shelton and found him wasting time. With commendable restraint he said: 'Brigadier Shelton, if you will allow yourself to be thus bearded by the enemy and will not advance and take these two guns by this evening, you must be prepared for any disgrace that may befall us. . . .'

But it was five o'clock and dusk was falling before the force finally took the field. One of the British guns got stuck in a canal while the advance body of infantry under Major Thain moved up the hill to close with the enemy. The Afghan cavalry charged and the infantry fired wildly at short range. When the smoke had cleared not a single

Afghan had fallen and they were charging furiously down upon the British bayonets.

To Lady Sale, watching from the cantonments it was terrifying. 'My very heart,' she wrote, 'felt as if it leapt to my teeth when I saw the Afghans ride clean through them. The onset was fearful. They looked like a great cluster of bees. . . .'

For a minute or two there was panic and confusion. The column gave way and friend and foe interlocked as the horsemen charged through the bayonets with a whirl of sabres. The British retreated down the slope, but rallied, and under cover of accurate shooting from Vincent Eyre's guns advanced again.

The British cavalry now charged the enemy's flank and scattered them. The infantry moved in, gained the height and captured the two Afghan guns. The enemy, says Lawrence fled 'with such precipitation that they abandoned their two guns and our troops might easily have followed them into and taken the city, had not the night come on. Brigadier Shelton thus gained a brilliant success against his own will, but his previous procrastination had rendered it impossible to reap any real advantage from the victory.'

One of the guns was now manhandled into the cantonment and when no volunteers could be found to help bring in the other—the Afghans were showering it with *jezail* fire— Vincent Eyre went out bravely with a gunner and spiked it.

The Afghans now began a small, but lively counter-attack upon the cantonment, and the British force hurried back to help repel it. It was done easily enough, but the hopelessness of having to retire to the cantonments and leave the Behmaru heights gained at such cost now became painfully clear.

Sooner or later the Afghans would reoccupy them and the British would again have to lose men in driving them out, thus paying over and over in blood from the initial mistake two years ago of not entering the Bala Hissar.

Casualities had been heavy on both sides during the action—some 200 British had been killed or wounded; Major Thain was hurt severely by a great sword slash,

Captain Paton's arm was shattered by a bullet and had to be amputated—anaesthetics were not in use by the British in India then; sometimes the shock of rough and ready surgery killed those who suffered it.

All night the defenders in the cantonment saw lights on the hillside and heard cries of lamentation from the women burying the Afghans who had fallen. Could this have brought home to a few of the British that the Afghans were not, after all, merely treacherous savages who loved to fight, but brave patriots dying to free their country from a ruthless invader?

So involved were these early-Victorian English with their empire and, unlike their eighteenth-century forebears—so race-proud, so certain of the rightness of their overseas policies, that practically none of them managed to look objectively, let alone with any sympathy at this primitive people whose land they had seized, ruined and drenched in blood.

Lady Sale made an attempt to do so. 'I often hear the Afghans designated as cowards,' she noted at this time. 'They are a fine manly-looking set, and I can only suppose it arises from the British idea . . . that assassination is a cowardly act. They never scruple to use their long knives for that purpose, *ergo* they are cowards; but they show no cowardice in standing as they do against guns without using any themselves, and in escalading and taking forts which we cannot retake. The Afghans of the capital are a little more civilised, but the country gentlemen and their retainers are, I fancy, much the same kind of people as those Alexander encountered.'

In the absence of Dost Mahommed in India, the Afghan chiefs leading this struggle for liberation, now chose a king in opposition to the British puppet Shah Shuja up in the Bala Hissar. He was Nawab Mahommed Zemaun, not Shuja's blind brother, but the son of an elder brother of Dost Mahommed, the same one who, at first opposing the rising, had tried to help Captain Trevor. The chiefs assembled in the mosque and read the prayer for the new monarch, whom some of the *moollahs*, or priests, refused to accept on the grounds of legitimacy. So while Shah Shuja sat tight in the fortress and lacked power in the country, Mohammed Zemaun, backed by many of the chiefs, took over and celebrated by minting his own money.

Macnaghten, all this time still hoped for the return of Sale's brigade, and almost daily was writing to his political assistant, Macgregor, with Sale in Gundamuk, imploring him to procure it. 'I have written to you four times, requesting that you would come up with Sale's brigade as soon as possible,' he protested on 12 November. 'Our force is so small that we cannot act on the offensive and we have not above a fortnight's supplies. We have lost a great many officers. . . .'. .

And two days later: 'Dozens of letters have been written . . . urging your immediate return with Sale's brigade to Kabul; and if you have not started by the time you receive this, I earnestly beg that you will do so immediately. Our situation is a very precarious one; but with your assistance we should all do well and you must render it to us if you have any regard for our lives or for the honour of our country. . . . The Ghilzye force being here I should conceive you will experience no opposition on the road.'

But there was to be from now on only bad news for the garrison. The next day, 15 November, at 3 a.m., two worn and bloody officers on horseback with a Ghurka soldier walking beside them crossed the Kabul plain in the darkness and entered the cantonments. They were Major Eldred Pottinger and Lieutenant Haughton, who had somehow managed to cross hostile country from Charikar, in Kohistan, 100 miles to the north, to report that the Ghurka regiment in an outpost there had been cut to pieces. Pottinger was wounded in the leg and Haughton's hand was cut off, while his head hung forward on his chest—his neck muscles had been severed by a sword cut. Wearing Afghan dress they had crossed the sleeping city of Kabul.

Pottinger's news was hardly cheering. Charikar had fallen —the Ghurka regiment no longer existed—a large force of

Kohistanee tribesmen would be marching to join the Kabul rebels. And worst of all, Macnaghten now learned that Sale's brigade, which he had looked upon as a lifeline, had instead marched westwards for Jellalabad from Gundamuk.

General Sale had held a council of war when he received the request. The outcome was a decision not to attempt to force the passes in a fighting return to Kabul.

The decision for Sale must have been a hard one—his wife and daughter were still in Kabul; it was opposed, too, by Broadfoot and some of Sale's best officers. Yet Sale had convinced himself that confined as he would be in the narrow passes while under attack from a nation in arms he risked a disaster—the annihilation of his entire force.

Also, to carry 200 wounded and sick back with him would have been impossible. He would have been forced to leave them guarded by a detachment at Gundamuk and for this and his own force he certainly did not have enough rations. In the event, his decision was the correct one, for he might have fought his way back to Kabul only to face starvation because the Afghans had seized the food supplies there and scattered them across the country.

But instead of staying at Gundamuk, where his force threatened the Ghilzyes in their traditional territories and discouraged them from seething into Kabul, Sale then launched his force another 80 miles west to Jellalabad out of the area of operations.

Macnaghten tried hard to bring it back and on 17 November sent a final appeal: 'I have written to you daily, pointing out our precarious state, and urging you to return here with Sale's brigade, with all possible expedition. General Elphinstone has done the same and we now learn to our dismay, that you have proceeded to Jellalabad. Our situation is a desperate one if you do not immediately return to our relief, and I beg that you will do so without a moment's delay. . . .'

But that same night his hopes were dashed. A letter he received from his political assistant Macgregor, dated 13 November, made it clear that the brigade would *not* return.

Typically, he put the best face possible on it. 'I perceive now that you could not well have joined us,' he replied, and went on to urge that the Sikhs should be brought in under the terms of the Tripartite Treaty to relieve them at Kabul. 'If there is any difficulty about the Sikhs getting through the pass, Mackeson should offer a bribe to the Khyberees of a lakh of rupees (£10,000) or more to send them safe passage,' he wrote, with as fervent a belief as ever in the power of money.

A forlorn hope indeed was this and Macnaghten now sent General Elphinstone a letter in which for the first time he objectively summed up their plight and how they might possibly survive. He himself thought it their imperative duty to hold on as long as possible. He thought they might even struggle through the whole winter by making the Mahommedans and Christians live chiefly upon horse and camel meat, supposing their supplies of grain to fall, by which means, as the essentials of wood and water were abundant, he considered their position might be rendered impregnable.

A retreat towards Jellalabad he went on, would teem not only with disaster but also dishonour, and ought not to be contemplated until the very last extremity. They should in such a case have to sacrifice Shah Shuja, to support whose authority they were employed by Government; and even were they to make good their retreat to Jellalabad, they should have no shelter for their troops in the march through the bitter winter snows, while the thousands of campfollowers would all be killed.

He had frequently thought of negotiating, but, he remarked with notable realism, there was no party with enough power and influence over the tribesmen to protect them. Another alternative would be to throw themselves into the Bala Hissar; but he feared that would also be disastrous. 'We would probably not succeed in getting our heavy guns and they would be turned with effect by the enemy against the citadel.' Food and firewood might be scarce, for a further supply of which they might be dependent upon sorties into the city, in which, if beaten, they might of course be ruined.

On the whole he was decidedly of the opinion that they should hold out; it was still possible that reinforcements might arrive from General Nott at Kandahar, or something might turn up in their favour; there were hopes, too, that on the setting in of winter the enemy might disperse. In eight or ten days, he concluded, it would remain for the military authorities to determine whether there was any chance of improving their position, and to decide whether it would be more prudent to attempt a retreat to Jellalabad, or to the Bala Hissar. If provision sufficient for the winter could be procured, on no account would he leave the cantonment, he ended, in contradictory fashion.

Macnaghten was playing for time, but events were now to move fast in another direction. Akbar Khan, Dost Mahommed's fiery and uncompromising son, was drawn to Kabul by news of the insurrection on 22 November. His hatred of the British, his powers of leadership, his blood relationship to the former king and the prestige born out of his refusal to surrender, at once combined to make him the leader the Afghans needed.

Chapter Twenty-three

Three thousand Afghan cavalry and infantry under Akbar Khan's command moved out of Kabul on 22 November and occupied the village and hills of Behmaru—the name meant *husbandless*—so-called after a beautiful virgin who was buried there. A crisis was now at hand for the British, for the next day they were to fight a decisive battle.

The Afghans had made frequent moves out on to the hill, often descending into the village below, where, lamented the commissariat officer, Captain Johnson, 'they destroyed the houses and plundered the inhabitants, and have expelled them from their homes on account of their aid to us in bringing in grain. . . . I am up daily long before gunfire and as soon as there is sufficient light commence purchasing as it is only in the morning that the villagers can venture to bring their stores for sale.'

Shelton decided to occupy the hill and on the morning of 22 November a weak force under Major Swayne, an officer who persistently avoided action in a crisis, marched out with a small body of cavalry. 'Major Swayne, whose orders were to storm the village, would neither go forward nor retire,' wrote Vincent Eyre, who was in charge of the single gun that Elphinstone allowed to support the force. 'But, concealing his men under the cover of some low wall, he all day long maintained a useless fire on the houses of Beymaru, without the slightest satisfactory result. . . . Thus we remained for five or six hours, during which the artillery stood exposed to the deliberate aim of the numerous marksmen who occupied the village and its immediate vicinity, whose bullets continually sang in our ears, often striking the gun and grazing the ground on which we stood.'

It was an absurd situation; the cavalry had many casual-

ties and two gunners were wounded; Eyre's left hand was
almost shattered by a bullet. Later in the day Swayne's
troops were withdrawn, having accomplished nothing.

Again, at Macnaghten's insistence, before daybreak next
day a force of about 1,200 infantry, 400 cavalry, 100 sappers and again only one gun, a 9-pounder, marched out and
occupied the north-east corner of the hills, overlooking the
village.

One gun, upon which Elphinstone had insisted as a result
of his imaginary shortage of ammunition, was a direct
breach of time-honoured artillery standing orders born of
the experience that it invariably became too hot to
fire.

From a commanding position, the gun fired grape-shot
down on to an Afghan camp in the village, revealed by
flickering fires. The enemy fired back from the houses and
towers until their ammunition was exhausted and Shelton
then sent the faint-hearted Major Swayne to carry the
village by assault at bayonet point. In his mole-like way the
Major again went to ground. He was recalled half an hour
later having done nothing but lose several men and receive a
slight wound in the neck himself.

At sunrise sounded the deep beat of drums—a stream of
several thousand Afghan cavalry and infantry surged out
occupying a nearby hill and part of the village. Leaving
five companies under Major Kershaw at the foot of the hill,
immediately above the village, Shelton now took the remainder of his force to an exposed position on the brow of
the hill where it was overlooked from the hill beyond just
occupied by the Afghans.

Here, as he had learned to do with Wellington in the
entirely different conditions of the Peninsular War, Shelton
formed his infantry into two squares and massed his cavalry
between them. It was an invitation to the enemy. A rain of
fire from the Afghan *jezails* struck this massed blue- and red-
coated target and men fell by the score.

Sergeant Mulhall fired the one 9-pounder as fast as it
could be loaded, killing many of the enemy in return until

the barrel became too hot to handle and he had to order his gunners to cease fire.

Undismayed by the sound and the fury, the intrepid Lady Sale carefully noted all that went on. 'I had taken up my post of observation, as usual, on top of the house,' she says, 'whence I had a fine view of the field of action, and where, by keeping behind the chimneys, I escaped the bullets that continually whizzed past me. The number of the enemy's foot men must have been upwards of 10,000 (some say 15,000) and, the plain, on the north-west of the hills, was swept by not less than 3,000 or 4,000 Afghan cavalry. . . .'

Taking advantage of a dip in the ground which hid them, a party of Afghans crawled up and hurled themselves in a furious hand-to-hand attack upon the British infantry, who, strangely, lost their nerve, wavered, turned and fled. The Afghans captured the gun and with shouts of triumph manhandled it towards their own position.

In the thick of the fire the stubborn Shelton now stood alone and vainly called his men to turn about and charge. ' . . . My own clothes were riddled, having been struck by no less than five balls, none of which did much harm; one spent ball hit me on the head and nearly knocked me down; another made my arm a little stiff,' he related.

At his command the bugles shrilled the *halt* and stopped the tearaway infantry in their tracks; the officers re-formed them and with a shout they again faced the attackers with levelled bayonets. The cavalry came to their rescue with a timely charge, scattering most of the Afghans, who abandoned the gun and rode off with its horses and limber.

At this moment one of Macnaghten's schemes for assassination of the chiefs bore fruit. Abdoollah Khan, one of the leaders of the rising, whose head Macnaghten had sought to buy through the efforts of Lieutenant Conolly and Mohan Lal, was in the thick of the fighting at the head of a party of Afghan horsemen. Suddenly he fell wounded—shot from behind a wall, it later transpired, by Abdool Aziz, one of Mohan Lal's assassins. Seeing their chief carried off, apparently dead, his men turned and rode in panic and con-

fusion behind him towards the city, with the Afghan infantry following them, streaming back across the plain towards the city walls.

Macnaghten, unaware that his hand had pulled the
trigger, was watching the battle with Elphinstone on the
cantonment rampart. Out of this Afghan confusion a fresh
force from the cantonment could now seize victory, with a
vigorous attack upon this disorderly rout. Macnaghten tried
strongly to persuade the General to do this, but Elphinstone
shook his head sagely and refused—'it's a wild scheme—it's
not possible', he said. And so while the Afghans were in
flight both from the Behmaru hill and the plain the chance
was lost.

The British infantry moved forward to their former position on the brow of the hill, a fresh supply of ammunition
was sent out for the gun and Sergeant Mulhall was soon
firing grape-shot and shrapnel at the diminished Afghan
lines, still two or three thousand strong. But again the British
muskets were outranged by the *jezailchis*, who mowed down
both infantrymen and gunners.

Colonel Oliver, the fat and pessimistic commander of six
companies of the 5th Native Infantry, ordered a party of his
men down the brow of the hill with him to attack a number
of Afghan sharp-shooters in a small ravine. Not a man
would follow him. Oliver said: 'Although my men desert me
I myself will do my duty.' He turned his back on them,
walked some paces into the thick of the fire and fell dead.

Still held in squares by the brave but stupid Shelton, the
British were falling on all sides—four of the gun-team of six
were dead. Finally Shelton ordered a retreat to the reserve
in position down near the village. The Afghans now attacked
with fresh vigour, a party of Ghazees, the religious fanatics,
leading a furious charge at the leading square. The square
broke, all order and discipline vanished and in a moment
first infantry then cavalry were running in a terrified rout
back down the hill towards the cantonment.

The Afghan horsemen dashed among them with whirling
tulwars and took a bloody toll. Major Kershaw in the Vil-

lage, seeing that he would be cut off, ordered a retreat, but he was too late, his small force was surrounded and only a few escaped. If Captain Trevor with some sepoys on the ramparts of the cantonment had not opened a heavy fire on the Afghans, and a troop of the 5th Cavalry under Lieutenant Hardyman had not emerged and charged them, the pursuit might have continued over the ramparts and into the cantonment.

Soon the enemy were so intermingled with the British that the cantonment guns could no longer fire. General Elphinstone stood up swaying on the ramparts trying to rally the men whom his failure in the past few days had so demoralised, but it was useless. 'Why, Lord, sir,' he said to Macnaghten, 'when I said to them "Eyes right," they all looked the other way.'

It seemed for a moment that the entire British force might be slaughtered, but one of the chiefs, said to be Osman Khan, suddenly ordered off his followers. In a short time they withdrew, 'astonished at their own success', says Lieutenant Melville, 'and after mutilating in a dreadful manner the many bodies left on the hill, they returned with exulting shouts to the city'.

The British had lost over 300 men. But for the action of Osman Khan these losses would have been greater. Of this Lady Sale noted: 'Osman Khan was heard by our sepoys to order his men not to fire on those who ran, but to spare them. A chief, probably the same, rode round Kershaw three times, when he was compelled to run with his men; he waved the sword over his head, but never attempted to kill him; and Captain Trevor says his life was also several times in the power of the enemy, but he also was spared.'

Most contemporary writers have blamed Shelton for this defeat, but the best military authority, Fortescue, points out that he was sent with a weak and demoralised force and one gun to a position where he could be surrounded, and that when as a result he *was* surrounded, no effort was made by Elphinstone, who had plenty of men near by, to rescue him. 'It would seem that the Afghan tactics were well con-

ceived, and skilfully and persistently executed; but Nott, in
the place of Elphinstone, would have turned the day's
fighting into a great and crushing victory.'

But Nott was 250 miles south, over the snow-blocked
mountain passes in Kandahar and with the demented
Elphinstone and the brave but foolish Shelton at its head the
demoralisation of the army was now complete. Physically
exhausted, under-fed, lacking the discipline, self-esteem and
cohesion that make an army out of a mass of men, it was
hardly fit for combat. One thinks of the ashamed, wretched
soldiers in the cantonment that night, without a pot of beer
or a dram of rum to console them, knowing above all that
with the present leadership they were at the enemy's
mercy. 'Who can depict the horror of that night and our
consternation, for we felt ourselves doomed men,' lamented
Lawrence.

The Shah, who had observed the rout through a telescope
in the fortress, now wrote in alarm to Macnaghten, urging
an immediate retreat into the Bala Hissar, as the only move
that could ensure the safety and honour of the British. Both
the General and Shelton objected and Macnaghten unhappily fell in with their views.

The next day came a letter from Osman Khan, the chief
who had called off his cavalry. He recalled this service, and
now suggested that the time had come for the British
quietly to leave the country. This letter and the fact of the
military leaders having left him no other way out than
negotiations for a retreat now made Macnaghten—doubtless with an eye on the record—ask the General whether in
fact his army could maintain its position in the country.

Elphinstone replied hopelessly that it was no longer
feasible to do so and that Macnaghten should avail himself
of the offer to negotiate. The Envoy wrote that day to
Sultan Mahommed Khan, saying he was ready to talk.

The next day, 25 November, Mahomed Khan and
Meerza Ahmed Ali, envoys of the chiefs, both in unassum-
ing dress, riding dismal horses and attended only by their
grooms, were met at the bridge over the Kabul River and

taken into a guardroom at the cantonments to meet Macnaghten.

Here, their unpretentious manners ended. Mahomed Khan, suddenly arrogant and offensive, declared that beaten in battle, the British should surrender unconditionally, giving themselves up with their arms, ammunition and money as prisoners of war.

Macnaghten rejected the terms out of hand. While the talks went on, crowds of Afghans armed with sword and *jezail* swarmed round the ramparts and with friendly smiles called out to the British that all was settled and the war was over.

Some of the troops went out unarmed among them, shaking hands, accepting presents of vegetables. Senior officers suspected that the cabbages might contain bottles of drugged spirits so that the garrison, flat on their backs, would be unable to ward off an intended attack. The cabbages were carefully examined, but found to be quite harmless vegetables.

Macnaghten now sent the chiefs a letter giving the conditions under which he was prepared to negotiate. 'I proposed to them,' he wrote, 'the only terms which could be accepted with honour; but . . . they returned me a letter of defiance the next morning to the effect that unless I consented to surrender our arms and leave his Majesty to his fate, we must prepare for immediate hostilities. To this I replied that we preferred death to dishonour and,' he ended piously, 'that it would remain with a higher power to decide between us.'

Little had been heard of the supreme Being so far in this campaign, though the British had no doubt that he was on their side against this heathen horde, but now while the Afghans waved sacred banners and swore on the Koran to put infidels to the sword, Macnaghten had introduced Him as the silent watcher of the British downfall.

On 25 November Shelton made a pretence at hostilities by again shelling the Behmaru Hills, to give cover to Captain Johnson, then in the village trying to buy supplies—a task which daily became harder and harder.

Akbar Khan had soon realised that if he could stop supplies reaching the cantonments he would have the British at his mercy. He threatened death to all the tribesmen within several miles of Kabul who were making small fortunes selling grain at fabulous prices to the commissariat.

Captain Johnson went daily during the last week of November to try to buy from the chief of Behmaru, but, he wrote in his *Journal* on 1 December—'notwithstanding my offers of the most handsome rewards to him, I cannot now prevail upon him or his people to give further aid. On going to his fort this morning I found merely two or three people inside who told me that Mahomed Khan had yesterday come with a party and destroyed every house in it, and threatened death to the Khoja (who had fled) and his family, in the event of his giving us further aid.'

Told of this, and that there were only eight days' provisions at half-rations in hand, Macnaghten refused to be downcast, insisting that they should 'wait two days longer', before deciding what to do 'as something may turn up'. Still hoping that the brigade from Kandahar would come to the rescue, he was also, through Mohan Lal, bribing any chief willing to sow discord or plant the seeds of treachery among the leaders of the insurrection.

Thus, while Elphinstone insisted that 'our position was becoming more and more critical', Macnaghten was declaring that 'our prospects were brightening'. In this vein he wrote to Mohan Lal on 29 November: 'The enemy appeared today in considerable numbers, but they did nothing and I am sure they will never venture to attack our cantonment. If we had only provisions, which, with due exertions ought to be obtained, we should be able to defy the whole of Afghanistan for the period.'

Elphinstone now pressed him almost daily to negotiate, but the realistic Macnaghten probably guessed unhappily that whatever terms were obtained they would amount to nothing. Once the force left the cantonments the chiefs would be unable to restrain their tribesmen. He still clutched therefore at any chance of hanging on.

On 5 December the Afghans cut off all chance for light-

ning retreat by destroying a vital bridge over the Kabul
River, and Elphinstone let them do so without having a
single shot fired to stop it. Continuing their offensive the
next day they surprised the British garrison of Mahomed
Shereef's fort, who, without resistance abandoned their
arms and 6,000 rounds of ammunition and fled from an
attack, which, in Lady Sale's words, 'a child with a stick
might have repulsed.'

Lieutenant Hawtrey, deserted by his men, stayed to
throw six grenades before escaping. Furiously, Lady Sale
called this defeat 'the most shameful of all the runaways
that has occurred'.

Lieutenant Hawtrey's company, ashamed at their un-
heroic flight, volunteered to retake the fort with him 'without the assistance of any other troops'. Elphinstone asked
Captain Sturt, the engineer officer, if the fort was practicable and tenable. Sturt replied with sarcasm: 'Practicable if
the men will fight—tenable if they don't run away.'

It summed up the whole situation of the British forces in
Kabul; but the demoralisation and despair from which the
troops suffered was almost entirely the fault of General
William George Keith Elphinstone.

Every day now the weather grew colder; and the troops,
the sepoys especially, shivered in the freezing barracks. On
8 December Captains Boyd and Johnson wrote to Elphinstone to report 'from personal knowledge of the country to
the north or north-east of cantonments, the utter impossi-
bility of obtaining, either by force or otherwise, the smallest
quantity of grain or forage of any kind . . '.

The transport animals, almost skin and bone, the British
and the Moslems now used for meat. A committee had chosen
all the useless animals to be slaughtered. 'So there will be
plenty of cheap meat,' Lady Sale commented, 'as tattoos
(ponies) and camels have for some time past been eaten:
even some of the gentlemen ate camel's flesh, particularly
the heart, which was esteemed equal to that of the bullock. I
was never tempted by these choice viands; so cannot offer
an opinion regarding them.'

Elphinstone, pressing the reluctant Macnaghten to negotiate, sent him a copy of the commissariat officers' letter. In reply, Macnaghten curtly asked him to state in writing whether or not it was his opinion that any further attempt to hold out would merely cause the sacrifice of the Shah and the British, and that negotiation for a safe retreat was the only alternative. Elphinstone hastily sent still another letter analysing their plight and ended with the request that Macnaghten 'should lose no time in entering into negotiations'.

Macnaghten, still no doubt hoping that the Bombay governorship was not yet lost to him, now had written evidence that what he believed to be a shameful surrender had been forced on him by the General. In India the inevitable inquiry would be bound to exonerate him and put the blame entirely on the General's shoulders.

His hope for rescue from Kandahar was now almost all that was left, for his efforts to weaken the rebels by assassinating their chiefs had brought the death of two chiefs— Meer Musjidi and Abdullah Khan—but none of the weakness or disorder in their ranks for which he had presumably hoped.

In fact, the event had harmed Macnaghten. Abdullah was only wounded by the shot fired at him, but he died a few days later from poison which Abdul Azeez claimed also to have administered.

Both assassins had demanded the balance of the blood money, but Mohan Lal refused it because, he said, they had failed to bring him the chiefs' heads, according to their contract. The facts of the case leaked, the blame was laid at Macnaghten's door and it was never forgotten. But Macnaghten still hoped bribery would succeed where assassination had failed, as we shall see.

Then on 10 December came the news from Colonel Palmer, who commanded the garrison at Ghazni, that the brigade which Nott had sent from Kandahar had been forced back by deep snows in the mountains.

Macnaghten's last real hope, it seems, was gone. It must

have been a bitter blow, for on 11 December one day's food only for the fighting-men was at hand in the cantonments and the camp-followers were already starving. Camels and bullocks were dying; food could be obtained neither by fighting—Elphinstone would not fight, nor by purchase, because the villagers were frightened to sell. Macnaghten could hold out no longer, but he by no means gave up. He still had more cards up his sleeve.

He drew up the terms of a treaty and met the chiefs by arrangement on 11 December about a mile from the cantonments on the banks of the Kabul River, Captains Lawrence, Trevor, Mackenzie and a few troopers going with him as escort.

Chapter Twenty-four

Afghan servants spread horse blankets on the river bank, and the leading chiefs, among whom was Mahommed Akbar, sat down, facing the British representatives. After formal expressions of goodwill on both sides, Macnaghten took from his pocket the white paper scroll on which he had written the draft treaty in Persian.

It must have been a grim moment for him, signalling as it did the total wreck of the great adventure of which perhaps more than anyone he was the architect. Even if he was lucky, and survived, the Bombay governorship in face of this surrender, would never now be his. Macnaghten's career had already been ruined, but he fought on.

The preamble for the treaty was a brilliant passage of diplomatic understatement and evasion—'Whereas it has become apparent from recent events that the continuance of the British army in Afghanistan for the support of Shah Shuja-ool-Moolk is displeasing to the great majority of the Afghan nation; and whereas the British Government had no other object in sending troops to this country than the integrity, welfare and happiness of the Afghans, and, therefore, it can have no wish to remain when that object is defeated by its presence. . . .'

Feelings of reluctant admiration for the wily envoy must surely have flashed behind the bearded faces—except probably that of Akbar Khan, whose bearing was according to Lawrence, 'very haughty'. Sir William went on to read out the first article—'that our troops should march with all practicable expedition to Peshawar'. Akbar interrupted— 'Why should you not march tomorrow?' The other chiefs checked him and he was silent for the remaining two hours of the meeting. They had better plans.

The treaty provided that the British should quit Afghanistan and return to India unmolested and with honour, taking with them supplies and transport which the Afghans would sell them; property left behind by the British would be taken care of and sent to India as soon as possible; Dost Mahommed and his family would be allowed to return to Afghanistan, Shah Shuja abdicating and returning to India with the British, or staying in Afghanistan on a suitable pension, as he wished; and without the consent of the Afghan Government no British force should again enter the country.

The articles were discussed with calmness and moderation and agreed in the main by the chiefs, who bound themselves to them on oath. Finally, they agreed to send in provisions at once and the British were to march out of the cantonments within three days. The meeting then ended, Captain Trevor accompanying the chiefs into the city, and Moosa Khan, one of Akbar Khan's followers, going with the British, both hostages for the mutual fulfilment of the treaty.

A shot whistled over the heads of Macnaghten and the others as they rode back to the cantonments and a large body of Afghan cavalry tried to ride them down until the chiefs warded them off. It was a significant mark of the doubtful hold the chiefs had on their followers.

The British garrison, on hearing of the agreement, looked forward with satisfaction to a speedy withdrawal to India, but they were soon to know the true worth of Afghan promises.

On 13 December the British rode out of the Bala Hissar—leaving it to the Shah and his army—and with as much grain as they could take with them were escorted across the plain to the cantonment by Akbar Khan.

As the last of them left, a number of Akbar Khan's troops tried to force their way inside. The gates closed abruptly and the Shah ordered his troops to fire. Many of Akbar Khan's men were killed. Lawrence 'heartily desired that similar energy might be shown by our own leaders, who appeared quite paralysed and incapable of adopting any measures to secure *our honour and our safety . . .*'

The three days stipulated in the treaty passed, the cold worsened, but none of the promised provisions or the transport animals were delivered. 'Forage had for many days been so scarce,' wrote Eyre, 'that the horses and cattle were kept alive by paring off the bark of the trees, and by eating their own dung over and over again, which was regularly collected and spread before them. The camp-followers were destitute of other food than the flesh of animals that expired daily from starvation and cold.'

To the commissariat officer, Captain Johnson, who had at last hoped to be able to supply proper rations, this trickery was infuriating. 'A lakh of rupees (£10,000) advanced to Mahommed Akbar for the purchase of camels—not one as yet forthcoming,' he noted. 'The Seeah Sung gateway, through which all supplies come in is daily infested by parties of Afghans calling themselves Ghazees, or fighters for religion. They are, without exception, the most bare-faced, impertinent scoundrels under the sun. Armed with swords, daggers and matchlocks they acknowledge no leader, but act independently—they insult and taunt the whole of us. . . ."

Afghan traders bringing in grain or boosah (bran) were plundered and beaten; the troops and cattle were both starving, yet no action was taken, though the ramparts were lined with troops and cannon. When these attacks were reported to the chiefs, their answer was: 'We cannot stop it —they are not under our control, but if they misbehave themselves fire upon them.'

Elphinstone forbade this—it might offend the Afghans. On 14 December Captain Johnson saw thirty donkeys loaded with bran for his cattle approach the gateway. The Ghazees insulted the drovers, beat them and drove them off, threatening them with death if they came again to sell food. Furious, Johnson reported the matter to the General. Nothing was done. The next day a flock of sheep Johnson had recently bought were grazing outside the cantonments, when two Ghazees attacked the shepherd. He fled and so did the two Ghazees with the sheep. Two British sentries with loaded muskets stood idly by. Johnson again reported this to the General, who replied: 'They had no business to go outside!'

'All this time,' fumed Johnson, almost at his wits' end, 'our garrison are starving!'

'They know that we are starving,' noted Lady Sale—'that our horses and cattle have neither grain, bhoosa (chopped straw) nor grass. They have pretty well eaten up the bark of the trees and the tender branches; the horses gnaw the tent pegs. I was gravely told that the artillery horses had eaten the trunnion of a gun. . . . Nothing is satisfied with food except the pariah dogs, who are gorged with eating dead camels and horses.'

On 16 December Macnaghten pressed the chiefs to carry out their side of the treaty. They then told him in writing in defiance of the treaty that so long as the British held the fort which contained reserves of ammunition and weapons and three other forts close to and commanding the cantonments, their people had no confidence in the British promise to leave the country and they would not furnish provisions until these forts were handed over.

Sir William took this reply to the General. He urged him instead to march out at once in order of battle and enter Kabul, or fight the enemy beneath its walls—'expressing his own earnest hope', says Lawrence, 'that the General, now that he had been reinforced by the fresh troops from the Bala Hissar, would adopt this clear and obvious course'.

But General Elphinstone would have no fighting. He gave up the forts the same evening. They were immediately occupied by the Afghans, and the entire cantonments were now at the Afghans' mercy.

'The envoy and I,' Lawrence recalls, 'stood on a mound near the mosque while the forts were being evacuated by our men, and I am not ashamed to say it was with eyes moistened with tears from grief and indignation, we witnessed these strongholds, the last prop of our tottering power in Kabul, which it had cost us so much blood to seize and defend, made over, one after another to our treacherous and exulting enemies.'

Food or no food, the chiefs now had the British at their mercy, They tauntingly sent in one day's supply of grain and promised 2,000 camels and 400 ponies for the march to Jellalabad. Then, on 20 December, continuing their cat-and-mouse tactics, they demanded the immediate surrender of all 9-pounder guns and ammunition, thus seeking to disarm the British of their one effective weapon.

Macnaghten refused, and reported the fact to Elphinstone, and still struggling to avoid disaster again proposed, says Lawrence, 'to break off all negotiations as futile and vain and to take our chance in the field, as he felt sure we would beat them if we only marched out boldly and met the rebels in the open plain'.

But the enfeebled old man argued that the abandonment of our position was the only solution. Lieutenant Sturt then tried to persuade him to start a fighting retreat to Jellalabad and hold it, together with Sale's force. 'But neither the General nor his immediate advisers could bring themselves to adopt a course which would have saved the national honour at the risk of sacrificing the whole force,' Eyre noted.

Snow began to fall next day and 'from morning to evening prayer it fell with frightful persistence and before sunset was lying many inches upon the ground'. The bitter winter had now joined the Afghans against the British.

On 21 December the chiefs put on the screw still more—they demanded four hostages as security for the British quitting the cantonments and retreating. This too was accepted, still further tying British hands. The chiefs first asked for Brigadier Shelton, but he refused flatly to go, so four other officers were handed over. Mrs. Trevor pleaded with the chiefs that her husband, Captain Trevor, who had been a hostage since the 11th, when the treaty was agreed, should be returned to her. The chiefs agreed. Trevor returned that day to his wife and to the last two days he would ever spend with her—for her plea was to cost him his life.

All this time the chiefs mulcted the British of huge sums of money for camels, bullocks and ponies, but never once delivered them. On 22 December Vincent Eyre revenged the British a little for this treachery. He was ordered to conduct an Afghan over the ammunition store so that this officer could choose what would be most useful to the chiefs. Eyre recommended a large pile of 8-inch shells, but the mortars for them were then in Jellalabad. 'He eagerly seized the bait and departed in great glee, with his prize laden on some old ammunition wagons,' Eyre relates.

Macnaghten all this time, still had not given up hope of avoiding what he knew would be a disastrous rout through the winter snows—he was now doing his utmost to sow strife between chiefs of the anti-British confederation—many of them traditionally hostile to each other. 'It is not easy,' Kaye writes with some truth, 'to group into one lucid and intelligible whole all the many shifting schemes and devices which distracted the last days of the Envoy's career. . . . He appears to have turned first to one party, then to another, eagerly grasping at every new combination that seemed to promise more hope than the last.'

Macnaghten realised that among the chiefs there was no unity, merely temporary allegiance, and that all of them thought first of themselves and their own tribal interests. This situation as time, and his available money began to run out, he began desperately to exploit.

He first tried to get the Ghilzyes to come out openly on the British side against the Barukzyes, the tribe which Akbar Khan and his father Dost Mahommed led, and whose rule the Ghilzyes feared. The treaty had been agreed with the Barukzyes and their allies, but since they had broken its terms by failing to deliver provisions and transport animals, Macnaghten seems to have felt himself free to negotiate with any of the other tribes best able to protect the helpless British. He therefore offered heavy bribes to the Ghilzyes and the Kuzzilbashes—the warlike descendants of the one-time Persian occupiers—to come out openly on the side of the Shah.

His secret correspondence with his tireless agent Mohan Lal at this time reveals his desperate last-moment efforts to sow the seeds of rebellion against Akbar Khan. On 20

December he wrote to Mohan Lal: 'You can tell the Ghil-zyes and Khan Shereen that after they have declared for his Majesty and us and sent in 100 kurwars (7,000 lb) of grain to cantonments, I shall be glad to give them a bond for five lakhs of rupees (£50,000). . . . I fear for Mahommed Shah that he is with Akbar; but you will know best. You must let me know before sunrise if possible, what is likely to be the effect of this proposal, as I must talk accordingly to the Barukzyes, who have shown no disposition to be honest. . . .'

But he apparently received no answer, for the next day in another note to Mohan Lal, he developed this plan for alliance with the Ghilzyes and Kuzzilbashes against the Barukzyes in more detail—it was his only hope now. 'In conversing with anybody,' he cunningly advised, 'you must say that I am ready to stand by my engagement with the Barukzyes and other chiefs associated with them; but that if any portion of the Afghans wish our troops to remain in the country, I shall think myself at liberty to break the engage-ment which I have made to go away. . . .

'If the Ghilzyes and Kuzzilbashes wish us to stay, let them declare so openly in the course of tomorrow, and we will side with them. The best proof of their wish for us is to send us a large quantity of grain this night. . . . If they do this and make their salaam to the Shah early tomorrow, giving his Majesty to understand that we are along with them, I will write to the Barukzyes and tell them my agree-ment is at an end; but if they (Ghilzyes and Kuzzilbashes) are not prepared to go all lengths with us, nothing should be said about the matter, because the agreement I have made is very good for us.'

Macnaghten, who seemed to have a premonition that time was more precious than gold now for him, had timed his letter 4 p.m. Desperately anxious about the danger of his scheming, he sent another note an hour later: 'Do not let me appear in this matter,' he warned, 'say that I am ready to stand by my engagement, but that I leave it to the people themselves.' And still more anxiously an hour later in another note timed 6 p.m.: 'If any grain is coming in tonight let me have notice of it a few minutes before. Anything that may be intended in our favour must appear before noon tomorrow.'

The sands were running out. By noon the next day, 22 December, no grain had arrived—nor had the Ghilzye chiefs declared themselves on the side of the Shah and the British.

There was still hope, but Macnaghten must have realised that he was on a knife edge—that his own life would be forfeit if Akbar Khan heard about his double-dealing. So that evening to lull Akbar's suspicions, he made him a lordly gift of his wife's splendid carriage, with a pair of fine horses.

Remembering too that the chief had said he would like a handsome pair of double-barrelled holster pistols belonging to Captain Lawrence, he asked Lawrence for them as a personal favour. 'I naturally demurred strongly to giving up my pistols,' Lawrence relates, 'as it was no time to part with such useful weapons; but as Sir William made it a personal favour I could not of course decline.'

Macnaghten sent the pistols to Akbar, and thus armed unknowingly his own executioner. Such was the savage irony of the presentation, for he had hoped that the gift would make him more friendly.

Hoping he had lulled Akbar's suspicions, Macnaghten then wrote to Mohan Lal asking him to warn the Ghilzyes not to send in any grain yet after all. 'The sending of grain just now would do more harm than good to our cause; and it would lead the Barukzyes to suppose that I am intriguing with a view of breaking my agreement; but I can never break that agreement so long as all the Khawanen wish me to stand by it. Pray thank our friends, nevertheless, for their kind attention to our interest. I wish very much to please them and am sorry my treasury is so empty.'

Scarcely was this ink dry than in a ferment he wrote again. 'I have already written to you begging that the Ghilzye chiefs should send no grain tonight. They should first openly declare themselves. . . . If they do not do so I must stand by my agreement. . . . If while our present agreement lasts I were to receive a large supply of grain from the Ghilzyes, suspicion would be raised that I intend to break my engagement, and wish to keep the troops here, in spite of the wishes of all the chiefs to the contrary.

'It would be very agreeable to stop here for a few months instead of having to travel through the snow; but I must not consider what is agreeable, but what is consistent with our faith. . . .'

Macnaghten the day before had asked that the Ghilzyes should first send grain and then declare themselves; and the very next day, on second thoughts, he begged that they should not do so until they had openly allied themselves with the British. The cause of this turn-about was a note from Mohan Lal warning him that Akbar Khan was now plotting against him and that he should place no faith in anything Akbar now said.

In his efforts to save the British force Macnaghten had overplayed his hand and had been warned, for Akbar Khan now suspected his scheme to set some of the tribes against him. He determined to test Macnaghten's honesty of purpose. No doubt recalling the rumour that the Envoy had already offered money for the chiefs' heads, he set a trap that would uphold Macnaghten's integrity or expose his treachery.

Chapter Twenty-five

Akbar commissioned two reliable followers to seek an audience with Macnaghten with details of a treacherous scheme, advantageous to the British, that would simultaneously advance Akbar at the expense of his fellow chiefs. To ensure that his two envoys would see Macnaghten, he had them escorted by Captain Skinner, a political officer who had been trapped in the city at the start of the insurrection and who recently had been living there under Akbar's protection. Skinner, says Colin Mackenzie, was 'commonly called "Gentleman Jim" from his more than usually pleasing manners and his cultivated mind'.

Macnaghten, who had recently left the tent in the cantonments in which since the start of the insurrection he had been living and had returned to the comfort of his own house just outside the ramparts, admitted them and talked privately to Skinner while the two Afghans waited in another room. In a jesting fashion, Skinner said that he was the bearer of a message from Akbar Khan 'of a portentous nature' and that he felt as one 'loaded with combustibles'.

Macnaghten, by now doubtless exhausted by the strain of his life-and-death intrigues no less than the appalling ruin of the whole situation, grasped as quickly as this hint as a drowning men at a piece of driftwood. The waiting Afghans were invited into the room to tell Macnaghten about Akbar's plot.

Akbar and the Ghilzyes, the envoys said, should unite with the British troops, seize Mahmoud Khan's fort and Ameenoollah Khan, one of Akbar's fellow rebel chiefs, decapitate him and present his head to Macnaghten for a large sum of money.

Macnaghten at once turned down this part of the plot—
it was against the customs of his country, he protested, to
pay blood money. The Afghans seemed to accept this, then
proposed that Shah Shuja would stay on as Shah, with
Mahommed Akbar as his Vizier, and the British too would
stay until the spring, when they would withdraw as though
by their own free will. Ameenoollah should be merely thrown
into prison.

Akbar Khan was to receive a cash payment of £300,000
and an annuity of £40,000.

The plot won over Macnaghten. It offered all the things
he wanted—the ultimate success of the policy of restoring
the Shah to the throne, with which he was so closely identi-
fied; avoidance of the threat of death in the snow-bound
passes that now hung over the army's head and his own;
and the chance of his own departure for India.

Without even stopping to consider whether it was treachery he staked everything on it.

Paper and ink were sent for; the Envoy wrote his agreement in Persian and signed it. The Afghans thanked him
profusely, took the paper and returned with it and Captain
Skinner through the snow to Akbar Khan in the waiting
city.

Dost Mahommed's son now had on this incriminating
document the name of the man whom he knew to be one of
the architects of his father's ruin and exile. Macnaghten had
given Akbar all the evidence he needed that he was capable
of double-dealing—that Akbar and the other chiefs had
repeatedly during the last few days broken their word to
Macnaghten and the British worried him not at all.
British confusion and ineptitude had enabled Akbar and his
friends to overcome them. Now they feared that at the last
moment the wily Macnaghten might still prevail against
them. So they planned their counter-action to prevent it, a
snare for the Envoy.

Macnaghten was to meet Akbar Khan next day to effect
the plan. He went in the morning to Elphinstone and let
him into the secret. The General asked vaguely what part

the other, the Barukzye chiefs, were to play and Macnaghten
answered that they were 'not in the plot'. To Elphinstone
the word 'plot' was alarming—he said he did not like the
sound of it. Was there no fear of treachery?

'Leave it to me—I understand these things better than
you do,' Macnaghten replied brusquely. 'I wish you to have
two regiments and two guns ready, as speedily and as
quietly as possible, for the capture of Mahmoud Khan's
fort. The rest you may leave to me.'

They parted, but at the eleventh hour a little of Elphinstone's good sense returned. He felt that something sinister
was afoot and at once sat down and dashed off a note to
Macnaghten setting out his fears. 'I hope there is no fear of
treachery,' he warned. 'The sending of two guns and two
regiments away would divide our force. . . . What guarantee have we for the truth of all that has been said? I only
mention this to make you cautious as to sending away part
of our force. Perhaps it is unnecessary with you, who know
these people so well. . . .'

Elphinstone's letter was for some reason undelivered; yet
it would have been ineffectual, for even the tearful pleading
of his own wife failed to keep Macnaghten from the meeting.
But there was to be a final encounter between the two
leaders. Macnaghten had asked Captains Trevor, Mackenzie and Lawrence to accompany him with an escort of ten
troopers to the meeting with Akbar Khan. As they were
leaving the cantonment, according to Lawrence, the General
met them and again warned of treachery.

Macnaghten answered: 'If you will at once march out the
troops and meet the enemy, I will accompany you, and I am
sure we shall beat them. As regards these negotiation, I
have no faith in them.'

Elphinstone shook his head. 'Macnaghten, I can't—the
troops are not to be depended on,' he said.

These were the last words that passed between them. The
two regiments and the guns were not available as the caval-
cade rode out of the cantonment, but Macnaghten rode on,
remarking how strange it was that although both the

General and Shelton knew the critical state of affairs they should have nothing ready. 'But it is of a piece with all the rest,' he added bitterly.

Not to have the troops and guns ready would turn out to be Elphinstone's most tragic blunder yet.

Macnaghten now remembered that the covetous Akbar had sought as another gift a fine Arab horse belonging to Captain Grant, one of Elphinstone's staff officials, who, for a large sum, had agreed to sell it to Macnaghten. Captain Mackenzie returned to cantonments and had the horse brought out, while Macnaghten now for the first time told Captains Lawrence and Trevor, who were also accompanying the party, the details of Akbar's scheme. Lawrence at once felt uneasy about it and he too warned of treachery. Macnaghten surprised them both.

'Treachery!' he answered. 'Of course there is, but what can I do? The General has declared his inability to fight, we have no prospect of aid from any quarters, the enemy are only playing with us and not one article of the treaty have they fulfilled, and I have no confidence whatever in them. The life I have led for the last six weeks, you, Lawrence, know well; and rather than be disgraced, and live it all over again, I would risk a thousand deaths. Dangerous it is, but if it succeeds it is worth all the risks. Success will save our honour and more than make up for the risks.'

The party had now reached a bank beside the swift-flowing Kabul river, 500 yards east of the south-eastern corner of the cantonment, where Akbar Khan, Mahomed Shah Khan, Sultan Jan, Khoda Buksh Khan, Azad Khan and several other chiefs awaited. The salutations—'Salaam Aleikoon'—'Peace be with you!' were uttered behind the heavy beards.

Macnaghten said cheerfully to Akbar Khan: 'Sirdar Sahib, here is Grant Sahib's horse for you, as you wished.'

'Thanks be to you,' Akbar said cordially, 'and also for Lawrence Sahib's pistols, which you see I am wearing. Shall we now dismount?'

Sir William agreed, some horse rugs were spread on a

small mound sloping towards the river, which was freer
from snow than the surrounding ground. Macnaghten,
elegant in his formal black frock-coat, black top-hat and
tight grey trousers, sat down between Trevor and Mackenzie, in brilliant red coats and tall black shakoes. The
chiefs, in high turbans and sheepskin poshteens, sat down
opposite.

'At first on dismounting I stood behind him,' says Lawrence, 'but on being importuned by Mahomed Shah Khan
to be seated, I knelt on one knee, the escort being drawn up
a short distance in the rear.'

A large number of armed Afghan retainers had by now
gathered round, and Macnaghten, at Lawrence's instance,
asked if they could be sent some distance away, as the
meeting was confidential. 'No, we are all in the same boat
and Lawrence Sahib need not be the least alarmed,' Akbar
Khan answered.

Akbar Khan opened the conference by abruptly asking
the Envoy if the were ready to carry out what had been
agreed the previous evening. 'Why not?' Macnaghten
answered. The crowd of armed Afghans now crowded round
more closely and Lawrence again remarked that if the conference were to be secret they should be removed. Some of
the chiefs made as if to lash out with their whips at them,
but Akbar Khan again objected—'No, we are all in the
same boat,' he repeated.

Macnaghten and the three officers were then suddenly
seized violently from behind. 'I heard Akbar call out,
"Begeer! Begeer!" (Seize! Seize!),' relates Mackenzie, 'and
turning round I saw him grasp the envoy's left hand with an
expression on his face of the most diabolical ferocity. I
think it was Sultan Jan who had hold of the Envoy's right
hand. They dragged him in a stooping posture down the
hillock, the only words I heard poor Sir William utter
being—"Az barae Khoda!"—"For God's sake!"'

The swords and pistols of Lawrence, Mackenzie and
Trevor were snatched from their sides. 'If you value your
life come along with me,' growled Mahomed Shah Khan to

Lawrence. The three were forced to mount each behind one of the chiefs while swarms of Afghans waving swords tried to attack them, yelling that they should be given up as a *koorban*—a sacrifice—in revenge.

The ten British escorting troops, frightened by the crowd of several hundred armed Afghans, galloped off back to the cantonments at the first sign of violence, Lieutenant Le Geyt had no choice but to follow them to try to get help, leaving Macnaghten struggling on the ground with Akbar, and Lawrence, Mackenzie and Trevor carried off on horseback. A few second later two pistol shots rang out.

Colin Mackenzie tells how, carried off behind Gulam Moyanud-din, a former chief of Kabul police, he ran the gauntlet of blows and sword thrusts from a mob mad for their blood. 'Ascending a slippery bank, the horse fell,' he relates, 'and I now received a heavy blow on the head from a bludgeon, which fortunately did not quite deprive me of my wits. . . .

'How I reached the spot where Mahommed Akbar was receiving the congratulations of the multitude I know not; but I remember a fanatic rushing on me and twisting his hand in my collar until I became exhausted from suffocation.'

But the chiefs struck out with their swords and drove Mackenzie's attackers back. Mahommed Akbar then turned to him and growled in a tone of triumph—'You'll seize my country, will you!'

No doubt in a fever of exultation at his triumph, he rode off on some urgent mission and Mackenzie's captor hurried him a few hundred yards west of the cantonments to Mahommed Shereef's fort. Here he was put into a room under guard and shortly joined by Captain Lawrence, also somewhat dazed and bruised from blows.

Ameenoollah Khan, the chief who was to have been seized and imprisoned under the terms of the plot suddenly blustered in. 'We'll blow you from the guns—any death will be too good for you,' he shouted. Not long after he had gone a blunderbuss was thrust through the window and fired at them—thrust aside just in time by their keepers. Then a bleeding human hand severed at the wrist was brandished at the window. 'We saw that it belonged to a European, but we were not aware that it was the hand of the poor Envoy,' says Mackenzie.

Seemingly it was Akbar's intention to capture Macnaghten with the other three, and hold him as a hostage or use him to force punitive terms on the Indian Government. But Macnaghten had reportedly thrown him to the ground and Akbar in a fury shot him with the pistols Macnaghten had given him as a gift.

So died Sir William Macnaghten, the scholar and administrator whom ambition led to turn man of action. There is something memorable in the cool courage with which he struggled on alone to try to save the British by sowing discord in the Afghan camp—to try to win by diplomacy after the General with an army had failed through incapacity.

Captain Trevor was killed, too—though he would have lived had he remained one of Akbar's hostages. A fanatical priest leading a rabble of Ghazee—religious fighters— heard an Afghan shout—'That dog is Trevor'—and cut at him with his sabre. Trevor fell a bloody corpse beneath a whirl of blows.

In the cantonments all this time, General Elphinstone had characteristically done nothing. Le Geyt galloped back, but the news of the attack on Macnaghten, noted Vincent Eyre, who was watching on the ramparts, 'instead of rousing our leaders to instant action, seemed to paralyse their faculties; and although it was evident that our Envoy had been basely entrapped, if not actually murdered before our very gate, and though even now crowds of Afghans, horse and foot, were seen passing . . . in hostile array . . . not a gun was opened upon them; not a soldier was stirred from his post . . .; treachery was allowed to triumph in open day; the murder of a British Envoy was perpetrated in the face and within musket-shot of a British army. . . .'

But not content with his death, the Ghazee fanatics hacked off Macnaghten's head, paraded it in triumph through the city, dragged his mutilated body through the streets and finally hung it up for all to see in the great bazaar.

Elphinstone, in face of this outrage, defiantly ordered the troops to stand to arms. They may have expected that at last their General had regained his sense and would attack the city by night to avenge Macnaghten and save their women and their children. But no such thing occurred. 'The garrison was got ready and remained under arms all day,' General Elphinstone wrote in his official report. And that, after letting the Envoy go to his death, was all. General Elphinstone was quite unmoved.

The Afghans, too, seemingly expected that the British would attack in revenge, for, as Lieutenant Melville noted, 'At 9 p.m. a great disturbance was heard towards the city, horrible shouts and cries, with rattling of musketry. . . .'

The Afghans were making psychological warfare—certain that before dawn the crash of musket volleys and the steady tread of the iron-shod boots of the redcoats would be heard in Kabul's streets.

But all thoughts of attack had long since left the minds of Elphinstone and Shelton. The defences were manned; nothing more. 'Our military chiefs,' says the historian Kaye, 'had settled down into the belief that now it had become their duty only to suffer.'

And from this date on, 23 December 1841, suffer they would for Elphinstone's feebleness, and suffer to the last man.

Chapter Twenty-six

Akbar Khan now became intransigent. Mackenzie and Lawrence were given Afghan turbans, tunics and baggy trousers to wear and taken under a strong guard to Nawab Zemaun Khan's house in the city, where they found Akbar waiting for them. In a transparent attempt to justify Macnaghten's murder by a violent tirade against the British he accused them of treachery and said that the terms must now include the delivery as hostages of all the married families and the surrender of all the British guns, ammunition and money.

After some argument he relented enough to agree that all the artillery but six guns should be handed over to him, and that married men and their families should be exchanged for the present hostages. In this form he returned the treaty that day, 24 December, to Elphinstone—together with a written accusation that Sir William Macnaghten had been guilty of a deliberate breach of faith that had cost him his life.

In a spirit both cynical and treacherous in view of what was later to occur, the document was headed:

'Agreement of peace that has been determined upon with the frank English gentlemen, to which engagement, if they consent and act accordingly, on the part of the heads and leaders of Afghanistan hence-forward no infractions will occur to their friendly engagements.'

The document—its contents were harsh—stipulated that 'the going of the gentlemen shall be speedy'—that General Sale's army at Jellalabad should march previous to the army at Kabul and proceed to Peshawar, Akbar Khan or Mahommed Oosman Khan would escort the army of the English to ensure that no harm came to it on the way. All cash, gold or silver must be surrendered.

It ended cruelly: 'If any of the Frank gentlemen have
taken a Musselman wife, she shall be given up. If there be
any questions about any article, send a note quickly by the
bearer.'

Then, as now, Christmas Day was celebrated by British
forces overseas no less heartily than at home, but, Vincent
Eyre noted lugubriously: 'a more cheerless Christmas Day
perhaps never dawned upon British soldiers in a strange
land; and the few whom the force of habit urged to exchange the customary greetings of the season, did so with
countenances and in tones indicative of anything but merri-
ment.'

But Christmas Day in fact brought good news. The
political officers Macgregor and Mackeson had written to
Macnaghten from Jellalabad and Peshawar respectively to
say that a relief force had already marched from India and
they urged Macnaghten to hold out to the last. As his
deputy, Pottinger received the letters. Elphinstone had
already requested him as senior political officer, to carry on
negotiations with the chiefs. Pottinger had reluctantly
agreed, but had at once found himself faced with terms
which would throw the whole army upon the mercies of the
bloodthirsty tribesmen and the killing winter.

Armed now with this letter, Pottinger—a tough, determined officer who had twice already shown his mettle—
now declared that the only honourable course would indeed
be to hold out to the last at Kabul or force an immediate
retreat to Jellabad. No confidence could in any case be
placed in any treaty with the chiefs, he said, and to bind the
hands of the Government of India by promising to leave the
country merely to save their own lives and property would
be inconsistent with their duty.

But Pottinger's dose of cold, honest realism did nothing to
halt the rush to self-destruction upon which Elphinstone and
his staff were bent.

Elphinstone called another council of war at which
Pottinger, still suffering from his wounds, urged that the
entire force and followers should sally out of the canton-

ments and fight its way up to the Bala Hissar and there hold out until the arrival of the reinforcements which they at last knew were on the march from India.

But if he hoped in this way to rouse the General from his invalid lethargy into acceptance of his plan, he was disappointed. The General was unable to make up his mind one way or the other, but Brigadier Shelton opposed it.

'We were prevented from going into the Bala Hissar by the obstinacy of Brigadier Shelton who declared the attempt impracticable,' says Pottinger in his official report. 'I pointed out the very doubtful character of any engagement we might make with the heads of the insurgents, the probability they could not make it good; and begged that they would spare us the dishonour and government the loss which any negotiations must entail.

'In a council of war held at the General's house— Shelton, Anquetil, Chambers, Grant and Bellew present— everyone voted to the contrary; so seeing I could do nothing, consented.'

So Pottinger began to make arrangements with the chiefs again, including the payment of $12\frac{1}{2}$ lakhs ($£125,000$) which they claimed Macnaghten had before his death promised them for safe conduct of the troops to Peshawar. 'I would willingly,' wrote Pottinger, 'have avoided the payment of such; but the enemy, by stopping our supplies obliged me to suffer the imposition, as the military authorities, were urgent to prevent a renewal of hostilities, cost what it might.'

Captain Lawrence, Macnaghten's military secretary, then a prisoner, was released on 27 December, for the purpose of preparing the money bills for the Chiefs for a final total of $£140,000$, but Lawrence refused to be tricked in this matter. 'I stipulated,' he writes, 'that the bills should be cashed only on the presentation of certificates from our political agent at Peshawar *of the safe arrival there of our troops* and took care to warn the bankers of the city of this part of the stipulation. This prevented the bills being marketable in Kabul, and the chiefs consequently could raise nothing on them.'

The ratified treaty was sent in to the British on New Year's Day, 1842, bearing the seals of the eighteen Afghan chiefs. 'At the present happy moment,' said the preamble, 'to put away strife and contention and avert discord and enmity, the representatives of the great British nation . . . have concluded a comprehensive treaty . . . which they have confided to the hands of the Afghan nobility, that by it the chain of friendship may be strenghened. . . .'

Thus rubbing salt into the British wounds it stipulated that the troops should 'speedily quit the territories of Afghanistan . . . and shall not return' and they must start twenty-four hours after receiving the animal transport. The troops at Kandahar under General Nott and at Jellalabad under General Sale were also to march out of the country immediately. The Kabul force would be allowed to take with them 'six horse-artillery guns and three mule guns, and the rest, by way of friendship, shall be left for our use. And all muskets and ordnance stores in the magazine shall, as a token of friendship, be made over to our agents.'

Elphinstone, who did at least refuse to hand over the women as hostages, had not only committed his own force to surrender and retreat but also the other two British forces in Afghanistan, both under the command of determined generals. It will be seen how these generals, Nott in Kandahar, and Sale in Jellalabad, reacted to this illegal act.

Meanwhile, warnings from Afghan friends began to reach the troops in Kabul that no trust should be placed in Akbar Khan's promise of safe conduct through the mountain passes. Mohan Lal warned Pottinger that unless the chiefs' sons accompanied the British as hostages they were all doomed.

An Afghan friend revealed to Captain Johnson that Akbar Khan had sworn to secure the English women as hostages for the safe return of his own wives and family— and to kill every British soldier except one, whom he would allow to reach Jellalabad to tell him his comrades had all been slaughtered.

'Whether we go by treaty or not,' Lady Sale wrote

realistically on 28 December, 'I fear but few of us will live to reach the provinces.' Her contempt for the treaty was swiftly justified. Armed tribesmen loitering around the defences still persistently attacked drovers bringing in grain and other provisions, against which robbery the British were ordered to take no action—the staff officers were frightened of offending the chiefs. Having surrendered under the treaty several hundred barrels of gun-powder, a great number of muskets and all but six guns, the British now received no food.

And in the cantonments the troops were already living from hand to mouth. To try to keep warm in a temperature which at night approached zero, furniture was broken up and burned. Lady Sale wrote of her last meals at Kabul being cooked on a fire of wood from their tables and chairs. 'We are to depart without a guard, without money, without provisions, without wood,' she lamented.

Shah Shuja still held out in the Bala Hissar with his 860 women, whom he was said to have warned that if the cantonment fell into rebel hands he would poison. Hearing now that the British had in effect capitulated, he made a final appeal to Elphinstone 'if it were well to forsake him in his hour of need and to deprive him of the aid of that force which he had hitherto been taught to consider as his own?'

But for all that it implied of British honour and his own life or death, he might as well have appealed to the 860 ladies. Elphinstone and Shelton were fixed in their determination to quit Afghanistan as soon as the chiefs provided the escort and to leave Shah Shuja to whatever fate befell him.

'The snow was falling heavily and all our Hindustanees looked cold and miserable,' Captain Lawrence noted. 'Crowds of Afghans were bartering all sorts of curiosities in exchange for articles the officers and men wished to get rid of to lighten their baggage.

'I gave my cocked hat to one fellow who instantly clapped it on his head and galloped off to the city, narrowly escaping being shot by his friends, who fired at him supposing him to be a British officer. . . . Few of the Afghans credited the report of our intended departure, not supposing we could be so insane as to leave our position. Many among them, friendly to us, freely expressed their amazement, or shook their heads doubtfully, when informed we were actually to retreat.'

Then came an offer of help that could yet save the army— from the Kohistanee tribe on 3 December to Captain Sturt, who had married Lady Sale's daughter during the halcyon days of the Kabul occupation. Sturt, though a junior officer, was in charge of fortifications and defences and so of importance. He had consistently opposed the policy of re- treat in favour of either an attack on Kabul or occupation of the Bala Hissar.

The Kohistanees' agent promised that if the British hung on for three more days they would supply rations and guarantee to attack and fire Kabul within this period. They also promised to escort reinforcements up to Kabul from Jellalabad, offering to furnish four of their chiefs as hostages for the implementation of their offer. Moreover, they swore that the Kabul chiefs were false and intended to destroy the British in the mountains. As for payment—the British word would do.

Sturt must well have seen this apparently safe offer as the silver lining in the grim and threatening cloud which had overhung them for the last few weeks. Here was their best chance yet of saving themselves, for a powerful attack on the city by this tribe, backed up by sorties both from the can- tonments and the Bala Hissar could not but succeed.

In a state of what must have been great hope and excite- ment he took the news to his military chiefs. Lady Sale said: 'The reply he received was, "It was better to keep the matter quiet; as in the present state of things it might, if known, cause excitement."'

The General and Shelton had now thrown away their last chance of avoiding disaster.

Orders were published on 4 January that the army would march for Jellalabad next day, but these orders were again countermanded because the Afghan escort was still not yet ready. Meantime, the cold grew worse—in Lady Sale's sitting-room at nine o'clock in the morning on 4 January the temperature fell to 11 degrees Fahrenheit even with a blazing fire of bits of the last chairs.

The next day Sturt made an opening in the cantonment defences through which the army and camp-followers could march out. Shah Shuja now sent a secret messenger to Lady Macnaghten urging her to withdraw from the army, who, he said, would all be destroyed, and come with as many other women as wished into the safety of the Bala Hissar.

Pottinger, when Lady Macnaghten told him of this, in a last effort to fend off disaster, proposed to Captain Lawrence 'to urge General Elphinstone when the force marched out of cantonments, to order them to move straight into the Bala Hissar, without previously saying a word to anyone, instead of proceeding by the road leading to Jellalabad, provided I thought the King would receive us into the Bala Hissar'.

It was a clever move and might have saved many lives.

'I replied,' says Lawrence, 'that I was sure His Majesty would be delighted at such a movement, and volunteered to ride on in advance and announce our coming. Pottinger and I then communicated with General Elphinstone.

'"Can you guarantee us supplies?" the General demanded.

'"We cannot guarantee, but we are pretty sure of sufficient supplies."

'"No, we retreat!" was the General's decision.'

It was final. Orders were issued for each fighting-man to take three days' provisions in his haversack and forty rounds of ammunition in his pouch and the force to be ready to march the following morning, 6 January, at daybreak.

Chapter Twenty-seven

The bugles blew at first light on this fateful day. It was clear, frosty and very cold, the thermometer well below freezing point and the snow nearly a foot deep. About 4,500 fighting-men and 12,000 male camp-followers, apart from thousands of wives and children, assembled ready to move off in the intense cold.

Sick or pregnant women and Lady Macnaghten were to be borne by Indian bearers through the deep snow in either palanquins or dhoolies. Lady Sale, Mrs. Sturt and one or two other wives, rode ponies; children would ride on the saddle in front or behind.

Lady Sale noted: 'Taj Mahommed (an Afghan friend) says that Mrs. Sturt and I must wear *neemchees* (sheepskin coats) over our habits—common leather ones—and turbans, and ride mixed in with the *suwars* (camel drivers); not to go in *palkees* or keep near the other ladies, as they are very likely to be attacked.'

Jellalabad lay 90 miles over the mountains to the west of Kabul, which was some 6,000 feet above sea-level. After crossing the Kabul River the route entered the Khoord-Kabul Pass, rising through this narrow precipitous gorge to about 9,000 feet for some five miles, to Khoord-Kabul. It then wound upwards for another 1,000 feet to Tezeen, a fort eight or nine miles to the west, through two more rocky passes and across several tributaries of the Tezeen River. The route then continued through some of the wildest mountains in the world, through the Jugdulluk Pass. Sourkab, Gandamuk and Futtehabad, descending gradually to 2,000 feet and the milder climate of Jellalabad—throughout, a stony, icy track rather than road, littered with boulders that had fallen or been heaved down from the peaks above.

General Elphinstone was now committing to this wintry hell a weak and dispirited force, encumbered by 12,000 undisciplined camp-followers, in face of the national uprising of a nation which traditionally lived on loot and murder.

He intended on the first day to march early to reach Koord-Kabul, and the next day another 15 miles to Tezeen, both to get out of the coldest and snowiest region quickly and to escape attacks by the tribesmen, believed not yet to have gathered along the route. But the General himself caused delays that upset these plans from the start.

Brigadier Shelton had ordered the baggage to be loaded by moonrise so that a start could be made by 8 a.m., but in the cantonments at this hour everyone still waited and shivered. Since dawn Captain Sturt had been struggling waist-high in the icy river water, directing the removal of boulders from the bed so that gun-carriages could be placed there to make a platform for a bridge—for this, though the river was easily fordable, the General had insisted upon.

Sturt had seen the river-bed cleared and had since been hindered by the General's foolish order that permission for the gun-carriage to be taken to the river must be obtained from him—even Shelton, his second-in-command, was not authorised to give this authority, and eventually he went to the General to obtain it.

'The order was for the baggage to assemble at 8 a.m.,' wrote Shelton in his report. 'At that hour I went to Elphinstone's quarters, to beg he would let the carriages of the gun-wagons go out to form a foot-bridge for the infantry over the Kabul River, about 300 yards from the cantonments—and got offended for my trouble. He was just sitting down to breakfast.'

Sturt and his men waited in their freezing clothes by the river. The vast crowd of troops and camp-followers froze in the cantonment parade ground in the snow and the General sat down to breakfast. Finally, he gave the necessary order, the gun-carriages were taken to the river, Sturt's men heaved them into place one beside the other in the swirling water and put the plants in place to make the bridge.

By half past nine the promised Afghan escort had still not arrived, and the vast assembly of men, women and children waited in a temperature below zero.

It was decided to march without further delay, presumably on Elphinstone's orders, and not long after half past nine, bugles rang out, drums beat and the advance guard marched out into the snowy plain, led by 600 redcoats of the British 44th Regiment, 220 Indian sappers, 100 sabres of Irregular Horse and three 3-pounder mountain guns, all commanded by Brigadier Anquetil.

Next followed Captain Lawrence, in charge of the party of women and children on ponies, and in palanquins on the shoulders of Indian bearers staggering under their burden through the snow. Remembering the warning they had received, Lady Sale and her daughter, Mrs. Sturt, without a word quickly left the other women, rode up to Captain Hay and mingled themselves with his Indian cavalry. Progress in the deep snow was slow. 'Mrs. Sturt and I rode with the horsemen through the river,' wrote Lady Sale, 'in preference to attempting the rattling bridge of planks laid across the gun-carriages.' By half past eleven the advance had gone barely a mile.

Now Afghan horsemen appeared and the mass of thousands of terrified camp-followers suddenly surged among the marching troops, so that officers could barely keep sight, let alone control of their men in the confusion. Frightened of fording the river, the camp-followers jostled and fought to cross by the bridge; many of them fell in the river and drowned at once...

The main column of troops under Brigadier Shelton now converged on this struggling mass—three Horse Artillery 9-pounder guns, 500 sabres of Captain Anderson's Horse, 650 bayonets of the 37th Native Infantry, 700 bayonets of the 5th Native Infantry, the sick, the wounded and the long, long column of several hundred bullocks and camels carrying rations, ammunition, gunpowder, equipment and baggage.

More Afghan horsemen appeared in sinister groups on the plain between the cantonments and the bridge. They were not, unfortunately, the promised escort—but tribesmen, mad with hatred and hot for plunder.

Firing a few shots to create terror among the camp-followers, they drew their swords and tore into them hacking at men, women and children alike, carrying off whatever baggage they could seize, dumping it out of sight, charging in again to rob and kill. The snow was soon stained and splashed with blood, dotted with the bodies of the fallen.

'From the opening in the ramparts to the bridge across the river,' related Kaye, 'streamed one great tide of soldiers and camp-followers, camels and ponies; and at the bridge there was an enormous mass of struggling life, from which arose shouts, and yells, and oaths—an indescribable uproar of discordant sounds; the bellowings of the camels, the curses of the camel-drivers, the lamentations of the Hindu-stanees, the shrieks of the women and the cries of the child-ren; and the savage yells of the Ghazees rising in barbarous triumph above them all.'

The Nawab Zemaun Khan, whom the Afghans had chosen as king in place of Shuja, now sent the General a warning that unless the British waited for the promised escort he could not guarantee their safety. General Elphin-stone therefore ordered that the troops then leaving the cantonments should stop, but Colin Mackenzie, still leading a score of *jezailchis*, saw that the garrison, half in and half out of the cantonments, was in danger of being butchered by the Afghans who were swarming round and beginning to fire at them.

Aware that the promised escort should have arrived three days ago and doubting now that it would come at all he informed the General he intended to tell Shelton the orders were to march on.

'Mackenzie don't—don't do it!' the bent old General in his sagging red uniform pleaded. Mackenzie galloped off in defiance of his pleas and conveyed the order to Shelton to

resume his march. A bold, if mutinous act, it at least saved
even more casualties at the time.

Through the horrible bloodshed and confusion at the
bridge, the march now continued. To Mackenzie one of the
most humiliating sights of that dreadful day was a beautiful
little Indian girl about two years old sitting naked in the
snow 'with its hair curling in waving locks round the soft
little throat and its great black eyes dilated to twice their
usual size, fixed on the armed men, the passing cavalry and
all the strange sights that met its gaze'.

He saw many other children as young and innocent
lying slain, and women with their long dark hair wet with
their own blood, such was the savagery of the tribesmen. 'If
an Afghan boy of twelve had passed he would have drawn
back the infant's head and amused himself with cutting its
throat,' he remarked.

Late in the afternoon, the rear-guard, prevented from
leaving at its scheduled time of mid-day, still manned the
cantonment walls. It consisted of the 54th Native Infantry,
630 bayonets; the Shah's 6th Infantry, 600 strong; two
squadrons of the 5th Light Cavalry, 250 sabres; and four
6-pounder Horse Artillery guns. The long train of laden
camels still poured out of the gate, the Ghazees thronged the
plain, attacking the baggage-train continuously, yelling
themselves hoarse with their lust for loot and blood.

When the rear-guard at last marched out it was dusk.
They had no sooner cleared the gate than the Afghans
swept inside and attacked them from the ramparts with
jezail fire. Lieutenant Hardyman and fifty men were shot
dead. In a blind fury, the Afghans then set fire to every
building in the cantonment and the flames rose hundreds of
feet, bathing the scene of death and destruction in a grim
pattern of flickering shadows.

Heaps of baggage were abandoned by the rear-guard
carriers at once. Food supplies, ammunition and equipment
were almost entirely lost.

The rear-guard fought continuously along the route to
Bagramee—it was here on the open plain that Elphinstone,

against the best advice, had established his first halt, only five miles from Kabul. They passed, says Lawrence 'through a continuous lane of poor wretches, men, women and children, dead or dying from cold and wounds, who, unable to move, entreated their comrades to kill them and put an end to their misery'.

The men of the rear-guard reached their camping ground at 2 a.m. having been under arms since early morning, and now, finding no food, fuel or shelter, they huddled together in the freezing snow. There was no system, nothing to alleviate hardship—not even any rum or brandy.

Regiments camped anywhere, soldiers and camp-followers huddling together on the snow with horses, camels and ponies. During this first night hundreds of Indian soldiers and camp-followers, unused to such severe weather, froze to death or were crippled by frost-bite. Over the whole dark scene there was total silence, not a voice was heard.

'In the morning,' says Lawrence, 'I found lying close to my tent, stiff, cold, and quite dead, in full regimentals, with his sword drawn in his hand, an old grey-haired conductor (*n.c.o.*) named Macgregor, who, utterly exhausted, had lain down there silently to die.'

Wrote Lady Sale: 'Captain Johnson, in our great distress kindly pitched a small Pal (tent) over us: but . . . we had few pegs; the wind blew in under the sides and I felt myself gradually stiffening. I left the bedding, which was occupied by Mrs. Sturt and her husband, and doubled up my legs in a straw chair of Johnson's, covering myself with my poshteen.'

So ended the first march of the retreat. It had already proved correct Sir William Macnaghten's contention that far from saving the army from disaster it would ensure its destruction.

The force—though it was now hardly that, for order and discipline were fast ending—moved off at 7 a.m., on 7 January, soldiers, camp-followers, baggage camels all together in one huge mob. More than half the Indian troops were too weak from cold and hunger to handle their muskets. They threw them away and mingled themselves with the thousands of non-combatant camp-followers. 'At starting,' noted Vincent Eyre, 'large clods of hardened snow adhered so firmly to the hoofs of our horses, that a chisel and hammer would have been requisite to dislodge them. The very air we breathed froze in its passage out of the mouth and nostrils, forming a coating of small icicles on our moustaches and beards.'

The Indian bearers of the palanquins and dhoolies carrying some of the women heroically floundered on through the snow for a mile or two, then, exhausted, dropped their burdens and cried out they could go no farther. The women were therefore found seats on horseback with the officers. Captain Lawrence took Lady Macnaghten up on his saddle for three or four miles, until, finding a camel with empty *kawajahs* (panniers) he lifted her into one side, balancing her with a bundle of clothes in the other.

The enemy now furiously attacked the rear-guard, though at first held in check by steady shrapnel fire from the guns. But they kept up a harassing fire on the troops, who soon found it almost impossible to put up a proper defence owing to the masses of panic-stricken camp-followers surging around them. Separated at one moment from the infantry, the three 3-pounder mountain guns drawn by mules were suddenly seized by a party of Afghans who sallied out of a small fort.

Lieutenants Green, White and a few artillerymen heroically charged as they withdrew and spiked the guns 'amid the gleaming sabres of the enemy', Lieutenant White being badly wounded in the face in this action. Weary and frost-bitten the troops were now hardly a match for the fierce, Afghan cavalry, swinging razor-sharp swords. Two more guns were spiked and abandoned when their horse teams became too weak from hunger to draw them. There were now but two 9-pounders left, and scarcely any shells.

At Bootkak, on high open ground near the head of the Khoord-Kabul Pass, which he hoped to penetrate that day, 7 January, the second of the retreat. General Elphinstone called a halt at about 1 p.m. to allow the hard-pressed rear-guard to close up. Major Pottinger then received an urgent letter from Nawab Zemaun Khan asking him to halt the army—promising if he did to send supplies of food and fire-wood and to drive off the attacking tribesmen.

Was there really a chance of relief in this offer—or was it a trick? Pottinger took the letter to the General, who said they would halt there for the day to allow the promised supplies to come up and march that night whatever happened. But at this, Brigadier Shelton argued that another halt on the open snow without tents or food would destroy the troops. Shelton wrote later: 'He was immovable, talked of the Sirdar's promises, and sending a letter to Kabul to know why they had not sent us a safeguard. Here was another day entirely lost and the enemy collecting in numbers.'

A body of several hundred Afghan horsemen now appeared about two furlongs away. Their leader was recognised as Akbar Khan. He sent a message to say he had been deputed by the chiefs to protect them from the attacks of the Ghazees and to escort them to Jellalabad—his instructions were especially to secure other hostages as security for the evacuation of that town by General Sale's force and to delay General Elphinstone's march until it was known that this had been done, supplying it meantime with all the food and fuel it needed.

No decision was taken then, but General Elphinstone decided to remain where they were not only for the day but also the night as well. Meanwhile, it later became clear, hostile tribesmen from all over this region of Afghanistan were mustering along the peaks of the passes ahead.

Night fell—the cold deepened—the icy wind—they were almost 8,000 feet above sea-level—howled across the exposed ground, cutting through thick uniforms as if they were thin cotton. But no food or fuel was sent in by Akbar Khan, and when anyone tried to fetch water from a nearby river the Afghans shot them. Men, women, children, horses, camels and ponies huddled indiscriminately together in the snow.

'For myself,' noted Lady Sale, '. . . I felt very grateful for a tumbler of sherry, which at any other time would have made me very unladylike, but now merely warmed me, and appeared to have no more strength in it than water. Cups full of sherry were given to young children three and four years old without in the least affecting their heads.'

Some of the sepoys burnt caps and equipment to stop themselves freezing to death. Lieutenant Melville and several other officers crowded round the glowing embers of a wooden pistol case, drank their few remaining bottles of wine, then threw themselves down together on the snow for warmth and went to sleep. Captain Lawrence recorded that the temperature that third night fell to 10 degrees below zero.

Colin Mackenzie spent the night in a little tent which his servant 'dear Jacob, got put up for me, I know not how. Pollock, a soldier of the 44th (the one who volunteered to follow me at Behmaru, where he got a ball in the thigh, the wound of which was not yet healed), lay close to me on one side for warmth and Major Scott of the 44th coming in, I asked him to lie down on the other.

'He said he could not, on account of the intolerable pain of his feet, which were frost-bitten. He sat in a chair. . . . I had two bottles of port, and admonished him to take some, which he did, and I believe that was the last wine he ever drank, for his body was afterwards found stripped and the chest cut open.'

Scott was only one of more than a thousand who died that night from the Afghan knives, or through freezing death.

Sharpshooters fired into the camp at sunrise, the third day of the retreat, 8 January, 'The confusion,' Lady Sale noted, 'was fearful. The force was perfectly disorganised, nearly every man paralysed with cold, so as to be scarcely able to hold his musket. . . . Many frozen corpses lay on the ground. . . . The ground was strewn with boxes of ammunition, plate and property of various kinds. A cask of spirits was broached by the artillerymen. Had the whole been distributed fairly it would have done them good; as it was they became much too excited.'

Several hundred Afghans now assembled to the rear of the camp in apparent readiness to attack. The 44th Foot who had somehow kept together in all the confusion, formed up facing them. Major Thain put himself at their head, ordered fix bayonets and led them, marching steadily, forward. The entire force of Afghans turned tail and fled, in no mood to face the bayonets.

This single event underlined a bitter truth—that given a bold and capable leader the British could even then have routed the Afghans. Instead, they were about to be led through a series of mountains passes and into ambushes whence few of them would come out alive.

Chapter Twenty-eight

General Elphinstone had not long after dawn sent Captain Skinner to Akbar Khan's camp to discuss the Sirdar's message of yesterday. But Akbar at once insisted that Major Pottinger and Captains Lawrence and Mackenzie should be given as hostages for the British halting at Tezeen until Akbar knew of Sale's having marched west out of Jellalabad for India, for Akbar was clearly determined to remove this additional threat if he could.

Elphinstone agreed without argument and the three officers went under protest, escorted by two of Akbar's men. They found him at breakfast on a nearby hillside and Akbar ordered his men to remove the hostages' fire-arms. Lawrence had to give up his rifle, slung at his back, and a pair of pistols, but was allowed to keep his sword. They then breakfasted, while Mahommed Akbar sent messengers allegedly to order the tribesmen to stop firing on the British camp.

Elphinstone, believing, with the delivery of these hostages, that a cease-fire had at last been achieved, had ordered the ragged force and its host of camp-followers to prepare to move. But the forty or fifty artillerymen had by now together drunk an entire barrel of brandy and truce or no truce, they wanted to fight. 'They were now fully primed,' relates Lady Sale. 'They mounted their horses; and, with the best feeling in the word, declared that they were ashamed at our inactivity, and vowed they would charge the enemy.'

One can imagine how aghast were General Elphinstone, Brigadier Shelton and the staff at this outburst of warlike feelings—it could have led to a pitched battle with the enemy in open terrain that favoured the British.

Captain Nicholl, commanding the artillerymen, rode up

and called them drunks, swore at them and promised severe punishment if they did not obey orders and go quietly. Probably open-mouthed with surprise at the rarity of being threatened for *wanting* to fight, the artillerymen put back their swords. 'They turned to Sturt shortly after their own officer had left them,' noted Lady Sale, 'having showered curses and abuse on them, which had irritated them dreadfully.

'Sturt told them they were fine fellows and had ever proved themselves such during the siege; but that their lives were too valuable to be risked at such a moment: but, if need were, and their services were required, he would himself go with them. This, in a certain degree, restrained their ardour; yet they still kept on talking valiantly.'

One can imagine them, clad in ragged sheepskin coats over their threadbare blue artillery tunics, hiccoughing brandy fumes over each other, astride weary, half-starved horses, and though ordered not to fight, soldiers enough as they rode off towards the Koord-Kabul Pass with the ragged multitude to know that a great foolishness had been forced upon them, for they might now have in any case to die without being able to fight back.

Only a few hundred serviceable fighting-men now remained on this third day as the ragged procession neared the mouth of the pass. Afghan bullets had killed or wounded hundreds, while two nights' exposure had brought thousands down with frostbite in hands and feet. 'Even cavalry, who suffered less than the rest, were obliged to be lifted on their horses,' Vincent Eyre noted.

General Elphinstone had decided to march through the Pass and push on to Tezeen as quickly as possible—through the five-mile-long Khoord-Kabul defile shut in by steep cliffs and threaded from side to side by a swift mountain torrent edged with layers of ice. So often had the British let the Afghans deceive them that despite the cease-fire they must surely have entered it with terror.

Lady Sale recalls that the march began about mid-day, with the 5th Native Infantry leading. 'The troops were in the greatest state of disorganisation: the baggage was mixed up with the advanced guard; and the camp-followers all pushed ahead in their precipitate flight. . . . We had not proceeded half a mile before we were heavily fired upon.'

Yet it now seemed as if Mahommed Akbar had been true to his word; he had certainly sent several lesser chiefs to march with the head of the column to order the tribesmen not to shoot, but not even the chiefs could stop the Ghilzye tribesmen's blood lust, their hunger for loot. From stone shelters at vantage points on the side of the cliffs, they poured in a destructive fire. While alternately floundering through the deep snow-drifts and splashing across the icy mountain torrent, camp-followers and troops alike were shot down in waves by the hundreds of hidden marksmen.

Lady Sale rode with her daughter and Captain Sturt, and Lieutenant Mein. 'The pony Mrs. Sturt rode was wounded in the ear and neck,' she relates. 'I had fortunately only one ball in my arm; three others passed through my poshteen near the shoulder without doing me any injury. . . . After passing through some very sharp firing, we came upon Major Thain's horse, which had been shot through the loins.'

When they were out of the danger zone Sturt rode back to try to find Thain. His own horse was then shot from under him, and before he could rise from the ground an Afghan bullet hit him in the groin.

Hearing later what had happened to his friend Sturt, Lieutenant Mein rode back, found him lying wounded in the snow and stood over him with the terrified horde stumbling and fighting their way to safety. Sergeant Deane of the Sappers arrived and helped Mein to drag Sturt through the Pass on a quilt. Finally, they mounted him on a pony and managed to get through to the camp on the far side of Khoord-Kabul. He was in much pain, had lost a lot of blood and seemed unlikely to live.

Also through the carnage rode the English wives on ponies or in camel panniers with their children. In one camel pannier were Mrs. Boyd and her youngest son Hugh, and in the other pannier Mrs. Mainwaring, 'a young merry girl' with her three-month-old baby and Mrs. Anderson's four-year-old girl, Mary. The camel with its two women and their children was shot and fell.

Mrs. Boyd was helped up out of the snow and on to his horse by a passing trooper, while another took her son up with him. Shortly after this the trooper was shot and the boy was seized by the Afghans.

Mrs. Mainwaring had scrambled up out of the snow with her baby in her arms to find that little Mary Anderson had disappeared. She stumbled on with her own child until an Afghan horseman rode up and threatened her with his sword. While she was pleading with him a sepoy forced his way through the melee and shot the Afghan dead. He then gave his arm to her and supported her along three miles of the pass until he suddenly fell without a sound—shot dead by a hidden marksmen.

Mrs. Mainwaring must have gritted her teeth then. She waded on through the deep snow, across the icy stream, picking her way with her baby in her arms over the bodies of the dead and the dying while the Afghan bullets droned through the air and fugitives all around her were struck down. 'She, however,' said Lady Sale, 'got safe to camp with her child, but had no opportunity to change her clothes; and I know from experience that it was many days ere my wet habit became thawed, and can fully appreciate her discomforts.'

Three thousand troops and camp-followers were shot down or knifed by the bloodthirsty Ghilzyes in this pass. The destruction of the army was following its inevitable course.

The hostages—Pottinger, Mackenzie and Lawrence, riding with Mahommed Akbar, Sultan Jan Fishar and about thirty horsemen—threaded their way among the dead and dying in the wake of the retreating forces. Already, the tribesmen—some of them boys—were stripping the wounded, then hacking them to pieces. Mackenzie saw children cut in two; men and women with their throats cut from ear to ear.

Mahommed Akbar himself now rode ahead to try to stop the firing. But Major Pottinger swore he heard him issue contradictory orders—'Stop firing!' in Persian which a few of the British officers understood too, and 'Slay them!' in Pushtu, the Afghan native tongue, which probably only Pottinger knew.

If this was so, and Mahommed Akbar was guilty of such treachery, it was contradicted in part by acts of kindness and mercy. He personally sent back first a wounded soldier of the 44th Foot to the safety of the hostages' party; later Captain Boyd's little son Hugh, whom he had found captured by the tribesmen—Lawrence took the boy up on his horse. Then Sultan Jan, who was with Akbar, up where the firing was hottest, sent back to them a Mrs. Bourke, wife of a private of the 13th Foot, whom he had rescued as a tribesman was about to cut off her fingers because her rings were too tight to pull off.

Mrs. Bourke was pregnant and so stupefied with fear and cold that she could hardly be roused enough to be hoisted up behind Mackenzie on his horse. He recalls that they wrapped a sheepskin coat around her, tying the sleeves in front, but it was only with the greatest pains that he could keep her petticoats from riding up, a point on which he was especially anxious on account of the Afghans.

Mrs. Bourke was terribly thirsty he recalled, and cried out every now and then: 'Och, Captain dear, for the love of God get me a dhrink of wather!' A heavy snowstorm began and Mackenzie felt her licking up the snow as it fell on his shoulders.

One of the Afghan escort now gave Mackenzie another precious burden—little Seymour Stoker, aged two, son of a private in the 13th Foot. He was found in the arms of his dead mother, all splashed with her blood—'a very fine young woman'—Mackenzie recalled.

That night the hostages and their escort spent in a small fort in a large room with a smoky fire in the middle of the stone floor. Mrs. Bourke was at last given a drink of water. 'Lawrence and I,' Mackenzie relates, 'pulled off little

Stoker's shoes and stockings, dried and warmed them, and made him nice, and then put him down to sleep.

'We all lay down with our heads close to the ground to avoid the smarting, blinding smoke. At midnight they brought in sheep's tail boiled in water, and half-baked indigestible bread, which we dipped in the broth. Poor little Stoker ate a mouthful or two but he was quite exhausted with terror and fatigue. Little Boyd lay snug under George Lawrence's poshteen and Mrs. Bourke crouched down a little apart from the circle of men.'

The carnage in the Pass had gone on until late in the afternoon. Companies of the 44th and 37th Foot had protected the rear, doggedly keeping up a heavy fire on the Afghans. At one time the Pass became completely choked— the rear-guard troops were stationary under a heavy flanking fire from the heights and they withdrew to higher ground, under the shelter of some rocks.

Here they were joined by General Elphinstone, Colonel Chambers of the 5th Light Cavalry, Captain Hay, a few troopers and the only remaining gun. They held the Afghans back while the remnants of the retreat straggled on out of the Pass. Finally as darkness fell, the rear-guard marched on, the soldiers heroically manhandling through the deep snow the gun which the horses were too weak to pull alone; and in this way they reached the camp.

But it was a halting-place in a snowstorm on high undulating ground, rather than a camp. There were no fires, no food—all reserve rations had been lost—and for most of the survivors no shelter. Four small tents only remained. One belonged to the General, two to the ladies and children and one to the sick and wounded. 'But an immense number of poor wounded wretches wandered about the camp destitute of shelter and perished during the night,' Captain Vincent Eyre relates. 'Groans of misery and distress assailed the ear from all quarters. . . . The snow was the only bed for all, and of many, ere morning, it proved the *winding-sheet*. It is only marvellous that any should have survived that fearful night.'

Lady Sale and her daughter and the dying Sturt rested on the side of a bank until a tent was pitched for her and the other women and their husbands and children. Lady Sale was an odd nineteenth-century mixture of brave stoicism and domestic incapacity. When the tent was pitched, she complains—'We had no one to scrape the snow off the ground in it.' She later faced painful surgery without anaesthetic or a word of complaint. 'Dr. Bryce, Horse Artillery, came and examined Sturt's wound: he dressed it; but I saw by the expression of his countenance that there was no hope. He afterwards kindly cut the ball out of my wrist and dressed both my wounds.'

Sturt, a brave and intelligent junior officer, who by virtue of his influence as the only engineer officer had more than once urged upon his seniors on the staff, action—such as a move into the Bala Hissar—that could have saved the force, was carried into the tent by Captain Johnson and Lieutenant Mein. 'Mrs. Sturt's bedding (saved by the ayah riding on it, whom we kept up close with ourselves),' Lady Sale relates, 'was now a comfort for my poor wounded son. He suffered dreadful agony all night, and intolerable thirst; and most grateful did we feel to Mr. Mein for going out constantly to the stream to procure water; we had only a small vessel to fetch it in, which contained but a few mouthfuls.

'To sleep in such anxiety of mind and intense cold was impossible. There were nearly thirty of us packed together without room to turn. The sepoys and camp-followers, half-frozen tried to force their way,' she complained, 'not only into the tent but actually into our beds—a poshteen or pelisse of sheep skin, half spread on the snow and the other half wrapped over one.'

At sunrise next morning, 9 January, the fourth day of the retreat, the camp-followers and sepoys moved off without orders, and the depleted British force followed an hour later. Sturt was dying, most probably through loss of blood, and since he was unable to ride, other transport had to be found for him. 'Mrs. Trevor,' Florentia Sale recorded, 'kindly rode a pony, and gave up her place in the *kajava* to Sturt, who must otherwise have been left to die on the ground. The rough motion increased his suffering and accelerated his death, but he was still conscious that his wife and I were with him; and we had the sorrowful satisfaction of giving him Christian burial.' He was the only one of all to receive it.

The British troops had gone about a mile next day at sunrise when the General ordered them to return. Akbar Khan had suggested that the retreat should halt for the day, in return for which he would send food and fuel. More important, he had offered through Captain Skinner to give protection to the handful of English women and children because the troops could no longer protect them; barely a thousand of them were left alive.

Akbar's promise of food and fuel had three times already failed the starving force, but again Elphinstone had believed him and had halted the retreat—though it would have been possible to send over the women and children without stopping the onward march to safety.

The delay caused despair. Shelton went to the General and protested that such a measure would cause the total destruction of the whole force. 'But he was not to be moved, replying that the Sirdar had sent to him to say, if he would stop there, that he would send him provisions, which, as I foretold, never came.'

A party of Afghan horsemen arrived to escort the women and children—and the husbands, for upon this Elphinstone had rightly insisted—to Akbar's camp in a fort near by. They must at this time have said goodbye to their compatriots, half-beaten as they were, with mixed feelings, for there was no guarantee of their security with Akbar.

Lady Sale was too upset about Sturt's death to note the reactions of the other women. 'Overwhelmed with domestic affliction, neither Mrs. Sturt nor I were in a fit state to decide for ourselves whether we would accept the Sirdar's protection or not,' she relates. 'There was but faint hope of our ever getting safe to Jellalabad; and we followed the stream. But although there was much talk regarding our going over, all I personally know of the affair is, that I was told we were all to go, and that our horses were ready, and we must mount immediately and be off.'

Apart from Lady Macnaghten, Lady Sale and Mrs. Sturt, the group included Mrs. Boyd and two children, Mrs. Mainwaring and one child, Mrs. Anderson and two children, one ten days old, the third having been carried off; Mrs Eyre and one child, Mrs. Waller and one child, Mrs. Trevor and seven children; Mrs. Ryler and two children, Mrs. Wade, Mrs. Smith and Mrs. Burnes.

They were accompanied by Captains Waller, Troup, Trevor and Eyre, all of whom were wounded; Captains Boyd and Anderson, Mr. Ryley and Sergeant Wade. Lieutenant Melville escorted them and returned to report their safe arrival. It was doubtless not forgotten to both the General and Akbar Khan, that the latter's father, brother, their wives and many members of their families were then in the hands of the British in India. Each group of hostages thus guaranteed the safe return of the other.

Mahommed Akbar received the ladies very courteously, according to Lawrence. He added, however, that 'it was distressing beyond expression to see our countrywomen placed in the hands of these ruffians, but there was no help for it. . . . Many of them during these four wretched days had tasted nothing but some dry biscuits and some sherry or brandy. With the exception of Lady Macnaghten . . . they had lost everything except the clothes they were wearing.'

Lawrence then explained, at Akbar's request, that they were the Sirdar's honoured guests, that they should want for nothing he could give them and that on the first favourable occasion he would have them escorted safely to Jellalabad. They were then distributed among three small rooms in the inner court of the fort, the men were assigned a fourth room and a sheepskin cloak was supplied to everyone who needed it.

The remnants of the troops and camp-followers began their hopeless struggle onwards to Jellalabad. In the various written accounts of the retreat there is no evidence that daily returns of casualties were made in the normal way—all military organisation had long since vanished and the official records of the force were lost or destroyed.

But it can be deduced that on this morning of 10 January, when some of the worst ambushes had still to be faced, that out of the force of 4,500 fighting-men which had left Kabul only four days earlier, some 3,750 had been killed outright, wounded or fallen sick and left to die. And of the pathetic camp-followers only 4,000 men, women and children were still alive out of the 12,000 who had left Kabul.

It is hard to imagine the tortured state of mind of the survivors. 'Every man among us,' Captain Johnson noted in his *Journal*, 'thought that ere many hours should pass he was doomed to die either by cold, hunger, or the swords of our enemies; for, if attacked, although we might for a short time hold out, nothing could eventually save us. . . .'

In the high mountain passes where the snow glittered brilliantly except where it was stained dark with blood, snow blindness now affected many of the troops on top of all their other terrors. 'My eyes,' Johnson lamented, 'had become so inflamed from the reflection of the snow that I was nearly blind and the pain intense.'

And they were not to feel the enemy's most savage attack so far.

After the Khoord-Kabul Pass, a series of narrow precipitous gorges followed, the first of which was Tunghee Tareekee, barely 50 yards long and 15 feet wide. Through it flowed a small stream and towards the heights numbers of Afghan tribesmen had been seen hurrying. The British troops were the only efficient ones left, the sepoys having nearly all suffered so much from frost-bite that they could barely hold a musket, much less aim and squeeze the trigger.

The advance, led by the British 44th Foot, with the 5th Cavalry troopers and the gunners with the remaining gun, a howitzer, forced their way with difficulty through the terrified camp-followers to the front of the column. Directly they approached the gorge they met with a heavy fire. By fighting back desperately they managed to get through, though with men falling continually. The mingled sepoys and camp-followers packed together in the narrow gorge met with even more deadly attacks.

'Fresh numbers fell at every volley, and the gorge was soon choked with the dead and the dying,' noted Vincent Eyre. 'The Afghans rushed down upon their helpless and unresisting victims sword in hand and a general massacre took place. The last small remnant of the Native Infantry regiments were here scattered and destroyed; and the public treasure with all the remaining baggage fell into the hands of the enemy.'

The advance pushed on to Kubbur-i-Jubbar, about five miles ahead and there waited to enable the rest of the force to join them. But only a few stragglers from time to time came up. Soon the awful truth dawned upon them. Of the troops, they were the sole survivors—about 50 men of the Horse Artillery, with one 12-pounder howitzer; 250 red-coats of the 44th, and 150 cavalry troopers.

Fifteen British officers and more than 300 men had died in the last deadly defile, and almost 100 camp-followers.

Akbar Khan and a party of heavily armed Afghan horsemen now approached this weary band of survivors and General Elphinstone at once sent Captain Skinner to protest at the attack made despite his promise of safe conduct. Akbar replied that he had been powerless to stop the tribesmen's savage fury—even their own immediate chiefs could not control them.

He then proposed that nevertheless the force should now lay down its arms, place itself under his protection and he would guarantee its safe escort to Jellalabad—though the camp-followers, being so numerous, would have to be left to their fate.

It is hard to arrive at a valid estimate of Akbar's actions towards the retreat. Remembering that he was an impetuous, primitive person it is very possible that there was no consistency—there were times when he encouraged slaughter and others when he tried to stop it, for example, when the restraining fact that his family were held as hostages in

India clashed with his revengeful urge to kill. Moreover, out of the 14½ lakhs promised the various chiefs by the British for safe conduct, the Ghilzye chiefs, in whose territory the retreat was now, were to receive only half a lakh, the smallest share of all. Akbar had no powers but persuasion over the Ghilzyes, who doubting that any of this conditional payment would ever be received now that the British force was all but destroyed, could well have opted for killing and plunder, despite Akbar's protests.

Thus his claim that he was powerless to stop the Ghilzyes seems to have been genuine, as well as his offer to escort the remainder of the force to Jellabad, but this, Elphinstone turned down probably because, in spite of all his defects, he had sufficient compassion not to leave the camp-followers to be slaughtered out of hand. So the retreat struggled onwards, a very much smaller body now, down a steep incline into another narrow gorge, the Halft-Kotil, about three miles long.

Again the tribesmen on the heights fired at them volley after volley. The rear was now commanded by Brigadier Shelton—in his element in such a dangerous situation—and about a score of picked redcoats. 'Nobly and heroically these fine fellows stood by me,' Shelton recorded, while Eyre noted that 'but for Shelton's persevering energy and unflinching fortitude . . . it is probable the whole would have been sacrificed.'

The force pushed on to the camping ground in the valley of the Tezeen. To save more slaughter, there was another attempt at negotiation with Akbar, but being faced again with the same demand for disarming, Elphinstone accepted Shelton's proposal that they should try by a rapid night march to reach Jugdulluk, 22 miles away. They could thus perhaps save themselves by crossing the pass at night, before thousands of Ghilzye tribesmen had gathered there.

Word was sent to Mahommed Akbar that they intended to march to Seh Baba, only another seven miles on—in the forlorn hope that he would be deceived. The last gun was spiked and abandoned. With it was left Dr. Cardew, one of the 'fighting doctors' of the Indian army, who was much loved by the men. They had lashed him to it when he was fatally wounded and too weak to walk in the hope of saving him on the only sort of transport left. They said goodbye now as his life ebbed and left him on the bare mountain.

Lawrence, who followed the retreat with the women and the hostages, next morning saw Dr. Cardew's body lying there. 'He had come to Kabul from Ghuznee, on his way to India to meet his betrothed, whose anticipations of happiness were thus for ever blighted by the stern vicissitudes of war,' he related.

The retreat, on a bright frosty night, had got as far as Seh Baba without being fired on, then a few shots were aimed at the rear. The camp-followers again surged forward, and into the dark mass of men the Afghans then fired with telling effect.

The retreat as a result failed in its night-long effort to reach Jugdulluk by morning, halting instead at 8 a.m. at Kutter Sung, 10 miles short of it, for the rear of the column to close up, and by now almost totally exhausted.

The few score fighting-men now wished the many sick and wounded good luck and left them, an act which appears merciless, but to which there was perhaps no alternative for men barely able to stagger along themselves. One of those left behind was Dr. Duff, the Surgeon-General. After a severe wound in his hand he had directed its amputation with a pocket-knife to avoid gangrene. Now exhausted, he was left on the roadway and was later found killed.

The few men of the advance, followed by the camp-followers, moved off on 11 January, the sixth day of the retreat, shortly after eight o'clock. But now all advantage was lost, wreaths of Afghan turbans crowned the heights on both sides of the Pass, a hail of bullets hit the column below. Brigadier Shelton with his diminishing band of redcoats again protected the rear with accurate short-range shooting which checked Afghan efforts to launch another murderous sabre-swinging charge.

The advance staggered into Jugdulluk at 3 p.m., and

halted in the snow behind some ruined walls on a height beside the road to await Shelton and the rear-guard. Here, where the Afghan bullets still droned past their ears, Elphinstone, with a crazy ineffectual gesture of defiance ordered some of his officers—about twenty were at hand— 'to form line and show a front'—that is, to stand up boldly in line, facing the enemy's *jezail* fire. One of his close advisers, Captain Grant of the 27th Native Infantry at once paid dearly for his bravado. A bullet smashed into his cheek and shattered his jaw and he fell forward in the saddle. Johnson lifted him to the ground.

But the remaining nineteen officers, led by the tottering old General, stood their ground bravely, until the rear-guard having appeared they received it with a cheer and took cover behind the heaps of masonry. There they hoped for rest, respite from Afghan *jezail* fire, and water, if no food, but they had none of these—only the whine and ricochet of the heavy $1\frac{1}{2}$-ounce rounds poured down from the surrounding heights.

'Our men were almost maddened with hunger and thirst,' Captain Johnson noted. 'Some snow was on the ground, which we greedily devoured; but instead of quenching, it increased our thirst.'

A stream of pure clear water rippled over the rocks 150 paces away; all were tortured by it, many no doubt poised themselves for a desperate rush to it, but no one ventured against the hail of well-aimed rounds that would have struck him.

Suddenly the firing ended. The General sent Johnson to see whether the camp-followers still had any bullocks or camels for food. Johnson and the men with him seized three bullocks, killed them at once and served out great doggets of flesh to the remaining troops—'instantly devoured, although raw and still reeking with blood'.

The Afghans opened fire again and again a party of horsemen appeared near by. Learning that Akbar was among them, Captain Skinner—'Gentleman Jim'—rode bravely out of cover to protest angrily about the continued shooting.

This now became so hot, with volley after volley hitting the packed fugitives in the small enclosure, that many of the camp-followers lost their wits and rushed out into the open where, like frightened deer, they were, one after the other, shot down on the run.

Captain Bygrave, paymaster of the force, called for volunteers to chase the sharpshooters from the hideout on a nearby peak. Fifteen redcoats of the 44th joined him in a brave dash up the hill in face of heavy fire. The hundred or so Afghans retreated at the sight of the gleaming bayonets—probably believing that the entire British force would at last come to its senses and occupy the height as well.

Not so. Elphinstone recalled Bygrave and his brave followers for some unaccountable reason. The Afghans thereupon reoccupied the height and once more picked off officers and men without fear of retaliation.

Why, at the earliest stage in the retreat, had not Elphinstone obeyed one of the basic rules of warfare in these circumstance—the detailing of small bands of skirmishers to move ahead of the force, seize the heights that dominated the route and thus prevent the slaughter? The answer can only be that while he had the officers and had the men capable of it, he himself must have lacked the fighting spirit, preferring instead the hollow pretence of gentlemanly negotiations with Akbar.

Late in the afternoon Gentleman Jim Skinner returned with a message to the General requesting his presence at a conference with Akbar and demanding Brigadier Shelton and Captain Johnson as additional hostages as well.

The force was now reduced to 150 redcoats of the 44th Regiment, 15 dismounted men of the Horse Artillery, 25 5th Light Cavalry troopers and not one single sepoy of the original 3,000. All reserves of ammunition had been lost or fired; and what remained in pouches had been taken from the bodies of comrades. In the circumstances, the General and Shelton felt that they had no choice but to attend the conference and try to make the best terms possible to save those who still lived.

They took Captain Johnson with them as interpreter and, relates Vincent Eyre, 'the troops witnessed their departure with despair, having seen enough of Afghan treachery to convince them that these repeated negotiations were . . . designed to engender confidence in their victims, preparatory to a fresh sacrifice of blood'.

Chapter Twenty-nine

Akbar received them with courtesy and kindness. A cloth was spread on the ground, mutton and rice, water and long draughts of tea were served, Akbar also promising Elphinstone that food and water would be sent at once to the famished troops and the General again believed him, but nothing was sent to them.

When the meal was finished they sat round a blazing fire in the darkness to discuss terms. Akbar now produced his bombshell. He required as hostages he said, not only Shelton and Johnson but Elphinstone as well, and though the General pleaded, said it would be dishonourable for him to leave his troops, promised if he were allowed to return to send Brigadier Anquetil instead, Akbar was adamant and the General was more or less a prisoner. The three officers were shown into a small tent for a night's sleep.

When the conference was resumed at 8 a.m. Akbar promised to do all he could to save the lives of the remaining troops, but at about nine o'clock, Johnson noted, the chiefs of the Pass and of the country towards Soorkhab arrived. 'The chiefs were most bitter in their expressions of hatred towards us; and declared that nothing would satisfy them and their men but our extermination, and money they would not receive. . . .

'From their expressions of hatred towards the whole race of us, they appeared to anticipate much more delight in cutting our throats than in the expected booty.'

Akbar tried to calm them as far as he could, but Johnson heard them say twice in reply—'When Burnes came into this country was not your father entreated by us to kill him, or he would go back to Hindustan and on some future day return with an army and take our country from us. He would not listen to our advice, and what is the consequence? Let us now that we have the opportunity, take advantage of it and kill these infidel dogs.'

The Ghilzye chiefs swore that they wanted blood, not money, but when the payment of 2 lakhs of rupees (£20,000) was promised them for safe conduct, their leader, Mahommed Shah Khan, hurriedly went off to consult the lesser chiefs. Akbar, when he had gone, remarked to Johnson that these chiefs were dogs in whom no faith could be placed—begged him to send to the force for three or four of his best friends, to save them from likely death.

Johnson answered that he would gladly do so, but his friends would be against leaving their comrades.

Akbar then proposed instead that at dusk that day each one of the surviving British troops should be mounted behind one of his men and brought away to safety in his camp, for the Ghilzyes would not fire for fear of hitting him or his men. But it was quite impossible, he said, for him to try to protect the crowd of almost 2,000 surviving camp-followers as well.

Akbar was obviously sincere in this offer. The 189 troops would present no problem as prisoners and could well prove a useful bargaining counter for him in the future with his own family.

'But', says George Lawrence, who was present, 'with the fatal indecision which adhered to all their measures, the General and Shelton demurred to the Sirdar's proposal on a point of honour.'

It was, as Lawrence remarks, a little late then to talk of honour, when seven days ago they had abandoned Kabul, where they had an army of 5,000 well-equipped men: when they had lost their stores, food and money, had allowed some 12,000 camp-followers to be butchered or taken into slavery, and had so commanded their troops that they were now less than 200. With certain annihilation now facing the weary officers and men down in the valley, surrender on Akbar's terms seems to have been imperative.

But at the moment, when these men's lives were at stake,

when a word to Akbar could have saved them—the General and Shelton preferred instead to talk of *honour*. What a fantasy this honour was if to sustain it men had needlessly to be left to die.

Having then declined Akbar's offer, the General asked again to be allowed to rejoin his troops, but once more Akbar refused and about mid-day rode off to Mahommed Shah Khan, the Ghilzye chief, to find out what had been arranged about payment. From time to time Elphinstone and his party heard bursts of musketry from the direction of the camp, but when they questioned it they were assured that all was well. They waited, fearing the worst.

Akbar returned at dusk, soon followed by Mahommed Shah Khan, who said that between him and his followers all was now arranged for the safe conduct of the troops to Jellalabad in the morning. Akbar said he would personally accompany them. General Elphinstone then wrote a note to Brigadier Anquetil informing him of this and ordering him to have the troops ready to move off at 8 a.m. next morning.

But at about 7 p.m., when the letter had not yet been sent, they heard a burst of heavy firing from the direction of the Pass and horsemen rode up with the news that the British had finally marched, followed by the attacking Ghilzyes. 'We were all in consternation,' relates Captain Johnson. 'At first the Sirdar suggested and the General concurred that we should follow them. In two or three minutes the former changed his mind and said he feared our doing so would . . . greatly injure the party, bringing after them the whole horde of Ghilzyes then assembled in the valley.'

From the time of the General's departure the day before the situation of the troops had been grim, with constant attacks. Early in the morning the tireless Captain Skinner —this time accompanied by Major Thain—had again set out for Akbar's camp to find out what was afoot.

A Ghilzye soldier, Bulund Khan, suddenly appeared, and passing Thain, who was slightly ahead, went close up to Skinner and shot him in the face. Skinner fell and was carried back to camp. Later in the day, behind the ruined wall he died, and all the surviving force mourned him.

At intervals throughout that day too, the Afghan sharp-shooters fired at the survivors from their hilltop, killing and wounding at will. The troops made repeated sallies and drove them off, but again and again the Afghans returned to shoot them down. Finally, it was decided at 7 p.m. to push on at all costs, necessarily abandoning the wounded.

Vincent Eyre passed by the ruined enclosure with the party of hostages an hour or two later. 'We beheld a spectacle more terrible than any we had previously witnessed,' he noted, 'the whole interior space being one crowded mass of bloody corpses. The carnage here must have been frightful.'

The force now descended into a long narrow defile some two miles long, closed in by precipitous heights. This the troops passed through without more than a few shots from the Ghilzyes. But towards the head of the Pass where the road sloped upwards they came face to face with two thick barriers of prickly hollyoak, twisted together, about six feet high, stretching across the whole defile.

The fugitives tore at the branches with naked hands and the hidden Ghilzye marksmen poured in a series of shatter-ing volleys. When all was confusion, they rushed in whirling sabres. The British met them with bayonets, killing and wounding many with savage ferocity, so glad were they at last to get to grips with their tormentors. But weak from hunger and thirst they were also hopelessly outnumbered. Falling bleeding by the score, they were massacred.

Their own casualties made the Ghilzyes eventually with-draw and as the clash of knives and bayonets ceased, the British still alive took up their wounded comrades, staggered on through the opening in the barrier and halted several miles on near Gundamuk just before sunrise. A small party of mounted officers and men rode on ahead.

Many wounded died during the night and when a count was taken there were but twenty officers, and forty-five men alive, apart from those who had ridden on alone. Brigadier Anquetil was dead and Major Thain, Elphinstone's friend who had gone out to India as his aide-de-camp to enjoy a little hunting; Colonel Chambers, who commanded the cavalry at Kabul, Captain Nicholl, of the Artillery, Captain Grant, who had still lived on after a bullet had smashed his jaw three days before, and more than 100 redcoats, cavalry troopers and artillerymen. Captain Dodgin, a very strong and active man who had lost a leg in some earlier campaign, sabred five Afghans to death before he was shot down.

Until daybreak there was a brief respite. Crouching together on the wintry plain outside the hovels of Gundamuk, the survivors, one can imagine, looked at each other with vacant eyes, bound up their wounds with any rags they had and wondered when they too would fall.

A messenger now came from the local chief to the senior officer, Major Griffiths of the 37th Native Infantry, suggesting a parley. Hopefully Griffiths descended a hill to a conference, with Lieutenant Blewitt. The Afghans surrounding the force now assumed a friendly tone, but one or two of them tried to seize the soldiers' weapons. Wild with despair and half-crazed now the men drove them off at bayonet point.

For this little group it was the end. The Afghans retired to a hill near by and picked them off one by one with unerring aim. Soon all were either dead or wounded, and Afghans rushed in and put them to the sword.

Only Captain Souter of the 44th and four redcoats were spared and taken prisoner. All five were badly wounded, Souter with a deep sword-cut in his shoulder. Earlier in the day, he had ripped the colours from their pole when the quarter-master sergeant carrying them was killed, and wrapped them round his body. He believed the Afghans thought he was a great leader and spared him so that he could be ransomed.

Another group of some fifteen officers and men who were still mounted, had ridden on ahead together after escaping the barrier of Jugdulluk. They, too, were shot down one by one on the road, until at Futtehabad, 16 miles from General

Sale's army at Jellalabad, only six still lived. They were all officers—Captains Bellew, Collyer and Hopkins; Lieutenant Bird and Doctors Harpur and Brydon.

Deliverance, it seemed, might now be at hand. If they could urge on their exhausted horses for these last few miles they could reach Jellalabad before night.

Just beyond Futtehabad, some Afghan peasants approached and offered bread. Having eaten nothing during three days of violent action, a little bread—even the half-baked lumpy Afghan bread—was irresistible. They stopped to eat.

A party of armed horsemen rode out and attacked them. Bird and Bellew were surrounded and cut down at once, the other four galloped off and Dr. Brydon, who was mounted on an exhausted pony, fell behind, left the road and hid behind some rocks while the chase went on.

Soon it occurred to him that there was no safety in delay so he turned his pony to the road again and drove him on. Not long after, he came up with the body of Dr. Harpur, terribly mutilated and bleeding. An Afghan horseman with upraised sword appeared and rode at him.

Brydon drew his own weapon and fought for his life. In the fight his sword was broken off at the hilt and a moment after he received a wound in the knee, the pain of which made him involuntarily lean forward. The Afghan, thinking Brydon was about to draw a pistol—or wounded himself—turned and fled.

Bleeding and weak, scarcely able to stay in the saddle, Brydon rode on blindly towards Jellalabad, not even sure that Sale's troops would still be there to save him.

Four days earlier on 11 January a party of Afghan horsemen bearing a flag of truce had brought General Sale a letter from General Elphinstone. It was dated 2 January 1842 and informed Sale that Elphinstone had agreed with Akbar Khan to evacuate the country and that this should start at Jellalabad. Sale was accordingly directed to march immediately for Peshawar—the force at Kabul had agreed not to march until it was known that General Sale and his force were beyond the frontier.

'Everything has been done in good faith,' the General had written. 'You will not be molested on your way; and to the safe-conduct which Akbar Khan has given, I trust for the passage of the troops under my immediate orders through the passes.'

The signature was genuine, the orders were peremptory, but Elphinstone had made it clear that he had capitulated —and that he was dependent upon Akbar Khan for the safety of his troops. Sale and his staff, believing that the letter must have been written under duress and that after all that had been done, Afghanistan should not be thus abandoned decided 'that it would not be prudent to act upon such a document; and that the garrison would abide where it was till further orders'.

Sale, who had great confidence in his troops saw no point in keeping this astonishing news from them and, says G. R. Gleig, their chaplain, they 'held up their hands in amazement when the capitulation of 5,000 disciplined soldiers to any conceivable number of barbarians was announced to them as an affair accomplished. Moreover, the men were ready to march, or stay where they were.' When told they would stay they received the news with a cheer and returned to the task of strengthening the fortifications.

On 13 January working parties were digging a ditch round the north-west angle. Their arms were piled near by and a squadron of cavalry with horses saddled were ready to go to their support if they were attacked.

There was a sudden shout from a sentry on the west wall, facing Gundamuk. He pointed into the distance—a mounted man was approaching. Officers levelled their telescopes and saw one of their own people 'faint, as it seemed, from travel, if not sick or wounded', noted Gleig.

A crowd of officers and men gathered. 'It is impossible to describe,' says Gleig, 'the thrill which ran through men's veins as they watched the movements of the stranger.'

A body of cavalry galloped out to help him. He was brought in supported in the saddle, covered with wounds, bleeding and faint, 'gripping in his hand the hilt and a bit of the blade of his sword'.

He looked like a messenger of death.

They lifted him gently off his pony. Between gasps and groans he said he was Dr. Brydon and that apart from a few hostages he believed he was the sole survivor of the Kabul force.

A shudder of horror ran through the assembled troops. It seemed to them beyond belief that Elphinstone's once magnificent little army had thus been slaughtered. 'What went wrong? How could this have happened?'—these were surely the questions everyone was asking.

General Sale sent out a squadron of cavalry along the road to Futtehabad to search for, or to fight and rescue any survivors in Afghan hands.

Sorrowfully at dusk they returned to say they found no one alive—only three mutilated bodies, those of Dr. Harpur and Captains Collyer and Hopkins, who had escaped with Brydon.

That night, and for several nights, General Sale ordered that lanterns should be hung on the ramparts, whose glimmer could guide any night-marching survivors to safety. Alert sentries peered into the darkness, bugles from time to time sounded the shrill notes of the advance, but they played a requiem for the fallen, for there was no one to answer. The Kabul force had been annihilated—a whole army had fallen.

What can be said in favour of this pointless and tragic war? Nothing. To India—and India paid—it brought oppressive taxation, the delay of reforms and the postponement of enterprises that would in time have made life a little easier. All this built up hatred for the English.

To England it brought not one single benefit, military or political—only loss of life and of military prestige, which she had to try to retrieve in a campaign of retribution.

Chapter Thirty

Lord Auckland received the news of the Afghan disaster on 30 January 1842. Characteristically he tried to minimise it by issuing a pompous proclamation saying that he considered it only 'a new occasion for displaying the stability and vigour of the British power and the admirable spirit and valour of the British-Indian army'.

Already, while the news of the insurrection was drifting in during December and January, he had sent a brigade to Peshawar and had ordered another 3,000 men to prepare to march. To command this relief force, he nominated another sick officer, Major-General Lumley. Just in time the doctors reported adversely on his health and spared the force the likelihood of still greater disaster. General Pollock, a capable and experienced soldier, was appointed instead, and he, as well as Nott in Kandahar, were given full powers to act as they saw fit.

Then on 21 February, Generals Nott at Kandahar, and Sale at Jellalabad, received letters signed by Akbar's prisoners, General Elphinstone and Major Eldred Pottinger, stating that the troops under their command should at once retreat to India. Both Generals had reported to the Government of India their intention of taking no action upon this letter.

Elphinstone's action was viewed 'with the most severe displeasure' by the Government. It directed that a full military inquiry should be instituted into all the circumstances connected with the direction of affairs at Kabul, superseded Elphinstone in his command by General Pollock and directed that Elphinstone's authority should wholly cease.

Whether news of his disgrace ever reached this broken

and pathetic man is hard to say. He was to die in captivity on 22 April. Meantime Nott was officially informed that it was of the 'highest importance that he should maintain his position in concentrated strength at Kandahar until he may receive further instructions'.

He replied that he had never for one moment contemplated retiring. 'And as to treating with these people, I never will, and I hope no Englishman will think of doing so. . . . I hope yet to assert the honour of Old England in this mountain land. . . .' After Elphinstone, what a stirring note.

General Sale's garrison of about 2,000 men had only 150 rounds each and were short of food as well. Pollock was known to have reached Peshawar by early February and optimistic expectations of his early arrival cheered the garrison, which at one time had been on the point of surrendering.

But Pollock was then unable to march. His army was not yet ready for the severe test of penetrating the Khyber Pass against a determined enemy.

On 15 February rows of white tents appeared a few miles away from the walls of Jellalabad. They were those of Akbar Khan and an army of 19,000 men. Having annihilated General Elphinstone's force Akbar had come to repeat his triumph. But the Jellalabad defences had been made ready by hard spade work of both officers and men to withstand the heaviest assault.

On 19 February an earthquake destroyed all that they had done in three months. It was vividly described by the force's chaplain, G. R. Gleig: 'Colonel Monteith, who happened to be the field officer for the day had ascended one of the bastions and was sweeping the horizon with his telescope, when all at once the earth began to tremble and there was a noise not so much like thunder as of a thousand heavily laden wagons rolling and jolting over an ill-paved street.

'The whole of the plain began to heave like billows on the surface of the ocean, and walls and houses, splitting asunder, came tumbling down upon the space which an instant before had been crowded with workmen. The whole of the parapets which had been constructed with so much skill and diligence were thrown down with a fearful crash into heaps of ruins. Happily very few lives were lost.'

Colonel Monteith was buried in the ruins. General Sale rushed to the rescue and laid hold of Monteith's head, which was the only part of him visible. Monteith, noted Macken-zie, was a great dandy and took most particular care of his wig, which he oiled and dressed throughout the siege with great tenderness and pains. When he felt someone tugging at his head he came round and cried: 'Let go of my head!' Sale in his joy at finding he was alive, tugged ten times harder, whereupon the Colonel exclaimed in wrath: 'Who is the scoundrel tugging at my *hair*?' which speedily caused his gallant old friend to let go.

The defences were restored with feverish energy, but the shortage of food was now dangerous. It was therefore decided to attack, and on 7 April Akbar's force was routed —baggage, artillery, ammunition, horses, arms of every kind and food were captured. With the remnants of his army the beaten chief fled towards Kabul. The British casualties were light, but the heroic Colonel Dennie died leading a charge.

Two days earlier, on 5 April, Pollock had finally march-ed from Peshawar to penetrate the formidable Khyber Pass. His troops were confident and well trained; the orders for the advance known in detail by all officers. The enemy were cleared from the heights by shrapnel; the heights were seized and held by skirmishers until the columns had passed. And so General Pollock forced this 28-mile-long defile for the first time in modern history.

The army relieved Jellalabad on 16 April. They were played in to the tune of 'Eh, but you've been a lang time o'coming.' A salute was fired and a great cheer burst forth.

General Pollock in Jellalabad and General Nott in Kan-dahar both now had the same ambition—to march to Kabul, enter the city and crush the group of chiefs who had slaughtered Elphinstone's force.

Another act of the Kabul tragedy now occurred. Shah Shuja was murdered as he descended from the Bala Hissar by the son of Nawab Zemaun Khan. A fierce struggle then broke out between Shah Shuja's sons, and Mahommed Akbar and his followers, for the right to rule the country.

A new Governor-General, Lord Ellenborough, had meantime succeeded Auckland, and he brought with him a new policy. It involved the removal of British forces as soon as possible, even if this meant abandoning the prisoners and hostages. He accordingly wrote to General Nott on 19 April ordering him to ruin the defences of Kandahar and march immediately to India, via Quetta, with his entire army. General Nott replied that the decision was regrettable, but he would do so as soon as he received money to pay his troops—they'd had no pay for three months—and much needed provisions and ammunition.

General Pollock, too, then received orders to withdraw from Jellalabad back through the Khyber to Peshawar. All responsible political and military officers in India vigorously attacked Ellenborough's orders, but despite this and the strong feelings which news of the Kabul massacre had created in England, Lord Ellenborough seemed fixed in his determination to retire both Nott's and Pollock's forces. October was fixed upon as the date.

Meantime, General Nott had defeated the Afghans decisively in a series of useful actions. He took good care that these were fully reported to the Governor-General.

Ellenborough then wrote directly to Nott congratulating him, but gave no indication of a change of mind. Nott fumed and fretted at Kandahar, certain that his army alone could vindicate British honour. 'Pollock's army was not necessary,' he wrote to his daughters in Calcutta. 'The troops under my command would have taken Ghazni and destroyed the Bala Hissar at Kabul. I told Lord Auckland so in December, last; but what is the good of talking of it? I am ordered to *sneak* away, though with my beautiful regiments I could plant the British banner on the banks of the Caspian.'

Nott was an outstanding military practitioner of *pax Britannica*.

Meantime, Mahommed Akbar had gained possession of Kabul and though he had been defeated by Sale at Jellalabad still revelled in his possession of captive officers, troops, women and children as well as the disastrous defeat British policy had suffered at his hands.

More and more Nott chafed at inaction as the summer wore on; soon he would have to prepare to 'sneak away'. Then on 22 July while out for an early morning walk a package from the Governor-General was brought to him. Nott read that now that his camel transport had been reinforced, Lord Ellenborough supposed that he could for the first time move his army with ample equipment for any service. He therefore left it to Nott to decide by which route he should withdraw his troops from Afghanistan.

'If you determine upon moving upon Ghazni, Kabul and Jellalabad, you will be . . . dependent entirely upon the courage of your army for the opening of a new communication by an ultimate junction with Major-General Pollock.'

Ellenborough told Nott in this remarkable letter which Kaye terms 'a masterpiece of Jesuitical cunning', that he must retire his army, but if he wished he could do so by way of Ghazni and Kabul. This was like ordering a retreat from Brussels to Strasbourg via a fighting advance to Amsterdam. And the responsibility for the decision was placed firmly upon Nott's shoulders.

General Pollock was also to be allowed to support Nott, though the Governor-General did not anticipate that he would move any troops to Kabul, but merely make a forward movement in that direction. Lord Ellenborough told him that if he did make this forward advance he would do so entirely on his own responsibility; and that in any case his instructions were to retire to Peshawar as soon as possible.

The Governor-General had thus manoeuvred both generals into a dangerous corner: if they took the easy way out and retreated into India without military action, theirs

would be the shame; and if they advanced and were defeated, the blame and disgrace would be theirs, not the
Governor-General's. But were they to win, Lord Ellenborough would share the praise and the awards at least
equally. History affords few if any situations so completely
based on 'heads I win tails you lose'.

But both Nott and Pollock were confident of the ability of
their troops to defeat the Afghans, and neither man gave a
damn for retreating first. Yet it was vital that they should
march so as to reach Kabul together from their different
directions so as to bring overwhelming force to bear. Correspondence from one side of Afghanistan to the other in
these conditions was risky indeed.

When his letters to Nott appeared to have been intercepted, Pollock—who had been to trying negotiate the
release of the prisoners with Akbar—sent a letter to Nott
through Akbar. Apparently a friendly greeting, secret information was written in rice-water, and when iodine was
applied it was revealed. Thus Akbar was used as the tool of
his own defeat.

Having meantime detailed the prisoners and hostages in
forts in and just outside Kabul, where, after great hardship
and privation they were now comfortable, Akbar occupied
himself, among other things by torturing Mohan Lal—to
make him produce 30,000 rupees. 'All my feet is wounded by
bastinadoing . . . red pepper is burnt before my nose and
eyes . . . he says he will pull out my eyes and burn my body
with a hot iron,' the unhappy British agent wrote to Pollock.
Just in time, General Pollock, in a severe letter telling Akbar
he would be held responsible for Mohan Lal's good health,
stopped this torture.

In August, the final battles in the campaign of retribution
occurred. General Nott quit Kandahar on 8 August 1842
and marched towards Ghazni. He engaged Shumsoodeen,
the Governor, in the field and defeated him, capturing
guns, tents, ammunition and supplies with moderate losses
to his own army. Soon after this the defenders of the fortress
of Ghazni surrendered without firing a shot. Nott destroyed

its defences and marched on towards Kabul.

Meanwhile, Generals Pollock and Sale marched on Kabul on 20 August with a force of 8,000 men full of hope and courage. Pollock had kept his final intentions secret—even General Sale—whose wife and daughter were still in Akbar's hands—was crazy with joy at the prospect. 'Hurrah!' he wrote to Pollock. 'This is good news. All here are prepared to meet your wishes and to march as light as possible . . . I am so excited I can scarce write.'

The first division of Pollock's army engaged the Afghans at Jugdulluk. Large bodies of the Ghilzyes thronged the hilltops ready to shoot down the British just as they had done in January. General Pollock ordered his howitzers to hit them with shrapnel, but well hidden in the rocky hilltops the Ghilzyes stood their ground even when the shells burst among them. They poured a hot *jezail* fire on to the British.

Pollock thereupon ordered the infantry to scale the heights and root out the Ghilzyes at bayonet point. The redcoats responded with a loud cheer, storming the steep hillside and scattering the enemy. The Ghilzyes retired to the topmost height, but even here they weren't safe—the redcoats stormed even this precipitous peak. 'Seldom have soldiers had a more arduous task to perform and never was an undertaking of the kind surpassed in execution,' Pollock wrote in his report. The victory was complete.

Then on 13 September the biggest army that Akbar Khan could put into the field was beaten even more decisively at Tezeen.

The battles were now over and the remnants of the Afghan force fled through the mountains to find safety wherever they could.

Pollock marched his army forward without delay, camped on the Kabul racecourse on 15 September and planted his standard high up on the Bala Hissar. General Nott continued his advance from the south, defeated the Afghans in two more engagements and camped outside Kabul two days later.

The great bazaar and many other buildings were destroyed; retribution was complete and national pride restored. Meantime, General Sale rode hard westwards, caught up with the prisoners at Bamian three days later and embraced his wife and daughter. Together with the other prisoners, Lady Sale and Mrs. Sturt had freed themselves when Akbar's defeat became known.

Nott and Pollock in due course led their forces back to India successfully and took part in a grand military parade to commemorate their victories. Both generals received the order of the Grand Cross of the Bath and in addition Nott was made British Envoy to the King of Oude, on the borders of northern India, a most cherished appointment. Lord Ellenborough, for his part in the final victories, was made an earl.

Lord Auckland had earlier been welcomed back in England with acclamations and in the new Whig government was rewarded for all the harm he had done with the post of First Lord of the Admiralty. Of the more deserving men who played a part in the war, both George Lawrence and Colin Mackenzie rose to the top of their professions, with the rank of lieutenant-general. Eyre became General Sir Vincent Eyre, but Shelton's career was short-lived. He returned to England and took command of his regiment, but soon after was killed when his horse threw him on the parade ground at Dublin. It is sad to record that his men cheered.

General Sir Robert and Lady Sale and Mrs. Sturt, who by now had borne her dead husband a daughter, sailed to England, where, as celebrities the General and his wife were received by Queen Victoria. One of the Queen's ladies-in-waiting was horrified by the stories of this 'red-faced man with a comical expression' and complained that he 'talked of cutting men down as if they were nettles'. Later Sale returned to India, and died in action in the Sikh War.

But events in Kabul only reached their full circle of absurdity towards the end of 1842. Dost Mahommed, having been freed by the British, was then allowed to return unconditionally to the throne of Afghanistan. He ruled until he died in 1863, a neighbour whom the British in India knew only too well would repulse invasion from whatever direction it came.

BIBLIOGRAPHY

For the main course of events I am indebted to Sir John Kaye's *History of the War in Afghanistan* (1851), which is the most comprehensive and best-documented contemporary source. But the following published books have also enabled me to add the depth, colour and individual reactions that only witnesses and participants could give to this account of an all but hidden tragedy in our military history:

Alexander Burnes: *Kabul, A Personal Narrative* (1842)

Major William Broadfoot: *The Career of Major George Broadfoot* (1888)

Colonel William Dennie: *Personal Narrative* (1843)

Sir Henry Durand: *The First Afghan War and Its Causes* (1879)

Vincent Eyre: *Military Operations at Kabul* (1842)

Colonel H. E. Fane: *Five Years In India* (1842)

G. R. Gleig: *With Sale's Brigade in Afghanistan* (1846)

T. W. E. Holdsworth: *The Campaign of the Indus* (1840)

Major William Hough: *Narrative of the Army of the Indus* (1841)

Dr. R. H. Kennedy: *Campaign of the Army of the Indus* (1840)

Lieut.-General Sir George Lawrence: *43 Years in India* (1874)

Lieut.-General Colin Mackenzie: *Storms and Sunshine of a Soldier's Life* (1884)

Mohan Lal: *The Life of Dost Mahommed* (1846)

Captain Henry Havelock: *The War In Afghanistan* (1840)

Major James Outram: *Rough Notes* (1840)

Lady Sale: *Journal of the Disasters in Afghanistan* (1846)

J. H. Stocqueler: *Memorials of Afghanistan* (1842)

J. H. Stocqueler: *The Life of Sir William Nott*

Also:

> *Political Proceedings of the Government of India* (India Office Library)
> *The Cambridge History of the British Empire*
> Vincent A. Smith: *The Oxford History of India*